CE

CUSTOMARY LAW OF THE HAYA TRIBE

Tanganyika Territory

HANS CORY AND

M. M. HARTNOLL

NEW IMPRESSION

First published in 1945, Cory and Hartnoll's Customary Law of the *Haya Tribe* was the product of detailed and thorough research under the direction of the late Dr. Hans Cory. It covers a wide range of topics, including Marriage, Divorce, Bride-Price, Inheritance, Property (immovable as well as movable), Personal Status and some contracts, as well as some notes on the customary courts and the way in which they functioned during the period of British administration.

In 1945 little was known about the indigenous legal systems of East Africa, and still less had been published. This study, now a classic in its field, did not receive wide circulation at the time of its publication (only three hundred copies were printed), though it has since become known to those engaged in work on the customary law of any part of Africa as a major contribution to the subject, and one of the most valuable works in this sphere. It remains so today, and this reprint which makes the book for the first time easily accessible, will therefore be especially welcome.

CASS LIBRARY OF AFRICAN STUDIES

LIBRARY OF AFRICAN LAW
No. 7

General Editors: NEVILLE RUBIN and EUGENE COTRAN
School of Oriental and African Studies, London

CUSTOMARY LAW
OF THE
HAYA TRIBE

CUSTOMARY LAW OF THE HAYA TRIBE

TANGANYIKA TERRITORY

BY

Hans Cory & M. M. Hartnoll

FRANK CASS & CO. LTD.

1971

Published by

FRANK CASS AND COMPANY LIMITED

67 Great Russell Street, London WC1B 3BT

by arrangement with the International African Institute

*The first publication of this study originally received
a grant from the then Tanganyika Government and
appeared in a limited edition of 300 copies.*

First published for the International African Institute
by Percy Lund, Humphries & Co. Ltd.

First edition   1945
Second impression   1971

ISBN 0 7146 2476 4

*Printed in Great Britain by Clarke, Doble & Brendon Ltd.
Plymouth and London*

C O N T E N T S

INTRODUCTION

The customary law of a tribe is built upon its experience and naturally alters to meet new circumstances as they arise. A new step in evolution affects the law, in that it may put existing laws out of date, and
equity demands that the judgments given should fit the changed conditions.
In time these changes pass into law by reason of being the accepted view
of all courts on the subject and the old rules are tacitly abandoned.
Where, as in Uhaya, the law was unwritten, the courts naturally had wide
discretion,and their interpretation and alterations were readily accepted.

Changes in customary law occur mainly for the following reasons:—

1. Owing to new conditions of life, superimposed on the people by
outside influences, which create new legal possibilities, e.g. bankruptcy.

2. Through the changing of a basic principle owing to modern influences, e.g. the inheritance of land by women.

Bankruptcy is solely the result of the effect of modern conditions
on the economic life of the people, and the law to deal with it can be
added quickly; but in the case of the second example, the change can
only be admitted when the ancient status of women has so far altered
that there is no reason to debar them from inheriting land and the people
themselves wish for the change.

Another effect of new conditions is to make the indirect effects of
jurisdiction heavier or lighter than they were intended to be, or justly
should be. For instance, in a community where land is abundant and
every man can easily obtain sufficient to bring him a livelihood, the
decision of a court with regard to real estate has no effect one way or
another on the citizen's social status; but in a community where new
land is not available and the livelihood of every man depends on his
land, a decision to take it away from him must involve a complete change
in his social status. Therefore when the latter conditions arise land
law must change from its original vague form, which left much to the

discretion of the courts in order to ensure that the consequences of its application are fair and cannot be affected by any personal bias or ignorance on the part of a judge.

In normal circumstances natural evolution and the adaptation of the law to fit it run at about the same speed but a sudden outside influence, such as the introduction of European culture, upsets the machinery, since the influences of civilization show quickly on the outward life of the tribe but reaction on its basic principles is slow; thus the law, itself the expression of those principles, accommodates itself but slowly to the changes, and until it has caught up must be deficient.

It is obvious that European culture will, as its influences go deeper, affect customary law more and more and therefore, apart from any other reason, this book can in no way be considered a code but is a collection of customary law as it stands at present.

The compilation of Haya Customary Law has been made over a period of nearly two years in the following way :—

1.) A first draft was made in consultation with two Native Court assessors separately.

2.) This draft was discussed in detail with 16 Court assessors, two from each Chiefdom, and additions made to it.

3.) A Swahili copy of the second draft was sent to every Chief for his comments. Each Chief discussed it in Baraza with his own selected assessors.

4.) The final draft was drawn up.

5.) Several hundreds of appeal cases were studied, of which over 200 have been used to illustrate various points.

It is recognised that some of the paragraphs in this book do not deal with points of law but refer to custom. The reason for their inclusion is that obedience or disobedience to the custom may have legal consequences though there is no legal punishment for its disregard; since the majority of the population still follows these customs, the Courts have often to deal with cases in which the back-ground has been formed by the mutual observance of a custom. For example, the bisisi custom (para. 187): a case about inheritance of land may arise wherein a man claims to have received his right to land by reason of his being a bisisi child.

No civil code was used as a guide in the compilation of this book and therefore it may be found that many points have been left out; neither was any attempt made to copy the form of a law book and the order of chapters was made with a view to the easiest arrangement for understanding by African Courts.

The use of a code might have meant that points foreign to customary law would arise and questioning the assessors on them might have resulted in the answers being their personal opinions and not rules of customary law.

It should be emphasised that Native Courts administering the customary law have hitherto had nothing written to which to refer, and with a written guide it may happen that a Court using it tends to follow too closely such small points as, for instance, the number of witnesses necessary to a transaction. Such a rigid observance of small matters has never been a rule in the application of customary law, which, when it states that 10 witnesses are necessary to a will intends to convey "approximately 10", thus 8 or 11 would equally suffice. In fact the assessors when giving such figures invariably stated " about 10 witnesses" etc.

H. Cory
M.M. Hartnoll

NOTE: The material of this book was, as indicated in the introduction, taken down from informants: inconsistencies in the spelling of vernacular words may be attributed to variations in pronunciation.

M.M.H.

INHERITANCE

THE HEIRS

1. Inheritance is patrilineal.

2. Three grades of heirs proper are recognised:

> A.   THE MUSIKA   — primary heir
>
> B.   THE MAINUKA   — secondary heir
>
> C.   THE KYAGATI   — minor heirs
>
> (in Kizeba, Kyabulabula, in Karagwe, Chagati.)

3. A.   THE MUSIKA. (male)   The Musika of a man who has one wife is the eldest son. The Musika of a man who has several wives is the eldest son of the first wife. The Musika of a man who has no sons by his first wife is the first born son of the family. The Musika of a man who leaves no descendants in direct line is one of his brothers.   x The Musika of a man who has no brothers is his father.

x NOTE   There exists a divergence of opinion on this point. Cases are known where the inheritance returned to the older generation, but usually it is considered preferable that the inheritance devolves on the younger generation, even if thereby it goes to more distant relatives.

QUOTATION: P.C's appeal No. 20 of 1934.
Sylvester v. binti Bukambanja.

```
                  Magangala
                      I
          Kente           Ilungami
            I                I
          Kaihula         Sylvester
            I
          binti Bukambanja
```

Kente died. His son Kaihula inherited his property. Kaihula died soon after and his grandfather Magangala inherited his property. It was stated in Court that there exists a difference of opinion as to the rigidity of the custom that in such cases the land should revert to the father or grandfather of deceased.

For division of property see para. 74 et seq.

The Musika of a man who has no brothers and no father is one of his paternal uncles. x The Musika of a man who has no near relatives is any relative however distant. If a man dies leaving no male descendents in the direct line and no paternal relatives, this is a case of Obuchweke. (see para. 67 et seq.)

> x NOTE Unless a man has sons his immoveable property is inherited by one of his relatives who is chosen by family council. Therefore, if he has brothers, the eldest need not necessarily inherit. For example: If there is a brother who has none or only a small plantation he may be chosen to inherit. If the plantation is capable of providing two families with livelihood it may be divided between two relatives.
> On this chosen relative's death the plantation is inherited by his heirs in the usual way.

4. B. THE MAINUKA. The Mainuka of a man who has one wife is his second son. (except Ihangiro and Kianja). The Mainuka of a man who has several wives is the eldest son of his family, excluding his children by his first wife. (except Ihangiro and Kianja).

IHANGIRO AND KIANJA. The Mainuka is always the youngest son of the family.

5. If a man has only one son,. this son is the sole heir.

> ILLUSTRATION: A leaves an only son B. He also has one brother C. B inherits the whole property. C having no claim to be Mainuka or Kyagati.

6. If a man has no direct descendents his Musika is his sole heir.

> ILLUSTRATION: A leaves no sons or grandsons in the direct line. One of his relatives B is chosen by family council as his heir. B inherits the whole of A's property. No one of the other relatives can claim to be Mainuka or Kyagati.

7. C. THE KYAGATI. The Kyagati are all sons, other than the Musika and Mainuka.

8. Should a presumptive Musika or Mainuka die before inheriting, his title passes to his eldest son. (except in Kiziba).

> ILLUSTRATION: A has three sons B,C,D who are respectively Musika, Mainuka and Kyagati. B dies and his title is inherited by his son.

KIZIBA. If a presumptive heir dies, his title is inherited by his next brother whose own title is inherited by the son of the deceased.

ILLUSTRATION: A has three sons B, C and D who are respectively Musika, Mainuka and Kyagati. B dies leaving a son. B's title is assumed by C.

9. If a presumptive Musika or Mainuka has no sons his title passes to the next heir below him whose own title devolves upon the next heir.

ILLUSTRATION: A has 3 sons B, C and D who are respectively Musika, Mainuka and Kyagati. B dies childless. His title passes to C. C's title passes to D.

10. Wives and female descendents of a deceased cannot inherit immoveable property under family tenure.

QUOTATION: Chiefs' Court Appeal No.44 of 1938
P.C's Appeal No.3 of 1939

The Bakama stated in their judgement "A daughter cannot inherit landed property from her father or her mother, with one exception: If the mother had bought the plantation or had paid kishembe, a daughter may inherit this plantation of her mother. But if the mother herself inherited a plantation, at a time when this has been permitted, she cannot nominate her daughter as heir."

NOTE: If a man has bought a plantation for his daughter he has the right to bequeath it to her, because since it is not under family tenure he is at liberty to sell or dispose of it as he pleases, and therefore may leave it to his daughter.

(For the property inheritable by females, see para. 81 et seq. For rules regarding maintenance of widows and daughters, see para. 260 et seq.)

11. Therefore sons of daughters are excluded from inheritance of the property of their maternal grandfather.

QUOTATION: D.O's appeal No.41 of 1933.
Kapia v. Barongo

Tagamaisho
I
Banyita
I
Kapia

Tagamaisho died and nominated his uterine grandson Kapia as his heir, probably in order to avoid obuchweke. It was held that he could not

be nominated heir because he was outside the circle of inheritance of
his grandfather.

NOTE: For rules with regard to inheritance from Nyarubanja landlords
and tenants see para. 9 et seq. "Nyarubanja Tenure".

KUSIKEKISHASI AND NINARUMI

12. Two persons who owing to their functions are entitled to remuneration by the estate, but who cannot rightly be named as heirs proper are
the following:

13. The Kusikekishasi is a man's eldest daughter or if he has no daughters
his next female relative.

The Kusikekishasi is given special items of the property, but her
share of money and cattle depends both on the size of the estate and the
number of heirs participating in it. She has no legal right to her share.
She usually receives:

a) in cash Shs.5 to Shs.20, either paid immediately or out of the
proceeds of the next harvest.

b) 1 cow providing the herd consists of more than 10 head of cattle.

c) 1 coffee tree and 1 bark cloth tree, both growing upon the
deceased's land.

NOTE: The Kusikekishasi has to perform certain ceremonies before the
body is buried. First she plucks in the front room of the house a
handful of straw from the roof. After this she breaks the water pot,
butter jar and the vegetable pan (nyabugio), which have been used by
the deceased. Then she goes to his bed and makes a hole in the wall
and through this hole she pushes the straw of the bed, which later she
will carry to the open grassland. Before this ceremony takes place,
the head of the family has placed one or two shillings on the bed.
This money the Kusikekishasi keeps for herself. She then leaves the
house and may not re-enter it for the next four days.

---

13. NOTE: IHANGIRO. The Ihangiro name is "omwisika atela ente emibazi".
She is the eldest daughter of the second wife. Her inheritance in Ihangiro is one coffee tree only.

14. The Ninarumi is the eldest maternal uncle of the Musika. He receives a spear or calabash and a piece of clothing given him by the Musika. The spear or calabash must be redeemed by the Musika, the price being agreed upon between them. It varies proportionally to the value of the estate. In the case of a rich cattle owner it may amount to one head of cattle, or anything from 1/10th to 1/8th of the money left. The cloth remains his property.

NOTE: The Ninarumi is given his share of the estate by the Musika, because he instals the Musika in the chair of the deceased, which means that he instals the Musika as the rightful and responsible heir of the deceased.

This ceremony is called kusikizo and is only performed if the Musika is a son of the deceased.

On the next morning after the father has been buried, everyone leaves the hut. The ninarumi takes several bundles of grass from the roof to make a grass-pathway from the door to the chair of the father which is placed in the middle of the hut. The Musika then enters the hut, followed by all present and walks along the path to sit in the chair. The ninarumi hands him his father's spear and other belongings. Finally he places a cloth of the deceased round the shoulders of the heir.

The Ninarumi has a legal right to his share.

15. A. Property of unmarried girls. All property passes to: the father, failing whom, the eldest brother (full blood) failing whom, the eldest sister (full blood) failing whom, the eldest brother (half—brother) failing whom, the eldest sister (half—sister) failing whom, the next paternal relative.

16. B. Property of married women **without children.**

a) immoveable property:

17. A woman may choose anyone to be in charge of her plantation during her lifetime, but at her death her property is subject to the same rules as those for property of unmarried girls.

18. b) moveable property:

The property of a wife is strictly separated from that of a husband. He has no claims on it unless in the case of her money it has been earned by the sale of produce from his plantation, when, at her death, he is entitled to claim half of it.

A woman's moveable property is subject to the same rules of inheritance as those for property of unmarried girls.

NOTE: A wife seldom deposits her own money with her husband. She usually prefers to give it into the care of one of her own relatives.

19. Property of married women with children.

a) Grown up children. They inherit the whole of the property of their mother in equal shares. There is no Musika or Mainuka of her property.

20. b) Children under age. A husband has full rights of disposition over his deceased wife's money. He becomes trustee for her cattle and immoveable property during the minority of the children who can claim it from him unless he can prove that he disposed it for their sole benefit.

21. Children who lived with their mother, but were not the children of

the husband, are taken away on her death by their own paternal relatives.

21a.   <u>Heirs of women's inherited land.</u>   With regard to the heirs of those women who did inherit land there are two possibilities, either an eventual heir was nominated by the testator to succeed on her death or no such heir was nominated, in which latter case the woman is free to chose an heir from among her father's relatives.   If she has children she will probably nominate them and there is no restriction on her doing so, because they are not of her clan.

NOTE: Although women cannot now inherit immoveable property, they may acquire it by the following methods:—

1.   By inheritance during the time when women were allowed to inherit land.

2.   By allocation in the usual way of paying "Kishembe" to the Native Authority.

3.   By purchase.

Some years ago the European Appeal Court allowed women to inherit real property.

QUOTATION: D.O's appeal No.25 of 1934.
            P.C's   "   " 10 " 1934.

Bibi Bajumuzi v. Mkungu Kezokia
Page 3   "Almost unanimous verdict of those present that, although by a properly executed will or by permission of the chief a man now may leave his property to a daughter . . . "
But as this was completely against Haya tradition the chiefs after a short time decreed that it would not in future be admissible.

QUOTATION: D.O's Appeal No.4/P.I/5 of 1937

Bibi Mukanyiginya v. Kayungi
Kailembo died without leaving direct descendants. He nominated Kayungi, a distant relative, as his heir. After Kailembo's death his niece Mukanyiginya claimed the inheritance. Her claim was refused because women are not entitled to inherit real property.

THE RIGHT OF THE BAKAMA TO CHANGE SEQUENCE OF HEIRS.

22. The heirs affected are Bashaya bomukama.   In every district there

exists a class of people called Bashaya bomukama (men of the chiefs).
To this class belong the following :—

BARANGILA: The members of the Bahinda, Babito and Bankango clans
to which the chiefs belong.

BARAMATA: Those who hold certain positions in the service either
of the chief himself or of the chiefdom:

1)   Members of the royal bodyguard, cooks, milkers,   cupbearers,
drummers, herdsmen, hunters, those in charge of the royal burial ceremonies
and officers of the soldiers (Rugaruga)

2)   All deputies (Katikiro), subchiefs (Bami), clan–heads, etc.,

3)   Anyone who has obtained a considerable gift (such as land or
cattle) from the chief in recognition of service or friendship.

23. The titles of the Barangila are hereditary and those of Baramata
usually go from father to son.   The chief can create new Baramata and if
he wishes to make their titles pass to the next generation he does so by
ordering the ceremony of Kwehonga.

24. Procedure of Kwehonga.   The chief must be informed if a Muramata or
Murangila dies when he sends two men with a shroud.   This is partly to
honour the deceased and partly because the chief deposits property (mostly
cattle) with these people and these messengers go to look after his interests.

As soon as the estate of a Muramata is wound up his children taking
a present, consisting usually of a cow, present themselves to the chief
who gives the Musika a present as a sign that he acknowledges him.   This
belongs to the Musika alone.

25. If there is any question about the inheritance, Baramata or Barangila
relatives go straight to the chief himself.   (See "Administrator", para.
196 et seq.)

26. In the case of Baramata the chief has the right to change the sequence

of heirs and depose the Musika in favour of another heir who thereby becomes Musika of his father's property and inherits his title of Muramata.

L A S T — W I L L. (kulaga = to make a will)

27. The institution of the making of a will is known and widely used.

NOTE: As the most important part of inheritance is land a Muhaya who talks about the provisions of a last will considers primarily the question of disposal of immoveable property. The disposal of moveable property may be included in a will but it may also be disposed of independently.

For separate disposal of moveable property see paras.81 et seq.

Examples of testaments which have been accepted by the Court as legal documents:

D.O's appeal No. 87 of 1936
D.O's   "   "   4/P.1/5 of 1937
D.O's   "   "   1/P 1/36 of 1938.

28. **Form of Will.** A will may be verbal or written.

NOTE: Should a man name in his last will a female as heiress of his immoveable property, even with the consent of the witnesses, such a testament would be considered void.

29. A. Verbal Will. The Testator must express formally before witnesses his last will.

30. B. Written Will. The testament may be written by the testator himself or by someone appointed by him, in which case this person must sign the testament as clerk.

31. **Nomination of Heir.** A testator can choose his heirs, but he must choose them among those who are entitled to inherit.

32. There is one exception to this rule: If a testator can prove that he has been completely neglected by his relatives, he may choose anyone as his heir. (except in Ihangiro and Karagwe.)

IHANGIRO AND KARAGWE. A man must choose his heirs from among his relatives however distant if he disinherits his near relatives.

QUOTATION: D.O's appeal No.102 of 1934.

Nsholo v. Kleofas.
Kabainda disinherited his relatives calling witnesses and declaring his intention. He quoted as his reason that his relatives had completely neglected him during his illness. The witnesses accepted the reason of the testator, who appointed as heir his friend Kleofas, the village headman, a man from another clan who had nursed him during his illness. A last will was made signed by 10 witnesses. It was held that the testament was legal and that Nsholo, a nephew of the deceased had no claim to the inheritance.

33. A man who has no direct descendants may nominate Musika, Mainuka and Kyagati for his property.

NOTE: This is contrary to the rule applicable to a man who dies intestate without direct descendants, when his property is inherited by a sole heir.

34. The man nominated to be Musika is always appointed guardian for widows and daughters.

35. If a man wishes to nominate as Musika or Mainuka a son who does not hold the title by reason of his birth, he may do so provided he can give adequate reason for the change.

QUOTATION: D.O's appeal No.69 of 1935.

Kwekaza v. Kyekuza.
It was held that a testator cannot disinherit a person entitled to inherit without giving sufficient reasons for the change of the rules.

QUOTATION: D.O's appeal No.17 of 1936.

Albert v. Byabato.
Mulumbe, the father of Albert and Byabato made a last will, which had been lost. Byabato, the elder brother, had inherited during his father's lifetime the plantation of his grandfather and Albert stated that the father in his will had nominated him Musika, as the elder brother had already a big plantation. It was held that that would not be an acknowledged reason for disinheritance. The eldest brother must have his share in the father's property. If the father made such a testament he was wrong. If the will was lost, that is as good as no will.

36. If property willed by a man is found on his death to have passed out of his possession, the clause in his will dealing with such property is

void.

37. **Witnesses.** The signatures of the witnesses in a written will constitute legal proof that the reasons for the change were valid.

NOTE: If the Court doubts the authenticity of the witnesses' signature it may adopt the following procedure:

The witnesses are called, separated and asked such questions as : time of day the document was written, name of clerk, kind of paper used for the document, means of writing, pencil or pen. etc.

The contents of the document are not necessarily discussed for fear of collusion between witnesses.

See case 3/P 1/3 of 1939.

38. The number of witnesses is not prescribed if the testament contains no change of the customary sequence of heirs.

39. If the will contains a change of the rule within the family, the testator must call for at least 3 reliable witnesses.

QUOTATION: D.O's appeal No.101 of 1939.

Hermani v. Stanislaus.
The father of these two brothers changed the sequence of heirs in favour of the younger brother Stanislaus. He called four witnesses.

40. Among the witnesses must be the testator's executor (ishento).

QUOTATION: P.C's appeal No.13 of 1934.

Ndyetabura v. Tibaikanya.
The Court decided, that the will not truly signed by witnesses is void.

NOTE: There have been cases in several districts where a man whose family has refused to witness has subsequently made a will witnessed by his chief, Mwami (subchief) or Mkungu (village headman). Such a will is invalid according to customary law and should be not allowed. Legal witnesses to a will have wide powers and represent public opinion watching that common sense and customary law are followed by the testator.

41. If the will contains a change of the rule and disinherits the family, appointing a man outside the family as heir, at least 10 witnesses must be

42. Among these witnesses must be either close relatives of the testator or the head of his clan or ihiga. (Ihiga is a subdivision of a clan. A clan has several mahiga. Each ihiga has its head who has certain duties within his unit.)

QUOTATION: Lukiko Kabale's decision No.8 of 1933.

Kabakaki v. Mutagaywa.
Kabakaki's bloodbrother nominated him as heir although he had a brother Mutagaywa. It was held that this will was void as the testator had not called the necessary number of witnesses. A bloodbrother with regard to inheritance is looked upon as an outsider.

43. The witnesses have to judge whether the testator is in full possession of his mental faculties or not. He must be able to speak clearly.

44. The testator must give an explanation to the witnesses for changing the rules.

45. This explanation and the discussion following it, will suffice as proof for the healthy state of mind of the testator.

46. If the witnesses think that the reasons given by the testator for a change in the rules are not sufficient they are bound to refuse to act as witnesses.

QUOTATION: D.O's appeal No.4/p.1/5 of 1937.

Bibi Mukanyiginya v. Kayungi.
Kailembo had no children. He disliked his relatives. He decided to nominate Kayungi, a friend of his, as heir. He called for the elders of his clan. When he explained to them his intention and the reasons for his decision, they refused to act as witnesses and went away. They thought his reasons for the disinheritance of all members of his family insufficient.

47. If the witnesses acknowledge the reasons for a change of heirs, this acknowledgment is binding. No discussion about those reasons is admissable in Court after the death of the testator.

QUOTATION: D.O's appeal No.102 of 1934.

Nsiima v. Kamuntu.
The judgment of the Provincial Commissioner confirms that a man can by will, legalized by sufficient witnesses who consider his reasons good, bequeath real property outside his circle of inheritance.

Disinheritance. (Kubachwa: disinheritance.   Kuchwa: to disinherit.)

48. Generally the following reasons are acknowledged for disinheritance

A. Assault of a man by his heir presumptive.

B. Sale of a man's cattle by his heir presumptive without his consent.

C. Neglect of a sick man by a presumptive heir, or neglect by an heir of his duties to share his luxuries such as beer, meat etc. with his father.

D. A long journey undertaken by a man's presumptive heir against his wishes.

(Confirmed, see D.O's appeal No.69 of 1935.)

E. General misbehaviour.

F. Illicit relations of a presumptive heir with one of his father's wives.

G. If a presumptive heir files an action in Court against his father.

H. If a presumptive heir transgresses the rules regarding marriage restrictions.

NOTE: Witnesses would not consider differences of opinion on religious matters to be sufficient reason for disinheritance.

49. When a presumptive heir hears that the testator has disinherited him, he can ask either the elders of his clan or the sub-chief as a private individual to try to persuade the testator to revoke his will.   Failing help from such private sources, he may ask for the intervention of the

NOTE: Disinheritance is considered in the same light as a curse, in the case of which also the son has the right to go to Court and ask for help if he thinks that his father treated him unjustly. The Court decides whether the malediction is appropriate to the deed. If not, the elders will try to induce the father to retract his word. As a native will never resist public opinion, the Court has in such cases considerable power.

50. Should it be proved that the heir knew of his disinheritance and undertook no such steps during the lifetime of the testator, he is not entitled to challenge the validity of the will after the testator's death.

QUOTATION: D.O's appeal No.87 of 1936.

Kleofas v. Nsholo.
Nsholo was disinherited by his paternal uncle and Kleofas, a man not belonging to the testator's family, was declared by the testator as his heir. Nsholo lived in the same village as his uncle and therefore the Court assumed that he knew about the disinheritance. As he brought no complaint before, it was held that he had no right to do so after the death of his uncle.

NOTE: It is generally assumed that the disinherited heir must know of his disinheritance. It is in fact usual and considered correct for the witnesses to inform him.

51. <u>Revocation of a Will.</u>

If a will is to be revoked its witnesses or the majority of them must be called and informed of the revocation.

52. Should this not be possible, at least 10 witnesses have to be called to make a valid revocation.

QUOTATION: D.O's appeal 1/P.1/29 of 1937.

Damian v. Magdalena.
Baitwa disinherited his son Damian for certain reasons. He nominated as heir his grandson, a son of his daughter-in-law Magdalena. Damian managed to reconcile his father, who in due course made a second testament, in which he nominated his eldest son Damian as Musika. This testament was signed by 10 persons as witnesses and acknowledged in Court as valid.

Lost Will.

53. If the will has been lost or destroyed, its contents may become legally valid if they are pronounced by the witnesses to the will.

54. This is not admissible if it can be proved that the testator himself destroyed the will.

55. If a will is lost and the witnesses to it are not unanimous as to its contents, outsiders may be called to give their opinions and the verdict of the majority will stand.

56. If a will is lost and cannot be reconstructed by its witnesses the distribution of the property is made according to customary law.

57. Deposit of Testament. If a man names no executor in his testament, the document is usually kept by himself. If the testator names an executor he usually places the document in his care.

58. Registration of Testament. (Kitabu ena wosia). There is a book kept in each Gombolola in which testaments may be entered. This can be done at will.

  NOTE: This book is intended merely as a register and has no effect on the validity or otherwise of the will. However there seems to be a tendency to consider such an entry as proof of validity by itself.

59. The entry is not a necessary condition for the acknowledgment of a testament.

Wishes and Legacies.

60. All wishes expressed in a will, unless they are at variance with the customary law, must be strictly followed, especially those with regard to burial, executor, maintenance of female dependents etc. The fulfilment of such wishes can be claimed in Court.

61. Legacies are paid before debts.

  NOTE: The incumbency on the heirs to pay out legacies before debts are paid, may seem unfair. But it should be remembered that legacies are usually very small sums, probably given for service rendered to the deceased during his last illness.

Disposal of Moveable Property.

62. A man may leave his moveable property as he wishes without restriction.

    ILLUSTRATION: A made a will leaving all his property to his sons B and C. He also left a book of wishes in which he bequeathed his money to his second wife who was childless. The wife received the bequest.

    ILLUSTRATION: A owed B Shs.20/- B stated in his will that A should be excused this debt. His heirs could not therefore demand payment from A.

63. It is not necessary for him to make a formal will to dispose of such property.

64. His unwitnessed signature is all that is necessary.

    NOTE: It is nowadays the custom for a man of any standing to keep a note book in which he enters details of his moveable property and his wishes regarding its disposal after his death. For such wishes to be binding his signature is necessary, but cases are mentioned where it has been dispensed with on account of sudden death, when it has been proved beyond doubt that the book and writing were those of the deceased.

Female Testators.

65. A woman is entitled to dispose of her property by will, with the exception of land that she has inherited.

66. She must nominate her heir among her relatives unless she is married, when an exception is made in favour of her husband.

67. The present form of obuchweke is applicable to a man who dies leaving no paternal relatives and a wife without, or with only female, offspring.

   NOTE: The old form of Obuchweke was that the property of a man who died without direct male descendants reverted to the Chief, together with his widows and daughters. This form of obuchweke still applies to a nyarubanja tenant whose holding reverts to his landlord, when he dies without leaving a direct male descendant. The only difference is that his widows and daughters do not become slaves.

   It is noteworthy that attempts are sometimes made by chiefs to revive this old form of Obuchweke.

QUOTATION: D.O's appeal No.24 of 1934.

Nyabuhoro v. Kalemera.
Chief Kalemera claimed, in an attempt to evoke the rigid form of obuch-weke, the disposition of a plantation of a man who died without sons, but left other paternal relatives. The chief lost the case.

   On the other hand there are also instances of the other extreme when the chiefs denied that any form of obuchweke exists today.

QUOTATION: D.O's appeal No.45 of 1934.
             P.C's appeal No.19 of 1934.

Bibi Bajumuzi v. Kezekia.
The Chief's Court in its judgment No.123 stated: "We cannot allow a renewal of the custom of resumption which has been abolished."

   Theoretically under the present day form there should be extremely few cases of obuchweke. These few being confined to strangers who have settled in Uhaya. In fact this is not the case because the chiefs, by virtue of their power, in every case where only distant relatives claim inheritance, try to refuse their claims. By distant relatives is meant people who claim by reason of being members of the same clan.

68. The property of a man who dies obuchweke reverts to the chief.

69. In districts where the bisisi custom (see para. 186 et seq.) is acknowledged, the bisisi son of a deceased who died obuchweke is entitled to inherit his bisisi father's plantation. If the plantation has al-

ready been re-allocated by the chief the present owner must give it up.

70. The chief has no duty of maintenance towards the widows and daughters of a man whose plantation has reverted to him.

71. The brideprice for the daughters is received by their mother.

72. Obuchweke refers only to immoveable property. The moveable property is inherited by the daughters; the mother is the guardian if the daughters are under age.

73. Attempts of a man to evade the custom of obuchweke by adopting a son or by nominating an uterine relative as heir by will are illegal.

QUOTATION: D.O's appeal No.41 of 1933.

Kapiga v. Barongo.
A testator nominated his uterine grandson as his heir, in order to evade obuchweke. It was held that the grandson Kapia could not be nominated heir because he was outside the circle of inheritance of his grand-father

DIVISION OF PROPERTY.

NOTE: This chapter deals with the property of a man who dies intestate.

For rights of disposal by will see chapter "Last Will" para.27 et seq.

LAND

74. The inheritance law does not allow an equal distribution of the property of the deceased among the heirs.

75. The principle of the division of land is that the Musika shall inherit enough land to provide him and his family with a livelihood. The interests of the other heirs are a very secondary consideration. If the father's plantation is not capable of maintaining more than one family the Mainuka and younger brothers are only entitled to receive nominal shares in it. If the father's plantation is big enough to give each of his sons a piece of land the limits of their individual shares are approximately fixed so that:

The Musika receives three parts of the whole, including the nyumba nyaruju (the big house) i.e. the house occupied by the deceased;
The Mainuka receives two parts of the whole;

The Kyagati each receive one part of the whole.

NOTE: In practice distribution is affected by many different circumstances, for instance in the case of one of the lesser heirs having a large family, he may be granted a larger share than is really his just due; or should a father have provided a plantation for each of his sons, each one will receive a property irrespective of the ratio.

76. It may happen that after division the plots are too small to maintain the respective owners and their families (except the Musika). This will not affect the manner of the division, but later negotiations may take place between the heirs.

77. Any heir who wishes to do so may offer to buy out his co-heirs and take over their shares either wholly or in part.

78. Conversely, any heir who wishes to do so may sell his share. He has in the first instance to offer it for sale to his co-heirs, and then if they refuse to buy it, he is at liberty to dispose of it to any bidder.

79. If any transaction with the land has been performed and the other heirs have not been informed, they have the right to invalidate such a transaction by filing an action against the seller or the buyer. (see para. 561 et seq.)

80. The seller must return and the buyer accept the earnest money. The buyer must then return the sold portion of the land.

CROPS.

81. Crops in the fields and in store with the exception of bananas and coffee are inherited in equal shares by the Musika and the wives of the deceased. Each wife receives as her share half that part of the harvest actually grown in her part of the plantation of the deceased.

NOTE: During her husband's lifetime each of his wives is given a portion of his plantation, the cultivation of which is her responsibility.

LIVESTOCK

82. The distribution of inherited livestock differs in the different Chiefdoms thus :—

82. A. A man dies leaving sons and daughters.

1. KIANJA, MARUKU, KIAMTWARA, KIZIBA, BUGABO. The livestock is distributed among sons in the same proportions as land. Of the daughters the Kusikekishasi only is entitled to a share.

83. 2. IHANGIRO, MISSENYI, KARAGWE. The livestock is distributed among all children, male and female. Among the sons the distribution is as with land. Among daughters the Kusikekishasi gets a larger share than the others, whose share is very small.

84. The Kusikekishasi is in all districts except Ihangiro entitled to 1 head of cattle if the herd numbers more than ten.

85. If the deceased had among his herd cattle or goats which he received as brideprice for daughters, the full brothers of these daughters inherit such animals and their progeny.

86. B. A man dies leaving daughters only.

The livestock is distributed between his heir and his daughters in the following proportions :—

86. 1. BUGABO, KIANJA, MARUKU, MISSENYE, KIAMTWARA, IHANGIRO. All livestock goes to the daughters.

87. 2. KIZIBA. The livestock is divided approximately in the proportion of seven to the heir and three to the daughters, unless the heir is a distant relative when the more distant his relationship the smaller his share.

88. 3. KARAGWE. The livestock is divided in the proportion of six to the heir and four to the daughters.

89. C. <u>A man dies childless</u>.

If his half—brother is his heir his full sister receives a share of the livestock, the proportion being seven parts to the heir and three parts to the sister. Otherwise full brothers and full sisters are treated like sons and daughters.

90. D. <u>A man dies obuchweke</u>.

If he leaves daughters all his livestock is divided among them. If he leaves no children it reverts to the chief.

MONEY.

91. The Kusikekishasi receives customarily a share of the money amounting to about Shs.5 to Shs.20 according to the size of the estate (except in Ihangiro). If there is no money to pay her immediately she receives her share out of the proceeds of the next harvest.

92. A. <u>A man dies leaving sons and daughters</u>.

1. IHANGIRO, KARAGWE, MISSENYI. All children share in the money, the shares of the daughters being decided by the Musika.

93. 2. ALL OTHER CHIEFDOMS. Except for the Kusikekishasi, the daughters are entitled to no share.

94. B. <u>A man dies leaving daughters only</u>.

1. KARAGWE, MISSENYI. The money is shared between the daughters and heir.

95. 2. ALL OTHER CHIEFDOMS. The daughters receive and share all the

24
money.

96. C. <u>A man dies leaving no children.</u>
His heir receives all the money.

97. D. <u>A man dies obuchweke without daughters.</u>

His wife receives all the money.

COFFEE IN STORE.

98. This is distributed among the male heirs.

TOOLS.

99. The Musika receives the greater number, especially any tools or arms which were personally used by the deceased. If any are left after he has taken his share, they are divided between the other male heirs.

CLOTH.

100. Cloth is distributed equally among the male heirs.

SONLESS WIDOWS.

101. Widows of the deceased are inherited by the Musika only and only with their consent.

NOTE: If Musika and widow agree, one of the minor heirs may be chosen to take her as his wife.

102. Should they refuse to be inherited they return to their families who are liable for the return of their brideprices.

NOTE: The Chief's Council proposed on 16th May 1939 that a rule be made that sonless widows should have the option of returning to their families or staying with the heir. Further that under no circumstances can an heir claim repayment of the brideprice.

Ref. letter No.126/35 contained in file No.275.

103. Wishes expressed by will with regard to maintenance of female dependants (before witnesses) must be observed by heirs and the former can claim in Court fulfilment of such wishes.

104. The rights of the Musika towards childless widows and those with female children only, vary in different districts.

105. IHANGIRO. The Musika inherits full rights of disposition over his father's widows. Therefore he can, if he wishes, return them to their fathers and demand repayment of their brideprices, irrespective of the length of time that they have been married to the deceased.

106. If the widows have daughters, these are not returned with them, but remain with the Musika, except when they are small, when they go with their respective mothers until the age of 3 to 4 years.

107. In practice the women automatically leave their husband's house on his death unless specifically told otherwise by the Musika.

108. MARUKU. This district makes a difference between a Musika who is a son and a Musika who is another relative.

109 A son alone has the right to return his father's widows, while it is the duty of any other relative inheriting to provide for their maintenance.

110 KIAMTWARA, BUGABO, KIZIBA. The Musika has the right to decide whether he will inherit any or all of the widows. He can reclaim the brideprice of a widow whom he returns.

111 KARAGWE. If the son is the Musika he cannot inherit his father's sonless widows. They are inherited by the deceased's brothers, failing whom they have to return to their own families who must repay their brideprice to the Musika.

If the Musika is a child.

112. IHANGIRO. The widows may remain on the estate as the Musika's wives.

113. If they do not wish to stay, the brideprice will be claimed by the heir when he comes into his inheritance.

114. ALL OTHER CHIEFDOMS. The mother of the Musika has the right to send away the widows or to tell them to stay.

115. If she returns them to their respective families, the guardian of the Musika must claim the repayment of brideprice immediately.

GENERAL.

116. A widow whom a Musika keeps holds the status of his legal wife and he cannot later return her to her family, unless he files a suit of divorce against her.

117. Daughters always remain with the Musika.

(For rules relating to reimbursement of brideprice see para. 295 et seq.; maintenance see para. 260 et seq; ex-slaves and their descendants see para. 335 et seq.)

ASSETS AND LIABILITIES.

General Rules

118. While a man's body is lying in his house awaiting burial his administrator (ishento) as far as possible claims assets outstanding and acknowledges debts outstanding.

119. The acknowledgment of these assets and liabilities by the persons concerned is considered binding.

120. There is no time limit for the presentation of their claims by creditors to the estate or vice versa.

121. Claims should be presented during the three months interim between the death of a man and the distribution of his estate, but a claim which comes in after this time cannot be disputed on the grounds that it is now too late. (cf. proverb 'Eibanja tilyunda' a debt cannot rot).

122. When the assets in hand are greater than the liabilities the latter are paid before the estate is distributed.

123. Both claims and debts are inheritable.

124. <u>Collection of assets outstanding.</u> Assets due to the estate after the distribution of property are distributed among the heirs in the customary manner, the Musika receiving the greater part, the Mainuka and lesser heirs receiving proportionately.

> ILLUSTRATION: After the winding up of an estate there remained to be collected outstanding assets to the value of Shs. 150/=, which were divided among the three heirs. The Musika received the right to collect Shs. 75/=, The Mainuka received the right to collect Shs. 50/=, The Kyagati received the right to collect Shs. 25/=. Each was responsible for collecting his own debts.

125. Such assets may be divided among the heirs at the distribution of the property, in which case it is the duty of the heir to whom a credit has been alloted, himself to collect his dues from the debtor in question.

126. <u>Repayment of Debts.</u> Debts acknowledged before distribution are repaid from the assets, which are used in the following order :—

> 1. Money in cash,
>
> 2. Coffee in store,
>
> 3. All claims either paid or outstanding,
>
> 4. Cattle,
>
> 5. Land.

127. Cloth, food stores and tools cannot be forcibly sold to repay debts.

128. If, after everything possible has been sold, debts still remain, the Musika, if he is a son, is responsible for them.

129. Debts which are acknowledged but not repaid before distribution are distributed among the heirs in the same way as are outstanding assets, provided that the total debts are less than the total assets.

130. Debts acknowledged after distribution of the estate are the liability of the Musika alone.

> ILLUSTRATION: after the winding up of an estate there remained debts to be paid off to the value of Shs. 96/=.

Assets to be collected amounted to Shs. 150/=.

Debts and assets were divided among the heirs thus:

The Musika inherited assets Shs. 75/=, and debts Shs. 48/=
The Mainuka   "   "   " 50/=, "   "   " 32/=
The Kyagati   "   "   " 25/=, "   "   " 16/=

Each was responsible for the collection of his assets and the payment of his debts.

131. Creditors who first present their claims are paid first.

132. When several claims are presented together, debts first contracted take priority.

As many debts as possible are paid and every debt is paid in full. The estate cannot be distributed pro rata among the creditors.

133. Business obligations. If the deceased was part owner of a business, his heirs cannot claim from his partner the capital put into the business by the deceased, but they inherit his assets and liabilities in the firm at the time of his death.

G I F T S.

134. A gift of land made by a father to an heir at any time prior to his death is counted in with his real property and after his death it must be divided among his sons.

> NOTE: Gifts of landed property which is under family tenure to persons who are not entitled to the inheritance of this real property are not legal. A father is therefore not allowed to make his wife or daughter or a friend etc. a gift of real property. Such a gift would not be acknowledged after his death, even if it should be confirmed in a last will or by witnesses (see para 31).

135. At such time the Musika has the right to decide whether he will take over the father's plantation or the plot that was given him.

136. The decision of the Musika is irrevocable.

137. Other presents made during lifetime are not counted in with the estate.

138. An exception is made in the case when the Musika has received as a gift Shs. 100/= or a cow for brideprice from his father. If the father dies and leaves enough money or cattle and one or more unmarried sons, one hundred shillings each must be handed over to the guardians of the unmarried sons to be kept until they have to pay brideprice.

138a. If a father makes gifts of land which is under family tenure or cattle to his sons, wives or daughters they are only considered the property of the recipients if presented formally before witnesses. If the gift is land the father must appoint a mutaya. If the gift is a cow see "kuhela kimoi" para 763 et seq.

STATUS OF CHILDREN.

139. As a rule no difference is made in the treatment of the children of a household whatever may be the reason for their membership.

LEGITIMATE CHILDREN

140. Children born in wedlock belong under all circumstances to their father and are his heirs.

STEP-CHILDREN.

141. Children of a women's first husband are usually left with their father or his family if, after his death or her divorce from him, she remarries. (For exceptions in cases of divorce see paras. 490 & 491.)

142. Such children can under no circumstances inherit any property from their step-father.

143. A step-father can never nominate such a child as his heir, even if he has no children of his own.

144. Such a child inherits property from his father and his father's family.

CHILDREN OF UNMARRIED WIDOWS.

The chiefdoms differ in their rulings.

IHANGIRO, MARUKU, KARAGWE.

145. 1. If the mother leaves her son's plantation and bears children. The first child is 'bisisi;

146. The second and following children belong to their father and he is not liable to pay compensation for them.

147. 2. If the mother bears children in the house of her deceased husband, the first child is 'bisisi;

149. For following children compensation must be paid by the father thus: Each male child — 1 bull or Shs. 30/=; each female child— 2 goats

or Shs. 20/=.

150. If the father does not pay the compensation, he can be sued in Court, but the children belong in any case to him.

BUGABO, KIAMTWARA, KIANJA.

151. <u>If an unmarried widow bears children whether in her deceased husband's house or away</u>, the first child is 'bisisi'; for each following child compensation must be paid thus: For a male child — Shs.20/=; for a female child — Shs.30/=.

152. If this compensation is not paid, the children belong to their father, but the Musika of the woman's first husband receives the bride-price for the daughters.

153. If a man pays compensation on his second child he need not pay on any further children. If however he neglects to do so until after the birth of a third child he must pay then on both these children and so on ad infinitum; but once he has paid on the number of children he has, he need pay on no future ones.

KIZIBA.

154. The father has to pay Shs. 30/= compensation for each child.

155. If the father does not pay the compensation, the children belong in any case to him, but the bride-price for daughters is received by the Musika of the woman's first husband.

QUOTATION: D.O's appeal No.3/P.1./10 of 1937.

Kawa v. Majerege.
A man died and left his widow with one son Majerege. After his death the widow had 3 children, one male Kawa and 2 females, by a man to whom she was not married. This man never paid any brideprice and the widow remained all the time on the estate of her deceased husband. When the elder daughter married, the two half-brothers, Kawa and Majerege started a law suit to decide which of them was entitled to receive brideprice. It was held in Court that as the father had not paid any compensation on the children, Majerege was entitled to his half-sister's brideprice.

156. KIZIBA, MISSENYI. All children belong to the woman's present husband.

157. ALL OTHER DISTRICTS. The first child of the marriage is mwana wa bisisi of the woman's deceased husband.

ILLEGITIMATE CHILD. (Mwana wa Luhoire).

158. A 'mwana wa luhoire' is the child of an unmarried girl, or a child born after marriage but at such a time that it would be impossible for the husband to be the father.

Mwana wa luhoire of an unmarried girl.

159. 1. If no one admits paternity. If the mother names a man as the father of her child, but cannot prove it, and the man refuses to acknowledge paternity, his refusal must be accepted.

160. However even in this case the child follows the taboo of this man. (The child cannot follow his mother's taboo as this would indicate incest).

161. If the mwana wa luhoire is a girl her brideprice is received by the mother or her relatives.

162. If several men are concerned, the mother names the first man to have intercourse with her and he is recognised as the father.

163. If the mother of the mwana wa luhoire subsequently marries her father receives such brideprice as is paid for a widow or divorcee.

164. 2. If a man admits paternity. The woman or her father can claim compensation:

165. a) If the girl is already betrothed: The seducer must pay to her father the amount of her brideprice as well as compensation and a fine. The amount is decided by the Court.

166. This payment of brideprice and fine does not mean that the girl be—

comes his wife.   If he wishes to marry her he has to pay   brideprice a
second time.

167. b) If the girl is not already betrothed: The   seducer   must   pay
Shs. 100/= compensation to her father.   If he wishes to marry her he
must arrange a separate brideprice with her father in the usual way.

168. Status of Mwana wa Luhoire.   A mwana wa luhoire is legal heir   to
his father.

169.   If the father has legitimate sons the mwana wa luhoire is one of
the minor heirs (Kyagati).   If the father has only one legitimate son
the mwana wa luhoire is Mainuka.   If the father has no legitimate sons
the mwana wa luhoire is sole heir.

QUOTATION: D.O's appeal No.78 of 1933.
            P.C's Revisional order No.1.

Ali v. Kyabalile.
Bibi Kyabalile's son John inherited from his mother's husband Byontamanyile, living in the latter's house as legitimate child. A few years
later a man Kashambwa declared before his death that John was his child
and that John had lived all the years in Byontamanyile's house as mwana
wa luhoire.   John's mother agreed and Kashambwa declared John as heir.
Thus John had the inheritance of two "fathers".   This being contrary
to all Haya custom John had to return Ali Byontamanyile's inheritance.

170. Marriage of a mother of a mwana wa luhoire.   If the mother of a
mwana wa luhoire marries, her father receives such brideprice as is paid
for a widow or divorcee.

171.   If she takes her mwana wa luhoire with her to her husband's house
the child is called mwana wa kishenshe.   Such a child has no right to
inherit from his step-father, even if there are no children of the marriage
nor can his step-father nominate him by will as his heir.

NOTE: Kishenshe is the old fashioned grass skirt of a woman, i.e. the
child is not any more in arms but follows Kishenshe. All children of
a mother in the house but not belonging to the husband are called
'mwana wa kishenshe'.

34

172. <u>A mwana wa luhoire born after marriage.</u> A husband has the right to file a suit of divorce because he can prove that his wife was pregnant when she married.

173. If he does not file a suit but allows his wife and her mwana wa luhoire to stay, his decision is not binding. He may at any later time send the child to its father or paternal relatives.

QUOTATION: Appeal No.95 of 1938. Lukiko Kalema.

174. If the mother takes the mwana wa luhoire to its father, who accepts it, without her husband's permission, the husband may, if he wishes, accuse the father of kidnapping another man's child for which he is liable to a fine.

175. It is acknowledged however that such proceedings by the husband would in no way prejudice his case if later, he changes his mind and decides to return the child to its family.

176. <u>Father's rights over a mwana wa luhoire.</u> A man can claim a child as mwana wa luhoire.

177. If a man claims a mwana wa luhoire and his claim is acknowledged, he has full rights over it and if it is a girl he receives her brideprice, even if he paid no compensation. (except in Kiziba.)

177. KIZIBA. The father must pay at least Shs. 30/= compensation to the father of the mother of the mwana wa luhoire, otherwise the brideprice for such a child will be received by its maternal relatives.

178. <u>Compensation for a mwana wa luhoire.</u> The father of the mother of a mwana wa luhoire can claim compensation.

179. If the husband of the mother of such a child does not file a divorce suit, the seducer must pay compensation which includes mbuzi ya ngozi and biabazaza (see para. 192).

180. If the husband files a divorce suit the seducer must pay the full brideprice as compensation and a fine. If he wants to marry the divorcee

he must pay a separate brideprice.

ADOPTED SON.

181. A man can adopt a child as his son.

NOTE: If a man wants to adopt a child who is not his heir presumptive he must call witnesses and explain to them the reasons why he has changed the customary sequence. If the witnesses do not consider his his reasons sufficient they refuse to act, as in the case of a will The heir presumptive can take the initiative and call elders to examine the reasons for the man's choice. If the elders definitely decide that the man's reasons are insufficient and he refuses to give up his adopted son, they will declare that he can do what he likes during his lifetime, but when he dies the adopted son will not be allowed to be Musika to his land.

182. He is bound in his choice by the same rules as those regulating his choice of heirs by will. (see para.31.)

183. An adopted son has no rights if a natural son is born later.

184. He must also leave his adopted father's property, if he has inherited it, when a real son who has been absent, returns and claims his rights to inherit, unless the father has by will disinherited his true son.

MWANA WA KIZARWA.   (KIZIBA).

185. A mwana wa kizarwa is a child who is conceived during the absence of the husband.   He can never become neir to the husband of his mother, but can become heir to the property of his true father.   (See para.424, et seq. "Absentee husband.")

MWANA WA BISISI.

(All districts except Kiziba, Karagwe and Missenyi).

186.   Mwana wa bisisi is a child acknowledged under certain conditions to be the offspring of a man who is not his father.

NOTE: Pressure of superstitious fear governs the adherence to bisisi custom.   This pressure is at present strong enough to ensure its rules being generally observed, but if fear is absent there is nothing to make it incumbent on anyone to follow them. As superstition decreases so will bisisi custom tend to disappear. Already there are a few cases on record where a husband has refused to allow a child to be presented as mwana wa bisisi to its bisisi father, but has filed a claim of adultery against him.

Judgments also have been given in which the judges refuse to recognise the rules of bisisi.

QUOTATION: D.O's appeal 101 of 1934.
D.O's "   37 of 1935.

Both these judgments are in direct contradiction to QUOTATION: D.O's appeal 43 of 1935.

The fact that bisisi is now sometimes denied by native judgments can lead to the use of this denial in cases where a man dies leaving his wife pregnant.   An heir who does not want a co-heir may try to declare his posthumous brother as not the son of his father and there-fore not entitled to share in the inheritance.

QUOTATION: D.O's appeal No.4/P 1/11 of 1937.

Bibi Kristina v. Paulo.
Paulo filed a case against his mother Kristina stating that Theonesti, the second son of Kristina, was the child of another man, born after the death of his father.   It was held that Paulo could not prove that Theonesti was born at such a time that Paulo's father could not have been his father.

NOTE: A parallel to bisisi is to be found in Sheik Ali bin Hemedi el Buhuri's "MIRATHI", a handbook of the Mahomedan law, in which it is stated with regard to a bequest to a child conceived but unborn that such a bequest is valid providing that the child is born not later than 4 years from the date of the bequest,because "a child cannot remain in the womb of the mother for more than 4 years in the ordinary way". Translation by P.E. Mitchell.

Situations in which bisisi custom comes into force.

187. a.) If a woman has illegitimate intercourse before her marriage but after puberty, the first child born after her marriage is the mwana wa bisisi of the first man to have intercourse with her.

b.) On the day of the birth of a child, a man who has obtained access to the mother can, if he goes through the action of touching her pudenda with his penis, make her next child his mwana wa bisisi.

c.) Following the birth of a child if a married woman sleeps with another man before her husband, her next child is bisisi.

NOTE: To avoid the consequences of paragraph b and c above it is customary for a husband to perform a ceremony of nominal intercourse with his wife immediately after child-birth.

QUOTATION: D.O's appeal No.37 of 1935.

Aloys v. Mumbeija.
See evidence given by witness Kalikwenda and bibi Itanisa.

d.) Following the birth of a child any man who urinates in a stream above the place where a mother is performing her ritual post-natal ablutions and then declares himself may be acknowledged as father bisisi of the next child.

e.) The first child born after divorce is mwana wa bisisi to the mother's ex-husband whether she is remarried or not.

f.) If a man dies his wife's first child born, in or out of wedlock, after his death is his mwana wa bisisi.

g.) If a husband is absent for any length of time and did not leave his wife pregnant, the first child born in his absence is his mwana wa bisisi.

188. If a bisisi child miscarries or dies at birth the next child is not bisisi.

189. Procedure for declaring a child bisisi. A bisisi father cannot claim his bisisi child during his life. However if the mother does not bring it to him according to custom he will probably spread it about that the child is his hoping to induce the mother when she hears the rumours, to bring it.

His other course is to tell his relatives that it belongs to him and in his will, claim it as his heir.

NOTE: The mother of a mwana wa bisisi will usually for reasons of superstitious fear take the child to its bisisi father. She need not necessarily take it at once. She may perhaps wait, if it is her first child,

38

until she has others, to avoid trouble with her husband, or until she attributes some ill luck which befalls her family to the fact that she did not confess the child to be bisisi. She may wait until the bisisi father's death, when even if he has not informed his relatives of its existence, they will probably acknowledge the child on superstitious grounds.

190. It is necessary before a child is acknowledged mwana wa bisisi for a man to admit that he is its bisisi father.

191. A man may refuse to acknowledge a child as his mwana wa bisisi in which case, unless its mother's husband tacitly acknowledges the child as his own, it is handed over to her relatives. In the latter case the child would become a member of the clan of the man nominated as bisisi father.

192. If a child is brought to its bisisi father, or after his death to his heirs, the husband of the mother of the mwana wa bisisi can claim the sum of Shs. 10/= called mbuzi ya ngozi (formerly it was a goat) as a present for bringing the child and a further Shs. 8/= called biabazaza as refund of expenses connected with its birth.

193. <u>Status of a mwana wa bisisi.</u> A mwana wa bisisi is the Musika of his bisisi father if the father has no other sons, and as such he may dispossess any heir rightfully installed before his appearance.

QUOTATION: D.O's appeal No.43 of 1935.

Kakyaija v. Maskini.
Igabundi bequeathed his property to his brother Maskini instructing him that if his wife should give birth to a male child he should become his heir according to the custom of bisisi. Maskini took over his brother's plantation giving up at the same time his own land. After a few years Igabundi's wife gave birth to Kakyaija. First she for her son and later her son himself claimed the whole plantation from Maskini. It was held that Maskini must return the plantation to Kakyaija, although he had given up his own plantation on account of the inheritance.

NOTE: The social position of children who are not legitimate.

Whether a mwana wa luhoire or mwana wa bisisi is acknowledged or denied by its father makes no difference to its treatment in the house in which such a child lives. On the other hand, however, should anyone, and especially a member of the family, use mwana wa luhoire or mwana wa bisisi as a term of contempt it would be taken by the person concerned as a deep insult. This is brought out by the words of a chief who said on this subject:

"In every hut a fire burns all the time. The roof of the hut is made of grass and if a flame catches the roof, the whole hut is burnt down."

This proved by the following case:

QUOTATION: Criminal Session Case 42 of 1939.

Rex v. Ngarazi.
When Ngarazi reached the age of about 20 years, his mother went to Kishunju and declared that Ngarazi was his mwana wa bisisi. Kishunju admitted paternity. Ngarazi gave up the small inheritance he had received after the death of his mother's husband and was given by Kishunju a plantation to live in. Kishunju had two wives, one of whom had 3 children by him. It seemed that Ngarazi developed an inferiority complex on account of otherwise unimportant events in the house. A hate grew in him which at last led to the murder of Kishunju's wife and her 3 children after a domestic controversy.

194. If the bisisi father has other sons, the legitimate sons are his main heirs irrespective of age and the bisisi child takes the place of a minor heir (Kyagati).

195. If a child is acknowledged mwana wa bisisi he has no claim to inherit anything from his mother's husband, and if he has already inherited from him he must give up his share. (For status of mwana wa bisisi in the case of obuchweke, see para.69).

QUOTATION: D.O's appeal No.3/P 1/39 of 1937.

Omari v. Ali.
There existed in a family the suspicion that the eldest son was actually the son of another man, but as the father was content to take no action, the matter did not arise. Several years later a man in the village became ill, called for the son and his mother and declared him before witnesses to be his mwana wa bisisi. He had no other children and claimed him as his heir. Some years before, the son had inherited the property of his father and thus as heir would become possessed of the property of two men of different clans, which is against the law. It was therefore held that he must give up the inheritance he had already received and take over that of his bisisi father.

NOTE: If a nyarubanja holder (mtwazi) acknowledges a mwana wa bisisi of his tenant (mtwarwa), the mwana wa bisisi inherits the tenants plantation, if he has no other sons.

QUOTATION: Chiefs' Appeal No.75 of 1938.

Banyenza v. Mwami Rugumamu.
Tirubaza, the father of Banyenza, was a mtwarwa of the Mwami. Banyenza was not his natural child but his mwana wa bisisi.   Tirubaza informed his mtwazi of this fact offering him one goat, which Rugumamu accepted. After Tirubaza's death Rugumamu refused Banyenza as heir.   The Court held that Banyenza was the rightful heir, (The Court remarked at the same time, that it would not discuss the custom of bisisi.) because Rugumamu had before the death of Tirubaza agreed that Banyenza was the son and heir of Tirubaza.

NOTE: The word 'Kisisi' (plural, bisisi) means a piece of charred wood which has been burned in the fire and gone cold; the inference being that if the fire is relighted it will be the first log to catch fire.

TWINS.   (Barongo)

Nomenclature.
195a.   The name given to the first born-twin is Ishengoma or Kakuru; that given to the other twin is Kato.

The names of children born after twins are affected:

The first male child after twins is called : Kaiza, Lwiza, Ngaiza or Kiiza; the first female child is called Nyamwiza; the next male is called Charuzi; the next female is called Mkabaruzi; the next male is called Kamara.

195b.   It is stated that twins have never been killed at birth except by the Bankango Clan (who perhaps brought this custom from Uzinza). The birth of twins is the occasion of many ceremonies. All parents of twins are members of a society called "kujeba barongo" (the dance of the twins.)

RULES.

195c.   The mother's family must supply a complete new household equipment, hoes, baskets, cooking pots, bark cloth etc.

Neither parent of the twins may enter the maternal grandfather's house until the father has paid him a sum of Shs.8/= to Shs.12/= called makula, when a ceremonial entrance is effected by the twins' mother.

If the mother's brideprice has not yet been fully paid the husband must complete payment on the day of the twins' birth. If he cannot find the money himself, his family lend it to him.

If he does not pay up one of his daughters becomes the property of her maternal grandfather who receives her brideprice.

ADMINISTRATOR. (Ishento)

APPOINTMENT OF ADMINISTRATOR

196. When a man dies it is the duty of his nearest relatives to come to his house. (See also para.22 et seq. re estates of Barangila and Baramata.)

197. If a man dies suddenly and his relatives are not near at hand, the village headman will immediately appoint a blood-brother of the deceased to bury him and to look after his property until relatives arrive, or failing a blood-brother the Native Authority buries him and takes charge of his property.

197. It is the right of the eldest brother to act as administrator. If there is no brother, or he is for some reason incapacitated from acting, the assembled relatives will choose from among them the one most capable of carrying out these duties.

198. If no paternal relatives exist, a blood-brother may be appointed as administrator. Otherwise the Native Authority (Mwami) appoints a reliable elder as administrator; but the claims of a very distant paternal relative are preferred before an outsider is appointed.

DUTIES OF ADMINISTRATOR.

199. The administrator must immediately make an inventory of the property of the deceased in the presence of two relatives as witnesses.

200. The property of the deceased is vested in the administrator as soon as this inventory is made and his responsibility lasts until the property is distributed.

QUOTATION: D.O's appeal No.27 of 1933.

Mugula v. Lyagoba.
Mugula was appointed administrator of the property of Ibrahim. When Ibrahim died he left a book which showed that two head of cattle were in the care of Lyagoba. Lyagoba refused to show these cattle to Mugula. 1 cow died and Lyagoba informed the son and father of Ibrahim, but not Mugula, who afterwards sued Lyagoba for two head of cattle. It was held that all property of the deceased is vested in the administrator,

and that Lyagoba should have informed Mugula and not the son and father of the deceased.

201. The property is distributed after three months.

(In Ihangiro and Karagwe the period is usually shorter.)

NOTE: The lapse of three months is insisted upon so that heirs who live at a distance have time to arrive before the distribution of the inheritance and further so that all claims and debts can be presented.

202. Nobody is entitled before this time to claim any payment of his share.

203. The distribution of the property by the administrator is not looked upon as final.

QUOTATION: D.O's appeal No.10 of 1938.

Lauriani v. Lugeyamba.
These men were brothers. Their father's property was distributed by the clan elders. Lugeyamba, the Mainuka, was not satisfied and filed a suit for re-distribution, which was granted.

204. Any heir may ask for a redistribution within a reasonable time, if he is dissatisfied.

He has two possible ways of procuring this:

a.) He can invoke the help of his Mkungu, Mwami or Omukama (village headman, sub-chief or chief.) as private arbitrators, in which case two elders are usually sent to make the new distribution.

b.) He can take action in Court against the administrator, in which case if it is proved that the administrator failed in his duty he will be made to pay the Court fees and a redistribution will be ordered.

QUOTATION: D.O's appeal No.1/P 1/15 of 1937.

Bibi Kokulamuka v. Lwilemera.
Kokulamuka filed a suit against Lwilemera, the Musika, in the interest of her son Theodor a minor, the Mainuka; the heirs were half-brothers She stated that the Musika received too big a share in proportion to that of her son. The Musika inherited 22 tenants and the Mainuka only 3. It was held that a redistribution should be granted.

205. The administrator has no claim to any compensation for his work except in Kiziba, Karagwe and Ihangiro.

206. KIZIBA, KARAGWE, IHANGIRO. The administrator has the right to claim a share of the moveable property in payment of his service. His share is called obusikisa and the amount is not fixed, but is in proportion to the size of the property.

> EXPLANATION: If there are 20 head of cattle for division the administrator may take one head.   If there are several wives left, he may take one.   If there are Shs.70/= left he may take Shs.10/= unless there are many children in which case he receives only Shs.5/=.   If there are only Shs.20/= left he gets Shs.1/=.

207. The administrator himself proposes the amount he may take on the day of distribution and the next of kin present consider his claim. He has no claim for any share of the real property.

208. In districts where the administrator is entitled to no reward for his service he is always an adult, but in Kiziba, Karagwe and Ihangiro, where he receives payment, a minor may become administrator. He will be represented by an adult relative, but the fees are due to him.

209. The administrator has the right with the consent of the Musika to take some money or a goat or a head of cattle from the estate for the entertainment of guests during the period of mourning. He has to prove that anything he takes is spent for this purpose. He can spend whatever he thinks necessary provided that he can account for his expenditure.

E X E C U T O R.   (Musigire. Karagwe: Mulagwa.)

210. The testator has the right to appoint by will any person he likes as executor.   This person need not belong to his family.

211. The property of a testator is vested in the executor as soon as the testament is made known and the executor installed.

212. If an executor dies before he has wound up an estate either the Chief or the family appoints a new executor.

213. If the executor appointed in the will is not present in the district at the time of the death, some one will be appointed by the Native Authority to take over the administration under the control of the N.A. until the return of the executor.

 NOTE: As it is clear from the fact that the testator has appointed an outsider executor that he did not wish his family to undertake this duty, no one of his relatives will be appointed by the N.A. to act for the absent executor.

214. If at the expiration of the usual time after the death of the test-ator and before distribution, the executor appointed in the will is still absent from the district, the person who has been put in temporarily under the N.A. will conclude the executor's duties.

215. For the rest the rules referring to administrators are to be applied with regard to the executor.

GUARDIANSHIP. (Musika Kulinda or Mlinzi.)

216. A male guardian is appointed:

    1. If the deceased leaves heirs under age.

    2. If a person entitled to inherit is absent.

    3. If a deceased leaves only female dependents.

(NOTE: As the Haya name for all persons who are in charge of property and wards is the same, we adopted the word "guardian" instead of differentiating between guardian and trustee.)

1. IF THE DECEASED LEAVES HEIRS UNDER AGE.

217. In cases where a man dies intestate or leaves no instructions in his will, if the heirs are all children of one mother, two guardians are appointed:

    1. The mother

    2. A male guardian.

218. If the heirs are children of different mothers, the guardians for each heir are

    1. His own mother

    2. A male guardian.

RIGHTS AND DUTIES OF THE GUARDIANS.

219. If a man leaves a widow with male children under age, she remains on the estate and is virtually responsible for its administration; even a divorced wife, unless she has remarried, usually returns. The male guardian for the children is more an advisor in decisions concerned with husbandry and field work. He occasionally receives gifts from the mother which are customary but not his legal due.

NOTE: The relationship between mother and guardian differs slightly in different districts. In Ihangiro the rights of the mother are strongest and in Karagwe they are extremely restricted, other districts ranging between these extremes.

ALL DISTRICTS (except Karagwe.)

220. The mother has full control of the proceeds accruing from the sale of produce including coffee.

NOTE: Should a mother be unable to continue guardianship (through re-marriage or death) her male co-guardian becomes sole guardian, while if a male guardian should die another male co-guardian will be appointed.

221. No heir can demand a statement of accounts of the monetary income during his minority, because he does not have to pay compensation to the guardian for his work and it is acknowledged that if an heir claims an account the guardian could make a counter claim for a salary.

QUOTATION: D.O's appeal No.30 of 1933.

Mujwanzi v. Rutakeburwa.
Mujwanzi administered as guardian Tutakeburwa's estate for 15 years during the latter's minority. The ward claimed in Court Sh.1162/= being the income during Mujwanzi's guardianship. The lower Courts awarded Mujwanzi Sh.1800 as wages at Sh 10 per month for 15 years. Thus Ruta-keburwa's claim was lower than that of Mujwanzi's. On appeal the parties were given one month to settle it between themselves, after which time neither appeared.

222. A guardian cannot legally claim compensation for any of his work, if he is not formally granted the right to do so according to para.221.

However at the discretion of the Court he may be granted compensa-tion, if when the heir comes into his inheritance, actual hardship is im-posed on the guardian by reason of the cessation of his office.

QUOTATION: D.O's appeal No.29 of 1936.

Kilibata v. Bibi Tingilakabi.
The guardian Kilibata asked compensation for maintaining and improving the estate from the mother of his ward, Tingilakabi. It was held that the guardian is entitled to a certain degree of compensation for the permanent improvements he has effected in the plantation, but not for maintaining them in good condition. The use of the products of the plantation is sufficient compensation for their maintenance.

EXPLANATION: the reason for the award of cattle in this case was that Kilibata was originally the Musika of the property and entered into possession of it as heir. Later the widow of the deceased bore a

48

bisisi   child and Kilibata's status changed from that of an owner to
that of a guardian.   The Court thus took into account the hardship for
Kilibata and made the award on these grounds.

QUOTATION: D.O's appeal No.27 of 1934.

Ndyanabo v. Ngemera.
Ndyanabo was the guardian of Ngemera.   When the latter came of age he
claimed the estate, but the guardian refused to hand it over until the
heir had paid him compensation for permanent improvements to the property.

EXPLANATION: Ndyanabo had no other property and spent many years as
guardian of Ngemera, neglecting his own interests.   Thus at the cessation of his guardianship the award was made to recompense him.

225. It is impossible to take away the control of the money from the
mother however necessary it may be to do so.

224. KARAGWE: The mother keeps the money but is accountable to the male
guardian for her expenditure.

225. The male guardian may, if he considers it necessary, take the money
out of her charge.

    However if the mother considers her co-guardian untrustworthy she may
ask for him to be supervised.

QUOTATION: D.O's appeal No.56 of 1936.

Rutikanga v. Mwami Samson.
Rutikanga's brother died and left a widow with two children one of whom
was a son. Rutikanga was appointed guardian.   As he was a man of no
property at all, the mother feared that he would squander the property
of her son and asked Mwami Samson to act as second guardian beside Rutikanga.   Rutikanga objected but it was held that Rutikanga was not a
suitable person to be guardian of the property of his deceased brother
alone.   The Mwami was appointed to supervise him.

226. An heir when he takes over his inheritance can demand a statement
of account of the income during his minority.

ALL DISTRICTS.

227. The mother may not sell land for which she is guardian.

    NOTE: It is obvious that while for land and cattle, which have always represented property, the law has no loophole, with regard to money, which is a new form of property, the law has not been brought up to date. (except to some extent in Karagwe.)

It was evident when the informants were questioned that they realised this and were aware that some legislation was necessary.

228. The mother may not sell cattle under her guardianship without the consent of her co-guardian.

229. If she does sell cattle under her guardianship on her own account her co-guardian can bring an action against her in Court, and the remaining cattle will be taken away from her and put in the charge of other people who will look after them until the heir comes into his inheritance.

230. A mother has no right to betroth her daughter without the consent of her co-guardian who undertakes all duties in the arrangements for the marriage as the bride's father would have done, but the brideprice is paid to the mother who after distributing the shares among the relatives entitled to them may keep the rest for her sons.

(In Karagwe the co-guardian distributes the brideprice in the usual way.)

231. A mother can take action in Court or in family council against her co-guardian if she considers he is neglecting his duties. If she proves her case he will be dismissed and another guardian appointed.

APPOINTMENT OF THE MALE CO-GUARDIAN.

232. The nearest paternal relative is appointed as male co-guardian with the consent of the mother.

233. Where there is no one suitable among the relatives for this office the next claimant is a blood-brother of the deceased. As a last resort the mother's eldest brother will be chosen.

DISTRIBUTION OF PROPERTY BY THE GUARDIAN AMONG THE HEIRS.

234. If the heirs are children of one mother, the property is not divided

until the Musika takes over his inheritance.   (See amplification in D.O. appeal No.12/1940).

234a. If the Musika on becoming adult turns out to be a fool or a knave the elders of the clan may postpone the division of the inheritance until the second son has become old enough to inherit, when he may if thought fit be made Musika.

QUOTATION: D.O's appeal No.12 of 1940.

Rutekaya v. Amdani.
Rutekaya was a minor when his father died.   Amdani was appointed his guardian.   Rutekaya sold one of the inherited plantations anticipating his position as Musika of his father   (he had some younger brothers). This was looked upon by the clan elders as an utter breach of native custom, therefore they decided to postpone the division of the inheritance, when Rutekaya became of age, until his brothers were old enough themselves to inherit.   Rutekaya objected, but the Court confirmed the decision of the elders.

235. If the heirs are children of different mothers the property is divided after the usual three months.

2.   IF A PERSON ENTITLED TO INHERIT IS ABSENT.

HOW THE ABSENTEE IS INFORMED.

236. If the domicile of the heir is known, the guardian must inform the heir.   If he neglects to do so the heir's mother or his maternal uncle should take the necessary steps to inform him.   Generally nowadays the Native Authorities are asked to inform the absent heirs.

237. If the domicile of the heir is unknown, the property to be inherited is placed in the charge of a guardian until such time as the heir returns.

238. If the heir does not return the guardianship is inheritable.   If the guardian dies before the heir returns, his son will go on as guardian and so forth.

NOTE: The law says:-   "Ezamugenda irai tisikirwa."

The property of an absentee is not inheritable.

QUOTATION: D.O's appeal No.33 of 1936.

Mkungu Kabete v. Lugilahe.
The parties were brothers. After the death of their father, Lugilahe, the Mainuka protested against the distribution of the estate stating that his share as Mainuka was insufficient in proportion to the share of his brother Kabete, the Musika. Kabete proved that a part of the inherited land he administered only as guardian for the brother of their father, who was Musika to the grandfather's property, but had left long ago for Uganda and never returned. The father was the guardian of his brother's (Musika) inheritance and the property remained all the years undivided until the first guardian's death, after which the son followed as guardian. The claim of the Mainuka was dismissed.

APPOINTMENT OF GUARDIAN.

239. The next heir to the property will function as guardian.

240. If a man leaves only one heir and there are no male members of the family, the mother of the absent heir becomes guardian of the property and she may select a co-guardian.

241. If the mother dies and the heir is still absent, the Native Authority appoints a new guardian.

RESPONSIBILITIES AND RIGHTS OF GUARDIAN.

242. If the mother of the absent heir is still alive she has the right to control the proceeds from his inheritance. She has the right to ask in Court for an account from the male co-guardian.

243. If there is no mother the guardian is responsible to the absent heir for his actual inheritance only.

The heir on his return cannot claim from the guardian anything except his actual inheritance at his father's death, even if he returns a few months after his father's death and there have been proceeds from the estate.

244. The guardian must pay the house tax in the name of the absent heir. If the estate does not bring in enough to pay the tax either the guardian pays the tax or he can refuse guardianship, in which case the Native Authority has to use its discretion.

245. A guardian can claim no compensation for any of his work during his guardianship when the absent heir returns.

3.   IF THE DECEASED LEFT ONLY FEMALE DEPENDENTS.

APPOINTMENT OF GUARDIAN.

246. The Musika of the property automatically becomes guardian. Whether the Musika is a near or distant relative his authority as guardian is the same.

GUARDIANSHIP OF WIDOWS AND WIDOWS WITH DAUGHTERS.

For guardianship of widows and widows with daughters, see paras. 101 et seq. "Sonless Widows."

GUARDIANSHIP OF DAUGHTERS.

247. If a daughter marries the guardian continues to look after the plantation.

QUOTATION: D.O's appeal No.26 of 1934.

Bibi Kokulora v. Balongo.
Kokulora was the niece of Balongo who after the death of his brother became guardian for her and her mother. Kokulora tried to claim rights to the estate but was refused. She was married and as it appeared that the husband had instigated her to claim, Balongo refused to allow him to enter the plantation. Balongo stated in Court that Kokulora should remain with her husband, adding: "She may come to me sometimes to ask for some requirements, which I will gladly give her. I will have her mother to live in the house". This statement was upheld by the Court.

248. If a female dependent dies the heir and guardian takes over the plantation without any restriction, but no heir can take full possession of a plantation until the death of his wards.

249. <u>Minor Wards.</u> For minor wards the next paternal relative becomes guardian.

250. <u>Adult Wards.</u> Adult daughters have the right to apply for a change of guardian, which will be granted to them if they can prove that their

present guardian does not fulfil his duties towards them.

QUOTATION: D.O's appeal No.21 of 1936.

Banyenza v. Bibi Tibilengwa.
When Kikaluga died he left only his daughter Tibilengwa so he appointed
a guardian for her.   The guardian died after a short time.   Another
relative appeared called Banyenza who claimed the guardianship.   Tibilengwa would not concur and choose a third relative to be her guardian.
It was held that she had the right to choose her guardian.

QUOTATION: D.O's appeal No.49 of 1935.

Kagaruki v. Bibi Batamaa.
Batamaa was allowed to choose a guardian from among her father's relatives.

QUOTATION: D.O's appeal No.45 of 1936.

Balikibona v. Mutanwa.
A father died and left two daughters, one of them is Balikibona.   On
the father's death his property was divided between his two daughters
for their lifetime, each daughter having a male guardian who would inherit on the daughters' death.   Balikibona wanted to change the guardian
because he cut beer banana on the estate of her father.   It was held
that she has no right to forbid the guardian to do this, neither was
it grounds for a change.   It was held that a guardian has mainly two
duties: 1. of providing the ward with the necessaries of life.

        2. of providing the ward with shelter in the father's house.

        Only for breach of these duties can a guardian be brought to Court
by his ward.

QUOTATION: D.O's appeal No.82 of 1934.

Kalongoro v. Lutananukwa.
Kalongoro's father appointed Lutananukwa, his nephew, as heir of his
property and guardian of his daughter Kalongoro. Kalongoro accused the
guardian of neglect of his duties, but as she had no proof for this
accusation the case was dismissed.

251. A change of guardian means a change of the heir, because heir and
guardian must be one person.

QUOTATION: D.O's appeal No.30 of 1935.

Bibi Bamaza v. Byontamanyire.
A man left two daughters, one of them Bamaza. The daughters chose a man Tiruberwa as their guardian. Tiruberwa was a remote relative. Byontamanyire claimed to be the next-of-kin of the deceased and therefore to be entitled to the guardianship of the two daughters. He stated that because the guardianship is connected with the subsequent inheritance of the property a remote relative would have no right to be guardian. The sisters were informed in Court that they are free to choose a guardian among their paternal relatives.

NOTE: It must be mentioned that contradictory evidence has been given on this point but the majority version is as given here. The minority agreed that the daughters have the right to change their guardian but stated that the heir remains unchanged in this case and that therefore it is possible for heir and guardian to be separate people.

The following quotation upholds the minority view.

QUOTATION: D.O's appeal No.25 of 1934.
          P.C's appeal No.10 of 1934.

Mukabankango v. Gregory.
Mukabankango disliked her guardian who was heir to the estate after her death. She asked in Court for a change and proposed another man as guardian. This was granted to her but the right of the first guardian to inherit remained unchanged. The clan elders were indifferent as to which of the male members should be the substantial heir, as long as he belongs to the clan. They also had no objection to the man whom Mukabankango chose as guardian, but they declared that the heir must belong to the clan, while the guardian may be anybody.

252. It is permissible for a guardian to resolve his duties of maintenance by giving the usufruct of a part of the bequeathed land to those entitled to maintenance during their lives.

QUOTATION: D.O's appeal 4/P 1/9 of 1937.

Bibi Tibakya v. Nyamubi.
Mwijage left his property to his relative Nyamubi, whom he also appointed as guardian for his daughter Tibakya. Nyamubi gave her a part of the inherited plantation to live in. The daughter claimed after some years, that this part of the plantation was not big enough to keep her. The Court sent an emissary to measure the plantation and it was held that the banana grove of 88' by 74' and 83 coffee trees allotted to her was quite enough for her maintenance.

253. The guardian has to pay the hut tax for the inherited plantation; the guardian is responsible for the cleaning of the inherited plantation. (D.O's appeal No.3/P.1./33 of 1937.)

254. If the daughters marry the brideprice goes to the heir, i.e. the guardian.

255. A man can by will name a guardian within or outside his clan.

QUOTATION: D.O's appeal No.57 of 1934.

Ndibaihukamu v. Mkungu Tibainuka.
The father of Ndibaihukamu called the village headman Tibainuka and entrusted him with the charge of his plantation until his son and heir became old enough to inherit it. No relative had any objection to this arrangement.

256. In the case of a guardian who is not of the testator's clan, he will have no claim whatsoever to inherit on the death of his ward.

257. Should a man bequeath the usufruct of a portion of his plantation to maintain his female dependents, the heir has to pay the tax.

258. Should a man bequeath the usufruct of the whole estate to his female dependents, the heir is still liable for the tax, but in this case he may claim the money for it from the women concerned.

NOTE: The majority of the elders state that it is illegal for a man to leave the whole usufruct of his estate to his female dependents by will. A guardian must receive at least part of the plantation to enable him to pay the tax.

259. In every case the tax is paid in the heir's (guardian's) name.

NOTE: When this has been omitted, the payment of house tax implies no right of ownership.

QUOTATION: D.O's appeal No.95. of 1934.

Kilize v. Alexander.
Kashumba the uncle of Alexander nominated Alexander as his heir and bequeathed the usufruct of a part of his plantation, including his house to his wife Kilize. Alexander allowed Kilize to pay the tax for two years in her own name. When Alexander came to harvest his coffee (on

his own part of the plantation) Kilize refused to allow him to do so, explaining that the entire plantation belonged to her because she had paid the tax. The Court held that the fact of paying tax does not constitute ownership of a plantation. Alexander was ordered to refund to Kilize Sh.24/= the amount of the tax she paid; but he remained the heir of the whole plantation while Kilize had the usufruct of the part bequeathed to her.

259a. It is the custom for the guardian to leave the harvest from one or two good coffee trees for each married daughter; the same custom exists where a son inherits his father's plantation and has sisters.

259b. A guardian has a right to enter the part of the plantation set apart for the maintenance of female dependents. The guardian has no right to take away any produce from their share.

259c. The guardian must build a house for the women in their part of the plantation if he himself has inherited the house of the deceased.

259d. If a woman neglects her part of the plantation, the guardian may ask the clan head to intervene; if this fails, he may apply to the Court. If she does not obey the order of the Court, the Court may decide that the whole plantation should revert to the guardian, who must then maintain the woman in the usual way.

(for rules relating to widows and daughters as inheritance see para. 101 et seq.)

260. <u>If a man makes no provision in his will:</u>   a female dependent can claim:

a.) a hut to live in,

b.) upkeep in the form of food, clothes and luxuries in the same degree as a wife may claim from her husband or a daughter from her father.

261. A female dependent cannot claim any share in the proceeds of the sale of produce from the estate.

QUOTATION: D.O's appeal No.1/P.I/43 of 1938.

Angela v. Morici.
Kaindowa had only daughters.   First he appointed in a testament a relative as heir.   This will he changed later nominating his daughter Angela as heir. Some of his relatives protested against this change of the law, explaining that a daughter cannot inherit real property. Kaindowa then nominated Morici, his nephew, as heir.   After his death Angela claimed the inheritance.   It was held that she has no right to it, but that Morici must provide her with all necessities of life and also give her a place to live in.

QUOTATION: D.O's appeal No.3/P.I/35 of 1937.

Bibi Tibahongerwa v. Tihairwa.
Tihairwa neglected the maintenance of the widow of a relative whose plantation he had inherited.   It was held that he must look after her until her death.   He is responsible for her welfare and also for the proper state of her house in which she lives and for the cleanliness of the inherited land.

D.O's appeal Court gave an appropriate order to the Native Authority to supervise the exact execution of the obligations by the heir.

261a. A sister may claim maintenance from her full brother whether he inherited property from their father or not.

261b. Any man or woman may claim maintenance from his or her next paternal relative if the need for it can be proved. The relative can refuse to maintain the applicant only if he can prove that he has not the means to do so.

261c. If no paternal relative exists, the duty of maintenance falls on the nearest maternal relative. If a person needing maintenance has no near relatives, the duty falls on the clan head.

261d. The next-of-kin to an insane person is responsible to the community for any damage done by the lunatic.

BRIDEPRICE. (Makula)

NOTE: Makula is derived from the verb kukura- to grow. This word gives an indication of the underlying reasons for the payment of the bride-price. Brideprice is distributed among both the father's and the mother's relatives. The neglect of this distribution is supposed to evoke the anger of the spirits of the family, who would punish the new couple with sterility: the brideprice is therefore given to ensure considerable offspring i.e. growth of the family.

METHODS OF PAYMENT.

262. Brideprice is a payment by the bridegroom (mushwezi) to his presumptive father-in-law (ishezara) on the occasion of the marriage.

263. Apart from the brideprice it is customary for the bridegroom to give presents in kind, called maliso, to his father-in-law and clothes, called kujweka, to his bride, which are not reclaimable in case of divorce, but are reclaimable if given after betrothal and the engagement is subsequently broken off.

264. The form of payment of the brideprice is solely a matter of agreement between the son-in-law and the father-in-law.

265. The amount of the brideprice is restricted by rules enacted by the Native Authority of Bukoba District under section 15 of the Native Authority Ordinance to:

Shs.100/= as a maximum

1 goat (kitema ilembo = to open the way to the house.) This is seldom paid in kind, generally Shs.20 — Shs. 30 in cash.

2 bark cloth (usually now clothes to the value of about Shs.3/=)

1 hoe (nfuka ye biboyo — hoe of anger)

2 calabashes of native beer.

In Ihangiro an additional payment of 90 cowries is made.

NOTE: It must be noted that despite the fixing, by rule, of the amount of the brideprice, these rules are frequently transgressed and a much higher brideprice is paid. A man pays his Shs.100/= and wants to fix his wedding day; the father-in-law under manifold pretexes tries to squeeze out more money; for instance the one goat is usually not a real goat but a sum of money to represent it, fixed by the father-in-law. Another method is the kishembe (bribe), which is a lump sum paid by the son-in-law to the girl's father for his consent or to the father's relatives for their help in persuading the father. If it comes to a divorce, officially the son-in-law can only claim the Shs.100/= etc. but in fact he usually gets his extra money back voluntarily from the father for superstitious reasons. Kishembe, being a bribe, is never repaid.

266. The brideprice can be paid:

       1. in full before the marriage,

       2. in instalments during married life,

       3. in instalments before marriage,

       4. A nominal brideprice is paid.

267. 1. Brideprice paid in full before marriage: This is the usual arrangement. The father-in-law and son-in-law are both held responsible for ensuring that the payment of the brideprice is performed before witnesses. The son-in-law appoints one man, called Musherezi, who is his deputy and later if necessary his witness for all negotiations.

NOTE: If a man pays brideprice to a person who is not entitled to receive it, he himself and nobody else is responsible for this mistake. He cannot claim that the girl for whom he wrongly paid brideprice, must become his wife.

QUOTATION: Chiefs' appeal No.50 of 1938.

Mwalamata v. Mufukuza.
Mwalamata wanted to marry the sister of Mufukuza and paid Shs.50/= to her uncle Rubare. Rubare died shortly after receiving the payment and Mufukuza refused to give Mwalamata his sister as wife. The Court held that Mwalamata had no right to claim the girl as his wife. He paid the brideprice to the wrong man. He knew that the girl had a brother, who as Musika was the rightful receiver of the brideprice.

268. 2. Brideprice paid in instalments during married life. A certain proportion is invariably payable before marriage. It consists always of

the one goat (the cash equivalent is now usually paid), barkcloth, hoe, beer and a part of the monetary sum.

269. Usually no period is fixed for the payment of the remaining instalments.

270. If a father-in-law finds it impossible to get the remaining instalments from his son-in-law he is entitled to recall his daughter, and to refuse to allow her to return to her husband until the latter has paid up. If after this the son-in-law still does not pay the woman's father can keep his daughter and refund the instalments already paid, thus making the marriage void.

271. If the brideprice is not fully paid and the wife leaves her husband, any children of the marriage remain with the husband, even if the sum already paid is refunded by the father-in-law.

272. If the brideprice is being paid in instalments and the wife dies before the full amount has been paid, her father cannot claim the remainder.

273. 3. <u>Brideprice paid in instalments before marriage.</u> If the father of a girl under age betrothes his daughter to a man, the man may start to pay instalments of brideprice at once.

274. If when the girl reaches marriageable age she or her father refuses to fulfil the contract, not only the instalments of brideprice but also the value of all presents made by the man to the girl or her family must be refunded. (see para. 344 and 368.)

QUOTATION: D.O's appeal No.22 of 1936.

Aliziki v. Makela.
Makela was betrothed to a girl named Justina, when she was only a child. For several years Makela made various presents to her father, to one of her uncles and to the girl herself. Further, Makela paid various instalments of brideprice. Eventually the girl and her parents refused to allow the marriage and the girl married another man. It was held that the cash value of all the presents must be estimated and this sum together with the brideprice-instalments must be repaid to Makela.

For instance:

Gifts to the girl:			Gifts to the uncle:		
1 shirt	Shs.	1/=	3 calabash beer	Shs.	6/=
1 shuka	"	2/20	cash	"	10/=
1 kikoi	"	2/=	meat value	"	1/=
1 cloth	"	0/40	fish "	"	0/40
1 pair shoes	"	2/=	2 sticks soap	"	0/80
1 soap	"	0/10	4 boxes matches	"	0/24
1 bottle oil	"	0/10	1 hoe	"	1/=
		=========	salt	"	0/10
	Shs.	7/80	cash	"	4/=
					=======
				Shs.	23/54

275. **4. A nominal brideprice is paid.**

NOTE: Such a nominal brideprice is only paid if a girl has a mwana wa luhoire (illegitimate child), if she is known to be of easy morals, or sometimes for widows or divorced wives.

The marriage laws are unaffected by the amount of the brideprice.

276. Sometimes a very small brideprice is paid but it will always amount to

Shs. 10/=
1 goat (kitema ilembo) or, more generally, the cash equivalent.
2 bark cloths or equivalent in money or cloth
2 calabashes of native beer
1 hoe.

Sometimes no brideprice, is paid (see para. 362.)

RECEIVING THE BRIDEPRICE.

277. The father or his deputy receives the brideprice.

NOTE: If a father-in-law takes brideprice for his divorced daughter for her re-marriage, without having returned his brideprice to the first husband, he is liable to pay a fine. The wife has then either to remain with the first husband, when the brideprice must be returned to the second, or vice versa.

QUOTATION: Chiefs' Appeal No.26 of 1938.

Byalyoruguru v. Lugereka.
Byalyorugu betrothed his daughter to another man and received bride-

price for her knowing that she was married to Lugereka. The daughter had deserted Lugereka probably on the advice of her father. The Court held that the father had to pay Sh.10/= fine. The daughter was asked whether she was willing to return to her husband, and agreed to do so.

278. If a father has cast off his daughter, he cannot receive her brideprice, nor can he claim it from anyone who has received it.

279. The father-in-law and son-in-law are both responsible for ensuring that the payment of brideprice is performed before witnesses.

280. In some districts the bride's mother, even if she has been divorced, must attend the ceremonial delivery of the brideprice; in others her presence is not necessary.

281. If the mother has emigrated or died, her next female relative takes her place.

282. If the father dies after receiving the brideprice his Musika inherits all his obligations and rights in the matter.

283. If the father dies before receiving brideprice for his daughters, he who receives it is responsible for reimbursement and maintenance;

    a.) If the bride has a full brother he receives the brideprice.

    b.) If the bride has no full brother, the Musika receives her brideprice. (except Ihangiro).

285a. IHANGIRO. If a father dies and leaves some married sons and some unmarried sons and daughters, the unmarried daughters are divided among the unmarried sons who will receive their brideprice and undertake the attendant obligations.

284. At the same time married sisters are also divided between all the brothers who thus share the responsibilities.

DISTRIBUTION OF THE BRIDEPRICE.

285. The father does not keep the full brideprice for himself. He is obliged to give a certain share to the mother of the girl, and he also

gives certain shares to his relatives and those of his wife; these latter are theoretically voluntary but for superstitious reasons are, in practice, obligatory.

286. The mother can claim her share by law; except in Ihangiro where she may not.

QUOTATION: D.O's appeal No.1/P.1/28 of 1937.

Bibi Bona v. Ibrahim.
Bona, a mother of two daughters, was divorced from Ibrahim, their father. When the daughters were married the mother claimed her share of their brideprice. It was held that she is entitled to a share in each brideprice. In this case the two brideprices amounted to Shs. 180/=. The mother received Shs. 53. 50.

287. The division of shares differs slightly in the different districts. Presuming the brideprice to have been paid in full, that is:

> Shs. 100/=
> 1 goat
> 2 bark cloths
> 1 hoe
> 2 calabashes of beer

the following table shows the recipients and the appropriate shares they receive:

RELATIVE	KIANJA BUGABO	IHANGIRO	KARAGWE	KIZIBA	KIAMTWARA	MARUKU	MISSENYI
	Sh	Sh	Sh	Sh	Sh	Sh	Sh
1. MOTHER	26/=	10/=	10/=	26/=	20/=	20/=	10/=
2. Eldest PATERNAL UNCLE	6/=	8/=	10/=	8/=	8/=	8/=	8/=
3. Second PATERNAL UNCLE	4/=	6/=	—	7/=	6/=	6/=	6/=
4. Third PATERNAL UNCLE	—	—	—	6/=	—	—	—
5. MATERNAL UNCLE	10/=	8/=	8/=	8/=	10/=	8/=	8/=
6. BROTHER	—	6/—	—	—	—	—	10/=
7. PATERNAL AUNT	8/=	6/=	6/=	8/=	10/=	8/=	8/=
8. MATERNAL AUNT	—	6/=	—	4/=	—	—	4/=
9. PATERNAL GRANDFATHER	2/=	4/=	4/=	1/=	2/=	2/=	1/=
10. PATERNAL GRANDMOTHER	—	—	—	1/=	2/=	2/=	1/=
11. MATERNAL GRANDFATHER	—	—	1/=		2/=	2/=	1/=
12. MATERNAL GRANDMOTHER	2/=	4/=	—	1/=	—	—	1/=
13. WITNESSES GUEST	2/=	2/=		4/=	—	—	2/=
14. CHIEF	—	6/=	—	—	—	—	—
TOTAL	60/=	66/=	39/=	74/=	60/=	56/=	60/=
REMAINDER FOR BRIDE'S FATHER	40/=	34/=	61/=	26/=	40/=	44/=	40/=

66

NOTE: (See table)

In all chiefdoms the mother receives in addition to the money, the hoe and one bark cloth, or their equivalent.

1. The mother's share is called lugoye rwekishenshe = girdle of the grass skirt, i.e. the mother let out the belt of her skirt when she was pregnant with the bride. The hoe is called nfuka yebiboyo = hoe of anger, i.e. the mother is angry at the loss of her daughter, who helped her in field and house work. The hoe signifies a compensation to the mother for her loss.

In Karagwe the mother only receives a share if she is a widow.

In Missenyi the mother not the father, receives the goat Kitema ilembo.

5. Maternal uncle: The mother's eldest full brother failing whom her half brother.

6. Brother: He has certain ceremonial duties to perform at the wedding.

7. Paternal aunt: She has certain ceremonial duties to perform at the wedding, in connexion with which some money has to be spent.

8. Maternal aunt: Mother's eldest full sister, failing whom half sister. In all chiefdoms, the maternal aunt receives one bark cloth.

9-12. Grandparents: Their shares are called kibundabudo = cover i.e. to keep the old people quiet. The money is given to them to stop them grumbling about the shares received by the others.

In addition to the money, the father keeps for himself the goat and the beer.

288. Should the brideprice be smaller than the maximum, the shares of the participants are in proportion.

NOTE: The question arises why do not all fathers prefer small brideprices thus avoiding the great risk of being responsible for refunding large sums, of which they actually keep only a part. The reasons are that fathers feel themselves bound to please their next relatives; that it is the character of Africans to think of today and not of tomorrow; finally, divorce is the exception rather than the rule, even in these days.

289. If a member of the family entitled to a share does not exist the bride's father keeps the money for himself.

290. If a member of the family, entitled to a share is dead the father pays his share to the Musika of the deceased.

REIMBURSEMENT OF BRIDEPRICE.

291. If a divorce has been granted the recipient of the brideprice has to refund it, in full or partially, to the husband. (see para. 283).

NOTE: Nowadays the different native courts sometimes treat questions of refund of brideprice either in full or in part differently, probably because of various modern influences.

QUOTATION: D.O's appeal No.78 of 1935.

Kalyesheza v. Ibrahim.
A man left two wives, one with a son Ibrahim, the other one with two daughters. His Musika was his son Ibrahim. The mother of the two daughters had lived with her children in her father's house during the last years of her husband's life without being legally divorced. Ibrahim asked Kalyesneza, her father, to return his daughter and his two grandchildren to Ibrahim which the old man refused to do. Ibrahim sued Kalyesheza for repayment of the brideprice paid by his father, because the wife had only borne daughters and refused to return to her husband's family. It was held that the father had to return not only the brideprice but also the two daughters to their stepbrother Ibrahim.

292. The recipient of the brideprice cannot legally demand assistance from the persons among whom he distributed the brideprice, if he has to refund it, except from the mother of the divorced wife, who is bound to repay her share. (In Ihangiro and Karagwe the mother is not obliged to repay her share.)

NOTE: The Chief's Council in letter d/d 12.12.36 proposed

      a.) The names and shares of the recipients of the distributed brideprice should be entered by the Native Authority on the marriage certificate.

      b.) In case of a subsequent divorce each recipient should be liable to return his share.

Reference is made to this proposal in the enclosure 2 page 5 of D.O's letter to P.C. Mwanza No.275/150 d/d 10.2.1939.

The payment of the shares to the relatives is at present theoretically voluntary (see para.285). If the repayment were made obligatory the payment would have to be made obligatory also. In the one case where payment is obligatory i.e. the mother's share (see para.286) repayment is also obligatory.

293. A wife has no claim whatever on the brideprice paid for her. Should the brideprice be cattle she has no share in the cattle or their offspring.

QUOTATION: D.O's appeal No.4/P.1/10 of 1937.

Elisabeth v. Joseph.
Elisabeth claimed from her brother Joseph the brideprice which her husband had paid for her. It was held that a wife never can claim her own brideprice either from her brother or from her father, whether her husband is dead or alive.

294. The question whether children belong to the paternal or maternal family has nothing to do with the payment or repayment of the brideprice. Children always belong to the father.

295. Reimbursement of brideprice: A.) In cases of divorce.

1. Childless women or women who have borne children who subsequently died: full brideprice i.e. money, goat, barkcloth, hoe and beer, has to be repaid.

2. Women with daughters: all brideprice except the ritual goat (Kitema ilembo) has to be repaid, except in Kiziba.

KIZIBA. Full brideprice has to be repaid.

3. Women with sons: all brideprice except the ritual goat has to be repaid, except in Kiziba.

KIZIBA. Shs. 30/= is deducted for one or more sons.

296. B) In cases of widows being returned to their homes.

1. Childless widows or widows who have borne children who subsequently

died: the heir can   claim the full brideprice.

2. Widows with daughters: the heir claims all brideprice with the exception of the ritual goat, except in Missenyi.

MISSENYI: the heir claims nothing.   KIZIBA, IHANGIRO, BUGABO: the heir can claim full brideprice.

NOTE: However there is a judgment in which the Bakama contrary to the ruling of the lower courts decided otherwise.

QUOTATION: D.O's appeal No.61 of 1934.

Mulokozi v. Rutaliga.
Rutaliga as heir to Mulokozi's son—in—law claimed from Mulokozi his daughter's brideprice.   Mulokozi was ordered by the lower courts to repay it in full.   In the Chiefs' Court part was deducted, because Mulokozi's daughter had a female child by the deceased.

3. Widows with sons: no brideprice is to be repaid.

NOTE: This is valid even if the widow refused to live with a member of her husband's paternal family.

297. C.) In cases of a wife's death or sickness.

If a wife dies, becomes insane or incurably sick no brideprice is to be paid back; exceptions being leprosy and epilepsy which are considered hereditary and therefore the father should have informed the husband before marriage.

NOTE: IHANGIRO. If with the help of soothsayers it is decided that the woman became ill or died through the influences derived from her own family and the husband, for this reason, sent her to her father's house, he can reclaim his brideprice.

Repayment of brideprice in excess of the legal amount.

298. If a man paid a higher brideprice than is permissible according to the rules issued under Sect.15 of the Native Authority Ordinance, before these rules were issued in the year 1930, he is entitled to ask for the full repayment of the sum which he paid.

299. If a man has paid a higher brideprice than is permissible according

to the rules under Sect.15 of Native Authority Ordinance after the introduction of these rules, he can only claim, in the case of divorce, the refund of such a sum as is allowed according to these rules. The remainder is, in practice, often claimed by the son-in-law as a common debt and several instances of Courts allowing such claims as valid are in existence.

QUOTATION: D.O's appeal No.38 of 1935.

Felix v. Tibolekwa.
Felix married the daughter of Tibolekwa and paid a brideprice of Shs.200/= in the year 1930. According to the then new marriage rules Felix received only a receipt for Shs.100/= and Tibolekwa was told to return Shs.100/= to Felix. He did not do so and when the marriage was dissolved later Felix could only ask for the repayment of Shs.100/=. The remaining Shs.100/= he was at liberty to claim as a common debt.

300. In certain forms of marriage, such as Kulehya and Kushutula, the son in-law pays a compensation to his father-in-law in addition to the brideprice. In the event of divorce the repayment of this compensation cannot be claimed by the son-in-law. (Kuleya, see para.349 et seq.; Kushutula, see para.364 et seq.)

QUOTATION: D.O's appeal No.1/P.1/19 of 1938.

Bampiga v. Kaumi.
Kaumi married the daughter of Bampiga by the form of Kulehya. He paid Bampiga Shs.200/= of which Shs.100/= represented the brideprice and Shs.100/= a punishment for the elopement. It was held that Bampiga in the case of a divorce had only to repay the Shs.100/= of the brideprice.

301. Refusal to receive repayment of brideprice. Should a man refuse to accept the repayment of brideprice, the Court may order him to do so. The Court can, if he does not obey this order, rule that as the man refused his father-in-law's offer of repayment of brideprice, he has no further claim to it. (see Note to para.505.)

QUOTATION: D.O's appeal No.3/P.1/6 of 1938.

Bibi Akola v. Nkokonjeru.
Akola was granted a divorce against her husband Nkokonjeru. She wanted to return the brideprice but he refused to receive it. It was held that a man must receive the brideprice back in the case of divorce. The

Appeal Court decided that the wife should be provided with a cheti cha talaka and be at liberty to marry. Her former husband had no further claim to repayment.

NOTE: The usual reason for a refusal is that the husband wishes out of spite to obstruct the execution of the decree of divorce thereby ensuring that his wife cannot remarry.

302. <u>Time-limits for actions in Court.</u> Action for refunding the bride-price can be brought before the Court at any time after the divorce has been granted. No time limit for such an action is fixed.

NOTE: A tendency among the people themselves to make limits for action in Court is noticeable. Chief Petro Mugunda has introduced in his area the rule that an action for repayment of brideprice must be filed within one year from the time of the granting of a divorce.

BRIDEPRICE PAID WITH CATTLE.

(All districts except Ihangiro and Karagwe).

303. Brideprice may consist of one cow or of one cow and money. It seldom consists of more cattle than one cow.

NOTE: In Karagwe the Banyambo as a rule have no cattle, therefore cattle as brideprice can seldom be used, while the Bahima, the cattle owners, do use cattle as brideprice. Ihangiro allows no cattle brideprice. The Chief of Ihangiro gave the following reason:"Cattle are valuable, wives are not."

In Ihangiro the son-in-law may give a cow to his father-in-law at the time of his marriage which the father-in-law keeps and uses but it never becomes his property. The cow is considered an earnest for good behaviour and remains with the father-in-law so long as the daughter lives with her husband.

If the son-in-law dies and his heir returns the widow, her father returns the cow and its descendents.

304. When cattle is brideprice it is a substitute for money. The other items have to be paid as usual.

NOTE: Nowadays it is usual for the monetary value of the cow to be fixed at the time of marriage, thus avoiding all complications which would otherwise arise if anything happens to the cow later on.

305. If the brideprice consists of one cow and money, the money is deducted from Sh.100/= and the remaining sum represents the value of the cow.

307. If the cow of the brideprice does not calve or dies before she could have been expected to calve, the wife's father can claim another in her stead. Thus until the husband sends another it is as if the brideprice were unpaid and the father can if he wishes threaten to take back his daughter.

> NOTE: In some parts of the country the payment of the cow is accompanied by a present of an axe, knife or Shs.5/=. If the father-in-law accepts this gift from his son-in-law, it means that the cow becomes the property of the father-in-law unconditionally. If she does not calve or if she dies he cannot ask for a substitute. The father-in-law has merely to send a piece of meat to his son-in-law if the cow dies; then all rights of the latter cease to exist.

308. The cow is the property of the father.

> NOTE: The father-in-law can sell the cow, but in case of divorce the son-in-law can claim the return of a cow and refuse to receive money instead. If the price of a cow should be higher than Shs.100/= the father-in-law cannot refuse to buy one by referring to the limit of brideprice. (see para. 320.)

DISTRIBUTION OF THE BRIDEPRICE.

309. The father distributes some of his own money among the persons who expect a share in the brideprice, or he may send them the cow from time to time so that they can share in its milk and manure.

310. The mother of the bride has certain rights in the cow and in all calves, except in Missenyi.

> NOTE: In Missenyi the mother receives the ritual goat and can claim no share in the cow.

311. The mother (unless she is divorced) naturally participates in the products of the cow. If the father sells the cow she is entitled to her proportional share of the proceeds.

312. If the mother is divorced the cow remains two months in the house of the father and one month in the house of the mother in turn; or the father pays to the mother her proportional share in money.

NOTE: Opinions differ as to whether a divorced wife can claim any share in the cow of brideprice, but the majority view is that she does participate.

313. If the father sells the cow he must pay to the mother her proportional share, except in Missenyi (see para. 310).

313. If the cow calves the divorced mother has her proportional share in the calf. If the cow calves a second time she gets one calf. She has then no further claims on future calves.

314. If the father has debts and the cow is impounded the mother is entitled to claim her share in money. Her share is estimated either on the proceeds of the sale or on the sum for which the cow was taken by the creditor.

Obligations of a father-in-law if the cow dies.

315. A father-in-law must notify his son-in-law if the cow dies after the period denoted in para. 307, and call him to share in the division of its meat.

316. If the son-in-law is not able to come at once the father-in-law must if possible dry all the meat and keep it until the son-in-law or his deputy arrives; except in Kiziba and Karagwe (Bahima).

317. If it is not possible for the father-in-law to inform his son-in-law himself, he may call for witnesses either to the death of the cow or to the amount of the proceeds of the sale of its meat, except in Kiziba and Karagwe (Bahima).

318. If the cow is slaughtered, the father-in-law must inform his son-in-law what price he received for it. (Paras. 317, 318 are only relevant if the monetary value of the cow was not fixed at the time of the marriage.)

318a.   KIZIBA AND KARAGWE (Bahima)   The father-in-law   must send one leg of the animal to his son-in-law stating when he does so how much it represents in cash value.   This sum, in Kiziba is called ebishambyo   and in Karagwe, maauzi.

REIMBURSEMENT OF BRIDEPRICE.

319. If a father-in-law complies with the rules stated in para.315, 316, he is not liable for any repayment.   If he complies with the rules stated in para. 317 and 318, he is only liable for repayment of the sum he received.

320. If a father-in-law did not comply with these rules he must return a cow similar to that which he received as brideprice or the monetary value as fixed at the time of marriage.

321. The same rules hold if any calf of the original cow dies.

322. An exception to rules para. 319, 321, exists in Kiziba and Karagwe (Bahima) where the son-in-law claims his cash share multiplied by three. (see para. 317 and 318a.)

> ILLUSTRATION: If the cow died and the father-in-law sent one leg to the son-in-law stating that the value of this leg is Shs. 15/= the son-in-law will claim, in the case of divorce Shs.45/= to be refunded to him as brideprice.

323. If the original beast is still in the herd of the father-in-law it must be returned.

324. All the descendents of the original cow must be returned.

325. Reimbursement of brideprice. A.) In cases of divorce.

    1.) Childless women or women who have borne children who subsequently died: the cow and all its descendants and the ritual goat must be returned.

    2.) Women with daughters: the cow and all its descendants must be returned but the ritual goat is kept, except Kiziba.

KIZIBA. The ritual goat has to be returned also.

3. Women with sons: the cow and all its descendants must be returned, but the ritual goat is kept except in Kiziba.

KIZIBA. One calf is kept for one son or more. If the cow did not calve at all the father-in-law keeps the hoe, barkcloth, ritual goat and beer.

326. B. In cases of widows being returned to their homes.

1. Childless widows or widows who have borne children who subsequently died: the cow and all its descendants and the ritual goat must be returned.

2. Widows with daughters: the cow and all its descendants must be returned but the ritual goat is kept, except in Missenyi.

MISSENYI: nothing is to be returned. KIZIBA, IHANGIRO, BUGABO: the cow, its descendants and the ritual goat must be returned.

3. Widows with sons: no brideprice is to be returned.

BRIDEPRICE PAID WITH GOATS.

(IHANGIRO AND KARAGWE (BANYAMBO) only.)

327. The equivalent of Shs.100/= is at the moment (1939) 16 goats.

328. When goats are brideprice they are a substitute for money, the other items have to be paid as usual.

329. If goats paid as instalments of brideprice bear kids before the marriage, such kids are counted towards the total number of goats required for the full brideprice.

REIMBURSEMENT.

330. An equivalent number of goats to that paid as brideprice must be returned, i.e. 16 goats maximum. Their kids are not returned but remain the property of the father-in-law.

331. If the goats die after the marriage, the father-in-law must still repay the total number received by him as brideprice.

332. For the rest the rules referring to "Brideprice paid with cattle" are

76

appropriately to be applied with regard to brideprice paid with goats.

THE RITUAL GOAT.   (Kitema Ilembo).

333. If the ritual goat dies, one leg has to be sent by the father-in-law to his son-in-law who must replace the dead goat by another one.

334. Any kids of the ritual goat have to be returned when it is returned.

BRIDEPRICE FOR THE DESCENDANTS OF EX-SLAVES.

335. <u>Sources of Slaves.</u>

1. War.

2. Obuchweke. If a man died obuchweke and left no daughter his sister if she had a daughter had to send her to the Chief, as a slave-girl.

3. As payment for the allotment of land a father sent his daughter to the Chief.

4. As payment of fines. A prisoner could buy his liberty by sending his daughter as slave-girl to the Chief.

5. As payment by the relatives of an executed man for permission to bury him, his daughter was sent to the Chief as slave-girl.

6. As payment for food in time of famine.

NOTE: The descendents of ex-slaves are completely free.   The slave owners cannot interfere with their liberty and have no rights over them other than the claim to share in their brideprices.

336. The slave owner is called Mukamawe.   The female slave is called Muzana.

All bazana were created by the Chief who had full rights of disposition over them and frequently gave them to his favourites or as presents for service.

NOTE: In IHANGIRO the only mukamawe was the Chief.

337. The children (female) of these slave-girls were also bazana   and

the men who owned their mothers were the Bakamabe. Only the first daughter of a muzana becomes a muzana. All following daughters are free and the mukamawe has no right in their brideprices.

Baramata or Balangira will never marry a muzana, but otherwise there exists no discrimination between a muzana and a free girl, although a man who marries a muzana knows that he will not receive the full brideprice for his first daughter.

338. Even today the descendants of these bazana are bazana to the descendants of the Bamamabe.

339: The status of muzana becomes extinct if a muzana has only male children. Daughters of sons of a muzana are not bazana.

340. On the death of a mukamawe all his bazana are inherited by his Musika.

341. Marriage. If a man intends to marry a muzana, her father when all arrangements are made, takes him to the mukamawe who gives his formal consent to the marriage.

342. When the brideprice is paid the father and bridegroom go again to the mukamawe with the full brideprice. The mukamawe usually takes half of it and returns the rest to the father for division in the usual way.

345. In the case of subsequent divorce the father has to refund the whole brideprice; he cannot claim as a right that the mukamawe shall help him.

MARRIAGE. (Bushwere)

GENERAL RULES.

344. The marriage of a girl who has not attained puberty is prohibited.

345. Younger daughters are not allowed to marry before elder daughters, and younger sons are not allowed to marry before elder sons.

346. A man is not responsible for debts incurred by his wife.

NOTE: In Karagwe the husband can be held responsible.

FORMS OF MARRIAGE.

347.
1. Bushwere
2. Kulehya
3. Kuteza omusika amajuta
4. Kunagisa ebigere
5. Kunywegeza or kukwasa amaguru
6. Kushutula
7. Kutahilira.

NOTE: The differences lie mostly in the ways in which the preliminaries are arranged.

No.'s 5 and 6 are now abolished but they are recorded here as cases may arise based on them.

1. BUSHWERE.

348. This is the common form of marriage in which the preliminaries and the ceremonies themselves follow the prescribed customary forms. (A description of these ceremonies and preliminaries is given in Appendix I).

2. KULEHYA. (Marriage preceded by elopement.)

349. The girl having failed to obtain her father's permission elopes in order to force him to consent to her marriage.

350. Both girl and man have to fulfil certain conditions. The girl must either tell one of her relatives of her intention to elope or when she runs

away leave a few shillings or a new hoe or some new cloth where her father must find it at once, which he will understand is proof that she has eloped but that the man intends to marry her.

NOTE: In Karagwe it is not customary to leave a sign of elopement.

351. The man must inform one of the girl's relatives that he intends to abduct her and when he arrives with her at his own hut he must call an old woman and one of his female relatives to perform a ceremonial washing of the girl called Kwogia.

NOTE: In Bugabo no Kwogia takes place.

As soon as possible he must try to establish communication with her family and offer to pay brideprice.

352. The father usually refuses to accept the first offers of brideprice. The sign that he is prepared to forgive the couple is that he agrees to accept one or two goats or a sum of money as atonement. This is called mirekiniga (the swallowed bitterness) or ey' okwata ebishare — (to cool the calabash.) In Karagwe it is called Mpongano (to pray forgiveness). In Ihangiro it is called mbusi ya bishare na ya baki.   In Kiziba it is called kulihya.   Afterwards negotiations for the payment of brideprice are opened.

NOTE: The girl who eloped goes to her brother taking a goat or a sheep (nowadays mostly money). If the father is ready to forgive her the brother accepts the gift.   The brother takes hold of the head and the girl of the tail while a third person kills the animal, after which brother and sister jump over the carcase. Should the brother refuse to accept the goat his sister is considered an outcast from the family. She may not visit or speak to her parents or any other relatives. This bann and the conviction that any misfortune however slight has been caused by her elopement makes life unbearable for her.

353. Marriage ceremonies are never performed.

354. During the time of negotiations a man cannot claim compensation for adultery if the girl has relations with another man.

NOTE: Opinions differ on this point. Some hold that a man can claim compensation for adultery before the marriage becomes legal. If we accept this point of view the status of the couple is difficult to define. If a girl elopes and lives with the eloper their status during negotiations with her father would be that of a married couple, but if after a short time the girl runs away to her own family and refuses to return to her eloper, he cannot claim her as his legal wife.

355. If the woman gives birth to twins before her brideprice is paid, this necessitates an obligatory reconciliation in order that the necessary ceremonies in connection with the birth of twins may be performed.

356. Should the woman die before her brideprice is fully paid, the man is not liable for further payments.

NOTE: If a man is living with a woman to whom he is not married and she dies he must send a goat (nowadays money) called mbuzi ya mabano to her parents so that they may attend the funeral. He would not dare to bury the woman unless members of her family were present; the reason being that the man is considered to be indirectly the cause of the woman's death because he took her away without the necessary ceremonies. The presence of her relatives at her funeral is an indication that her family have forgiven him.

357. If a man who has eloped does not offer a brideprice or makes an insufficient offer, the woman's father cannot legally insist on a payment or on the return of his daughter against her will providing she was not already betrothed to another man.

NOTE: Superstitious fear of the consequences of disobeying parents usually makes such a situation impossible. It is conceivable that in the future such cases may become more frequent, which would be a danger to the institution of marriage and to the family generally; especially as paternal rights over widows are not legally defined.

358. A man who elopes with a girl betrothed to another man is liable to pay to her father compensation amounting to the sum of her agreed bride — price. It is irrelevant whether the father has already received the brideprice in full or in part.

359. This payment of compensation is not a payment of brideprice by the eloper. He must pay a separate brideprice to legalise his marriage.

360. Compensation must be paid in all circumstances even if the woman should die.

3. KUTEZA OMUSIKA AMAJUTA. (To smear oil on a girl)

361. A man would meet a girl whom he anointed with butter or smeared cattle dung on her or he placed in her father's house a small arrow and the fruit "ibono". The girl was not allowed henceforward to enter her father's house for superstitious reasons.

Her father had two possibilities open to him:

1. He could send her to the man, in which case the situation was as in kuleya.

2. The girl was taken to the man's house where she urinated; after which she could return to her home as there were no superstitious reasons why she should not enter.

The girl's consent was not asked.

NOTE: This form of marriage has now been abolished. The man using this method forced the father's decision because by the ceremonies of butter and cattle dung he performed a religious rite invoking the aid of the spirits. This method was often chosen by poor men as probably many fathers driven by fear gave their consent and even accepted a nominal brideprice. Out of this form of marriage originated many long-lasting family feuds with frequent scrapping because the family of the girl dared not show their anger to the spirits but considered that taking their revenge on the man's family had nothing to do with the spirits.

4. KUNAGISA EBIGERE.

362. After all the usual preliminaries, such as goat, brideprice etc. have been settled according to the bushwere form, the bride is taken by her paternal aunt to the bridegroom's hut. Generally the bride does not know that she is going to be married on that day. She has not been informed of the date.

NOTE: In Karagwe it is called luhabura amatai; in other districts kuhaugura.
This form of marriage is chosen if the bride's family is afraid of a public wedding ceremony on account of superstition, i.e. fear of witch-

craft etc.

NOTE: A woman who is taken by her relatives to the house of her bride-groom is the man's legal wife even if no brideprice has been paid for her. The fact that her relatives accompanied her is proof of their consent to her marriage. Under such circumstances the man cannot later claim that she is merely a concubine. Cases of such a claim being made are on record, the man's reason usually being the hope of thereby avoiding the plural wives tax.

5. KUNYWEGEZA OR KUKWASA AMAGURU.

363. A father refuses to accept the choice of his daughter, or the father of the young man is a miser and refuses to help his son with the bride-price. In such a case the young man may make friends with the brother of the girl and ask him if he would agree to a marriage between his sister and himself. If the brother agrees a goat is brought and slaughtered on the spot. The brother of the girl then goes to his father and informs him of the situation.

The would-be bridegroom also informs his father. The couple then ask the help of the elders of the village who go to the obstructive father and try to persuade him to agree to the betrothal, in which they are usu-ally successful.

If all parties agree the marriage rites are performed in the usual way. The usual brideprice is agreed upon. If the girl's father con-tinues to withhold his consent and the marriage does not take place, the goat brought by the suitor to the girl's brother must be returned.

NOTE: This form of marriage is not used in Ihangiro. The purpose of these proceedings is to make the situation public. A presumptive son-in-law cannot argue with his father-in-law, and a son cannot argue with his father. Through kunywegeza the help of the elders is obtained. They can talk bluntly with a father.

6. KUSHUTULA.

NOTE: This custom has its origin in very ancient times when it was a wide-spread custom to capture women from another tribe. The study of this old custom among many primitive tribes led John Ferguson Mclennan to the discovery of the rules of exogamy. See also J.G.Frazer "Totemism and Exogamy": "The form of pretence of capturing wives must everywhere have been preceded by the reality of it."

This may be also the reason that a bride is carried to the house of her bridegroom and does not walk.

364. A man abducts a girl by using force, but he fulfils certain conditions.

365. These conditions are: the presence of assistants, the intention to marry the girl and the approach to her father.

NOTE: The custom of kushutula is forbidden.   Tangazo ya daima Ref. 811/27 of 22.12.27.

Despite this rule the lower Courts still at times acknowledge this form of marriage if the conditions which distinguish, in their eyes, kushutula from rape are fulfilled.

QUOTATION: D.O's appeal No.2/P II/1 of 1938.

Bibi Kimbakiza v. Kabitina.
Kabitina seduced Kimbakiza against her will and kept her for one night in his house.   The girl's mother, being a stranger in the village (she came to the dispensary with her daughter for treatment) got no help from the villagers, of whom two men assisted Kabitina.   The mother of Kabitina went at last into the hut and asked her son, what he was doing. He answered: "I am marrying".   The Native Court fined the accused with Shs.30/= not on account of the seduction but because the girl was married, which fact Kabitina did not know. There was no appeal against this judgment: but the A.D.O. on inspection reopened the case, as it appeared to be a case of rape.   Kabitina was then sentenced to 6 months hard labour and a fine of Shs. 30/=.

366. If a bridegroom abducts his own bride, he is then married, but is liable to pay a compensation to his father-in-law.   It is irrelevant whether the father has already received the brideprice in full or in part.

NOTE: The reason for kushutula in such cases is that a father is dil-atory in fixing the date for the wedding ceremonies after all parties had agreed upon the marriage.

Sometimes a father arranges with his son-in-law to abduct his daughter.   The future son-in-law has usually in these cases already paid the brideprice and the father is afraid that the marriage may be upset by a third person.   This form of kushutula is considered by the natives strictly legal.

367. As in the case of kulehya a man, when the father is reconciled, has to pay in addition to the usual brideprice an extra amount as compensation.

368. Seduction without the consent of the girl is considered by Government under all circumstances to amount to a crime which cannot be tried by Native Courts. Kushutula is seduction without the consent of the girl.

NOTE: See Tangaso ya daima Ref. No.41/91 of 18.8.39. It may be useful in this connection to state the stand point of the Customary Law with regard to seduction.

SEDUCTION.

I. No age limit is fixed below which sexual intercourse is considered criminal. Some assessors mentioned puberty as such an age limit, but others refused to allow that puberty is the criterion. European Law with regard to the age is now sometimes invoked, but not on its own merit; rather as a means of revenge by a father.

II. A man who has sexual intercourse with an unmarried girl, whether she is betrothed or not, is not liable to pay compensation.

III. A man by whom an unmarried unbethrothed girl becomes pregnant is liable to pay compensation to her father, not exceeding the sum of Shs. 100/=.

IV. A man by whom an unmarried betrothed girl becomes pregnant is liable to pay the amount of her brideprice as compensation to her father in addition to a fine as decided by the Court.

QUOTATION: D.O's appeal No.4/P 1/16 of 1937.

Mushumbusi v. Nestor.
The daughter of Mushumbusi became pregnant by Nestor. She was betrothed to another man. It was held that Nestor must pay the amount of the brideprice plus Sh.15/= fine.

V. The character of the girl (in the last two cases) is no excuse, but it may be considered in the computation of compensation.

VI. A man who deflowers a girl with her consent is not liable to pay compensation to her father.

85

QUOTATION: D.O's appeal No.1/P 1/41 of 1938.

Baitani v. Kasharabaita.
Kasharabaita, a betrothed girl, became pregnant by Baitani. It
was stated that the girl was aged 10 years. Though this statement was
accepted by the Gombolola Court and a bare mention of it made in the
judgment, no consequences accrued from it. (see para I above). Both
Lukiko and Gombolola Courts held that Baitani must pay compensation to
Kasharabaita's father amounting to the brideprice he had already received
for her plus a fine. (See para IV above). The Appeal Court held that
no fine should be paid because the girl encouraged Baitani's attentions.
(see para V above). Baitani had to pay the brideprice as compensation
according to the judgment of the Lower Courts. The Appeal Court had
asked the M.O. for an attest with regard to the age of the girl. The
M.O. estimated her age as 16 years.

REMARRIAGE.

1. Sonless widows and all divorced women.

369. These are allowed to remarry.

370. There are no marriage ceremonies, except that the bride is taken to her new husband's hut by her paternal aunt as in kunagisa ebigere, (see para. 362.).

371. The first child of the new marriage is a mwana wa bisisi to the former husband's family: except in Kiziba and Missenyi.

KIZIBA AND MISSENYI: All children born of the new marriage belong to the new marriage.

372. A widow who remarries and is subsequently divorced has no right to claim maintenance from her former husband's relatives.

373. If a divorced couple wish to remarry each other the man refunds the returned brideprice and customarily adds one goat, called mpongano.

2. Widows with sons.

374. A widow with a son cannot remarry.

375. If a widow who is her son's guardian leaves him in order to live with another man, she must leave her child under the care of her co-guardian.

376. Should she leave this other man, she has the right to return to her son.

377. It is illegal for the woman's father to receive brideprice for her.

378. If the woman has children by the man with whom she is living, see para 145 et seq.

379. A woman living with a man under such circumstances cannot claim status as a wife, nor can the man claim status as her husband.

3. Inherited widows.

380. There are no marriage ceremonies, except that the widow is taken

to her new husband's (the heir's) hut by her paternal aunt as in kunagisa ebigere. (See para 362.) A wedding without ceremony with an inherited widow is called kutahilira.

381. The first child of the new marriage is mwana wa bisisi to the deceased husband; except in Kiziba and Missenyi.

   ILLUSTRATION: A died and his widow B was inherited by his brother C. B bore a son D to C. D is the mwana wa bisisi to A and therefore his heir. As such D ousted his own father C from the inheritance into which he had rightfully entered as heir presumptive on A's death. Should B give birth to a second son, he would be heir to his father C.

KIZIBA AND MISSENYI. All children of the new marriage belong to the new marriage.

382. An inherited wife holds the position of the heir's wife whether she is so in fact or is merely under his protection.

383. Once the heir has accepted her as inheritance and been accepted by her he cannot send her away unless he is granted a divorce from her.

   NOTE: It is stated that this law is often disregarded by heirs. It is seldom however that the women affected bring the matter to Court. If the heir takes a widow to his house as his wife and subsequently wants to get rid of her he will probably follow the law and divorce her because both he and she will in such case consider themselves man and wife.

   On the other hand the position of a widow who remains on the estate as the nominal wife of the heir is very unstable if any quarrels arise. She will probably in such case be sent away and neither she nor the heir would think of asking for a divorce because they would never have considered themselves married.

   The object of this point of law is not to safeguard the woman's interests. It is only concerned with the question of the heirs' claim to repayment of brideprice. No husband can claim repayment of brideprice unless he is first granted a divorce and therefore an heir can either refuse to become the widow's real or nominal husband and claim brideprice at once or he can accept her and then his only way to obtain repayment of brideprice is to be granted a divorce.

   ### 4. Widower and his deceased wife's sister.

384. If a wife dies leaving children it was once customary for her father

88

to give one of her sisters in her place.

NOTE: This custom is now practically obsolete.   A widower usually arranges for the children to be cared for by his own relatives.

385.   The widower paid a small brideprice on the sister.

386.   No ceremony was performed except that she was taken to her husband's hut as in kunagisa ebigere.   (para 362.)

387.   In case of divorce the husband could only claim the amount he paid for the sister.

LEGALITY OF MARRIAGE.

388.   Marriage is legalised :—

1.   In the case of bushwere by the ceremony of kubukara.

2.   In the case of kulehya by the payment of brideprice or the first instalment of it.

NOTE: Some people consider that the marriage is legal after the conditions of this special kind of elopement have been fulfilled.   (See note to para. 354.)

3.   In the case of kuteza omusika amajuta by the payment of brideprice or a first instalment of it.

4.   In the case of kunagisa ebigere by the bride being taken to the bridegroom's hut.

5.   In the case of kunywegaza by the ceremony of kubukara.

6.   In the case of kushutula by the payment of brideprice.

7.   In the case of remarriage by the bride being taken to the bridegroom's hut.

8.   In the case of inherited wives by the bride being taken to the bridegroom's hut.

CHRISTIAN MARRIAGES.

389. Certain parts of Haya marriage ceremonies (kubukara, kumukwenza, akatikeilembo, payment of brideprice) are performed as well as the Christian ceremonies.

REGISTRATION OF MARRIAGES.

390. There is now a law that marriages shall be registered by the native Authority. (Rule enacted by Native Authority under Section 15 of the Native Authority Ordinance No.18 of 1936.)

391. The registration does not affect the legality of the marriage. Neglect to register is punishable but the marriage is legal.

QUOTATION: D.O's appeal No.95 of 1936.

Stefano v. Salapion.
Salapion married Stefano's niece. He paid brideprice to Stefano, because her own father was dead. The marriage failed and during the following quarrel about the amount of the brideprice the Lower Court ascertained that the marriage had not been registered. The two parties were punished with a fine of Shs.2/= each but the legality of the marriage was acknowledged.

RESTRICTIONS OF MARRIAGE.

A marriage may be prohibited by 1. exogamy, 2. consanguinity, 3. affinity, 4. blood-brotherhood, 5. custom, 6. obwiko.

392. 1. <u>Marriage prohibited by exogamy.</u> A marriage between two members of the same clan is prohibited. (See also Appendix III, para. "Exogamy" and Appendix IV, para. "Exogamy".)

NOTE: The Bahinda do intermarry if the relationship is extremely distant but such marriages are infrequent.

In Karagwe a wife sometimes changes her totem to that of her husband after she has given birth to a son. The appropriate ceremony is called kukaraba and consists in the summoning of a mfumu who prepares medicine which he mixes with the flesh of the animal which has been up to now the wife's taboo, and gives to her to eat. Thus a wife enters completely into the family of her husband. She can do this without fear because she has borne a son and therefore even after the death of her husband she

will depend on her son and not on her own family.   The husband will
consider her step as a sign of great affection,particularly as divorce
would create a very difficult situation for her,   since she would have
to return to her family and keep a different taboo.

393. Several different clans have the same totem.   Therefore it   is
necessary for the person concerned not only to ascertain the totem but
also the name of the clan.

395. Nobody can marry into the clan of his mother.

396. 2. Marriage prohibited by consanguinity.   A man may not marry:

> A. his mother or grandmother;
>
> B. his daughter or grand-daughter;
>
> C. his sister whether full, consanguineous or uterine;
>
> D. his niece or great nieces;
>
> E. his aunt or great aunt, whether maternal or maternal.

NOTE: A man can marry:

> A. his step-mother after his father's death,
> B. his sister-in-law after his brother's death,
> C. his foster mother,
> D. his wife's sister after several years have passed since his
> marriage with the first sister.

397. 3. Marriage prohibited by affinity.   A man may not marry:

> A. His wife's mother or grandmother;
>
> B. his wife's daughter or grand-daughter.
>
> C. His son's wife or the wife of his daughter's son.

398. 4. Marriage prohibited by blood-brotherhood.   A blood-brother is
considered with regard to consanguinity as a natural brother.

ILLUSTRATION: A blood-brother may marry the widow of his blood-brother.
A blood-brother is not allowed to marry a sister of his blood-brother.

QUOTATION: D.O's appeal No. 77 of 1936.

Petro v. Mashenshe.
Mashenshe accused Petro of adultery with his wife.   But Petro was a blood-brother of the wife's brother and the Court held that such a breach of custom is so improbable that it acquitted Petro.

In order to marry distant relatives of a blood-brother a ceremony kwita omukago is performed between the parties wishing to marry which dissolves the prohibition.

398. Generally the descendants of blood-brothers do not marry each other until the third generation inclusive.

399. <u>5. Marriage prohibited by custom.</u>   The daughters of Chiefs were not allowed to marry while their father was alive. In former times this crime was punished with death.

NOTE: This rule is falling into desuetude.   The reason why daughters of Chiefs may not marry is to avoid the possibility that a Chief may make a favourite of a son-in-law who would perhaps try to become a Chief himself.

400. <u>6. Marriage prohibited by Obwiko.</u>   Obwiko is the name given to an unfriendly relationship between two persons, two families or two clans, which may have its origin either in the belief that it is possible for a living person to influence the spirits to the detriment of some one else, or in historical events.

NOTE: In the case of the first a man who has suffered misfortune by reason of sickness, failure of crops, loss of money etc. may go to a soothsayer who attributes his bad luck to the ill will of someone.

The second case is illustrated by the following example: About 70 years ago a member of the Bagiri clan intended to leave Bugabo secretly. His wife who was of the Bajubu clan gave away his intention to her lover who informed the Chief and the Mugiri was prevented from leaving. The Mugiri killed his wife for her treachery and cast off her clan; since when obwiko has existed between the Bagiri and Bajubu.

401. All persons between whom obwiko exists refuse to speak or eat to-gether; neither can they nor their children marry.

402. A reconciliation is always possible.   The Chief has the power to

92

remove the obwiko by certain ceremonies called "kuchwa obwiko" (to cast off the ban.)

QUOTATION: D.O's appeal No.1/P 1/18 of 1938.

Bibi Koburungo v. John Birama.
In the judgment it was recommended to the Chief to remove the Obwiko.

CONSEQUENCES OF TRANSGRESSION.

403. Transgressions of the law with regard to prohibited marriages are not brought before the Court. (Exception: see para.417.)

404. With regard to prohibitions No.2 and 3: a man who has married a woman prohibited to him is not punishable, but the marriage is void; therefore an action for adultery is impossible.

NOTE: Such a transgression is called "kuzira kitazirurwa eihano lita-hanurwa" (to be sullied by an inextinguishable ignominy.) In former times both parties were cast away on Musira island with their eyes bandaged and hands tied behind their backs. Another method was to tie them up and tie a stone to them and throw them in Lake Victoria Nyanza.

405. With regard to prohibitions No.1, 4, 5 and 6.

A. a father may disinherit his son,

B. a father may banish his daughter,

C. the clan may ostracise a member who has so transgressed.

406. The same consequences befall two people who are not married but transgress the restrictions by having illicit relations.

POLYGAMY.

407. The number of wives is not restricted.

NOTE: A man usually builds for each wife a separate house. The first wife he marries, called omukazi mkuru, lives in the nyumba nyaruju (the big house.) All houses built later are called maju'g enyuma (the houses which are at the back). There live the other wives. Each wife, at any rate nominally, has a certain part of the plantation under her special care. Even coffee trees are distributed among the wives in this way.

408. A man may not choose a second wife without consulting his first wife. He cannot marry a second wife if his first wife is not present to receive her into the house.

409. A husband has to give his first wife a present when he marries a second wife. The present is called ihangiko in Ngiba; akikeiba in Ihangiro and Karagwe, and amounts to Shs.2/= to Shs.6/=.

410. A man may not bring a concubine to the house without the consent of his other wives.

411. A woman cannot be accused of bigamy. If she marries a second man, knowing that she has not been divorced from the first, no charge lies against her.

QUOTATION: D.O's appeal No.35 of 1934.

Abdullah v. Jonasani.
Jonasani met a woman on the road whom he married. It was found later that she was already married to Abdullah who claimed compensation from Jonasani. The woman admitted Abdullah to be her legal husband. She was not accused of bigamy. The charge was solely against Jonasani.

D I V O R C E.   (Kutambya).

NOTE: Kutambya means to drive away. The use of this word illustrates the native point of view on divorce.   Kwangana,   another word often used, means to disagree with each other. It is used if the wife leaves her husband and goes to her father, expecting that her husband will follow her and that she will eventually return.

GENERAL PROCEDURE.

412. The contract of marriage can be dissolved:

a) by mutual consent of the persons concerned without the intervention of Court, but before bagurusi (elders).   (The name in this connection has nothing to do with age; it means an arbitrator in a case.)

b) by a judical decree at the suit of the husband or wife.   (re divorce of Christian marriage see Permanent Notice No.811/58 of 27.3.39.)

413. The decision of the elders is only arbitrary and if either party is dissatisfied he (or she) may reopen the case before the Native Court.

414. Should the decision of the elders be accepted by both parties and subsequently one of them fails to fulfil a condition of the decision, an action could be filed against the delinquent before the Native Court, in which case the decision of the elders would be recognised.

ILLUSTRATION: A and B were granted a divorce before a council of elders B's father did not return the brideprice, so A filed an action against him in the Native Court, quoting the elders' decision as his proof that he was entitled to reimbursement.

415. In all cases where a divorce is granted brideprice must be repaid.

RECOGNIZED GROUNDS OF DIVORCE.

For a Husband.

I. ADULTERY.   (Busiani)

NOTE: In pre-european times, adultery was considered a petty offence. The Bahima did not recognise adultery among themselves. If a man found that another man had committed adultery with his wife he could complain to the authorities but the only redress allowed was their permission to cohabit with the wife of the adulterer.

416. Adultery by a wife is grounds for divorce but adultery by a husband is not.

417. The exception to the above is if a husband commits adultery with a woman within the prohibited degrees of affinity.

418. A charge of adultery can only be brought to Court by a woman's husband. Only a woman's husband, father, brother or blood—brother may collect evidence of her adultery.

419. It is unknown for a father to lay a charge of adultery before the Court citing his son or a son his father. A brother may charge his brother except in Karagwe and Kiziba.

NOTE: In Karagwe custom allows that a brother may visit his sister—in law.   The situation was summed up by an assessor of a Native Court in Karagwe who asked a young man accused of adultery: "Why do you go to to strangers? Have your brothers no wives"? The recognised indication by a husband that he acknowledges this custom was that he ordered one of his wives to wash and anoint the feet of a visiting brother which meant that during his visit this woman was at the brother's disposal. This rather official sanction is becoming obsolete, but the fact that it existed explains some points of the inheritance law with regard to sonless widows. (see para.101—111.)

420. There are two acknowledged forms of adultery :—

1. Adultery in flagrante delicto.

2. Adultery of a wife under certain circumstances during her husband's absence.

1. Adultery in flagrante delicto.

421. Direct proof by more than one witness is necessary in order to lay a charge.

422. The witnesses must declare their presence to the guilty parties at the time.   Their proof is not considered sufficient if they have watched the occurence from a hiding place.

423. The following types of evidence are not accepted as proof of guilt

without corroboration:

        a.) circumstantial evidence,

        b.) production of property of alleged adulterer,

        c.) confession by a wife.

NOTE: It is the duty of the Court to decide how far circumstantial evidence should be taken as proof of guilt.

QUOTATION: D.O's appeal No.4/P 1/18 of 1938.

Byabato v. Nyeme.
Witnesses found Nyeme at 4 a.m. in Byabato's house in conversation with the latter's wife. Nyeme stated that he had only come to fetch a calabash of beer. His defence was not accepted by the Court which refused to belive him owing to the time of his visit. Byabato stated that his wife had confessed to him that she had committed adultery. Her confession is not mentioned in the judgment though it was evidently taken as corroborative evidence. Nyeme was sentenced to a fine of Shs.40/= and ordered to pay Shs.20/= compensation to Byabato.

QUOTATION: D.O's appeal No.53 of 1935.

Ngemera v. Libalio.
Tibamalana was first married to Libalio by whom she was divorced. She married Ngemera as her second husband. Witnesses proved that she spent a few days with her former husband which she herself also admitted On this evidence the Lukiko and Gombolola Courts both found Libalio guilty and ordered him to pay a fine of Shs.30/= and Shs.20/= compensation to Ngemera.

QUOTATION: D.O's appeal No.4/P 1/17 of 1937.

Leonard v. Ishengoma.
Witnesses saw Leonard's wife enter Ishengoma's hut during the daytime. No witness brought evidence of adultery. Ishemgoma and Leonard's wife were both ordered to pay fines because she went to his hut without her husband's permission. As there was no proof of adultery the Court did not award compensation to the husband.

QUOTATION: D.O's appeal No.53 of 1936.

Filippo v. Simoni.
Filippo found Simoni and his wife in the house of the latter's aunt. They were alone, but the Court held that this was not sufficient evidence to support a conviction of adultery.

QUOTATION: D.O's appeal No.26 of 1934.

Abdullah v. Ntinabo.
Ntinabo taking witnesses with him went to Abdullah's hut at night and searched it.   They found Ntinabo's wife there but not Abdullah. It was held that a conviction of adultery could not be made on this evidence alone without further proof.

2. Adultery of a wife under certain circumstances during her husband's absence. (All districts except Kiziba and Missenyi.)

424. If a husband who has made proper provision for his wife during his absence, finds proof on his return that she has been living consistently with another man but has had no children, he can obtain a divorce.   Occasional lapses are not grounds for divorce.

425. If however she is pregnant on his return or has borne a child during his absence he can claim neither compensation nor a divorce.

426. If she has borne more than one child or has borne one child and is again pregnant, a husband can claim a divorce and compensation on account of the second child.

KIZIBA and MISSENYI.

427. If a husband who has made proper provision for his wife during his absence returns to find proof that she has been living consistently with another man, a divorce is granted to him.   Occasional lapses are not grounds for divorce.

428. If he finds her pregnant on his return no action can be taken until the child is born, when a husband claims divorce and compensation of 30/= from the child's father.   During the pregnancy the woman lives with her own relations.

429. If he finds that his wife gave birth to a child or children during his absence and he did not leave her pregnant a husband can claim a divorce and Shs. 30/= compensation for each child from its father.

NOTE: The reason for the difference in this law between Kiziba and Missenyi and all other districts is that these two districts do not admit the custom of bisisi. Where bisisi is in force, the first child born in a husband's absence belongs to him irrespective of the time of birth, and therefore its birth cannot be considered as grounds of divorce.

All Districts.

430. If a man's wife during his absence, has lived with more than one man he must cite the man with whom she last lived as co-respondent.

431. If she died during his absence, while living with another man, he can claim the return of her brideprice.

432. If a man goes away and makes no provision for his wife during his absence he cannot when he returns claim either compensation or divorce on the grounds of her adultery. (In Karagwe he can get a divorce.)

NOTE: It is customary for a wife, if she returns to her husband, to bring a goat (called mbuzi ya kitabo) which is used in the ceremony of the ritual cleansing of the bed (kwogiama).

433. The Court shall not dissolve a marriage if it finds :-

1. that the petitioner has,with full knowledge of the facts,forgiven the matter complained of and continued or resumed cohabitation.

2. that the petitioner had unreasonably delayed the presentation of the petition after he had full knowledge of the matter.

433A. Kurubuni i.e. a case where a man persuades another man's wife to leave her husband and to live with him, is treated in the same way as an adultery case.

NOTE: Permanent Notice 811/22.

433B. A man, not a relative, living under one roof with a woman is considered her temporary lover, unless he has informed his Mukungu or Mwami of another legitimate reason for her presence in his house.

QUOTATION: D.O's appeal No.29 of 1933

Mafili v. Nyantaza.
Nyantaza brought Mafili's wife into his house where she remained 14 days.

Nyantaza was ordered to pay fine and compensation.

QUOTATION: D.O's appeal No.2/P 1/12 of 1937.

Simeon v. Abdrahman.
Abdrahman gave Simeon's wife shelter without informing the village headman.   The Court found Abdrahman guilty and fined him Shs.50/= of which Shs.10/= were fine and Shs.20/= compensation to the husband.

QUOTATION: D.O's appeal 1/P 1/10 of 1938.

Nyamaishwa v. Klemens.
Klemens' wife deserted him and lived for a considerable time with a man Shabani.   Trouble arose between her and this man and she went to the Mukungu Nyamaishwa and remained in the latter's house for some days.   Shabani informed the husband where she now was.   Klemens had not known during all this time where his wife lived. He found her in Nyamaishwa's house.   It was held that Nyamaishwa was not guilty, because the woman did not come to him from her husband.   The judgment says: "To have a prostitute in the house is not a crime but a shame".

QUOTATION: D.O's appeal No.10 of 1935.

Simeon v. Merewoma.
Merewoma gave Simeon's wife work on his plantation.   She slept in his hut.   Merewoma had informed the Mukungu, who took them both to the Gombolola to obtain the consent of the Mwami, as is the custom.   The Mwami was absent and the clerk told them to come on another day. Simeon arrived on the scene before the Mwami had returned and found that Merewoma had not obtained the official consent.   The Court held that Simeon had no case to accuse Merewoma of kurubuni.

ONUS OF PROOF OF A WOMAN'S ELIGIBILITY.

434.   It is a man's duty to ascertain that a woman with whom he lives or whom he marries has no living husband.

435.   The word of the woman herself is insufficient evidence.

QUOTATION: D.O's appeal No.52 of 1935.

Kahimukirwa v. Mohamadi.
Kahimukirwa's wife ran away and lived with Mohamadi who stated that he thought he was married to her as she came to him from her parents' house and he did not know that she was married to another man. It was held that as previously Mohamadi had lived for ten years within 150 yards of Kahimukirwa's house he must have known that the woman was

100

his wife.   Mohamadi was ordered to pay a fine of Shs.20/= and Shs.60/=
compensation to the husband.

QUOTATION: D.O's appeal No.29 of 1935.

Petro v. Festo.
Petro accused Festo of committing adultery with his wife. Festo's defence
was that the woman told him that she was not legally married to Petro
and that she did not come from Petro's hut, but from her father's house.
It was held that Festo was guilty of adultery because he should not have
relied on the woman's word alone.

436. If circumstances prove that it was practically impossible for a man
to obtain the truth he cannot be charged with adultery.

ILLUSTRATION: I. A lived with a woman of an alien tribe believing her
to be free.   Subsequently a man of her tribe arrived and claimed her as
his wife.   A could not be charged with adultery.

ILLUSTRATION: II. A visited a prostitute* and while he was with her a
man appeared who claimed to be her husband.   A could not be accused of
adultery.

437. Should a man live with a woman under the assumption that she is free,
it is his duty if he subsequently finds he was mistaken to send her away
immediately.

QUOTATION: D.O's appeal No.103 of 1936.

Nathan v. Augustini.
Nathan was a lorry driver whose work took him away from home.   During
his absence his wife Margareta,while visiting a market in a neighbouring
district approached a group of young men asking for "work and wages".
Augustini agreed to take her on as his concubine, later they appeared
together at a wedding in Margareta's family. The Court held that though
it was possible that Augustini might not have known in the beginning that
Margareta was Nathan's wife, he must have known after meeting her relatives
at the wedding. Augustini was found guilty and fined Shs.15/= and
ordered to pay Shs.45/= compensation to Nathan.

_____

*The word prostitution is difficult to define here because the taking of
money is no criterion as many women living with their husbands take payment from time to time from other men. It must be left to the discretion
of the Court to decide the circumstances which constitute prostitution.

438. If a man has had no communication with his wife's family it indicates that there is something suspicious about his marriage.

QUOTATION: D.O's appeal No.35 of 1934.

Abdullah v. Jonasani.
Abdullah claimed that he thought he was legally married to Hamina who was proved to be Jonasani's wife. It was remarked in the judgment that Abdullah had not informed the village chief of his marriage nor had he been to pay his respects to Hamina's family as is the custom. It was therefore held that he must have known that she was already married.

439. <u>The penalty for adultery.</u> A fine must be paid and compensation must be paid to the husband. The amount of the fine and compensation does not depend on the circumstances of the case, but on the economic status of the convicted man.

II. DESERTION. (Kusigao).

440. Desertion by a wife is grounds for divorce.

NOTE: There are frequent cases in which a husband does not want a divorce but wants his wife to return to him. If the wife refuses to do so, the Court usually fixes a time limit for reconcilliation. If the woman remains adamant she cannot be forced to return to her husband (See Permanent Notice 811/22 and para.445.)

441. A husband is entitled to file a suit of divorce, providing one condition is fulfilled. He must know where his wife is living before he files his petition; except under the circumstances mentioned in para. 442.

442. If the wife goes first to her father or a near relative and after staying a short time with him, leaves and goes elsewhere, her husband can file a petition if he can prove that she has been in her father's house. He is then not obliged to state where she went on leaving her relations.

NOTE: The Chief's Council in its letter of 27.4.39, Ref.No.126/31 recommended the following :

a.) If a wife runs away to her father her husband must follow her within seven days.

b.) The wife's father should not be allowed to keep his daughter in his house for more than 7 days without discussing the matter with his son-in-law.

c.) If a husband wishes to separate from his wife, he should inform his father-in-law within 7 days.

d.) Transgression of these rules should be punishable by a fine of Shs.5/=.

The above rules are framed to force the husband to follow his wife if she deserts him, because in many cases the husband takes no steps to enforce his rights. Attention is drawn to the effect of the Plural Wives Tax in cases where a man has two wives or marries a second one after the first wife has deserted him. The demand for plural wives' tax induces the husband to keep his domestic affairs in order.

443. If a father keeps his daughter in his house he becomes liable to pay compensation to his son-in-law and may be ordered by the Court to expel her if he insists on keeping her. (Exception see para.270.)

QUOTATION: D.O's appeal No.12 of 1935.

Mugoa v. Bamanyisa.
Mugoa's wife went to her father Bamanyisa and did not return. Mugoa sued his father-in-law for the return of his wife. The Lower Court ordered that she should return. She did not obey the order. It appeared that Bamanyisa undoubtedly countenanced and encouraged her desertion. It was therefore held in the Appeal Court that it was Bamanyisa's duty to insist on his daughter's return to her husband and that unless he insisted, even to the point of turning her out of his house, he would not be deemed to have done his duty. If she continued to live with him, he was liable to punishment.

QUOTATION: D.O's appeal No.26 of 1937.

Augustini v. Kakoko.
Kakoko's daughter left her husband Augustini and went to her father. Augustini followed her and took her home, but she escaped again to her father. Her husband discovered when he fetched her the second time that she was suffering from syphilis. He tried, probably by force, to ascertain who had infected her. She ran away again to her father who refused to send her back until she was cured. The Court held him guilty of retaining his daughter and he had to pay Shs.15/= compensation

to Augustini and to return his daughter to him at once.

444. A husband cannot take action against his father-in-law merely for giving shelter to his daughter for a few days.

445. If a divorce suit is filed but no divorce is granted and the wife refuses to return to her husband, the Chiefs now sometimes order punishment of anyone who gives her lodging.

445. Desertion by a husband is not grounds for a wife to claim a divorce.

NOTE: A wife whose husband has completely deserted her is in a very unfortunate position. She cannot divorce him however long he has neglected her and therefore cannot marry again. Thus nobody is responsible for her maintenance. This injustice is explainable by the fact that a man's reason for leaving his wife is completely different from that of a wife who leaves her husband. A man has no need to run away in order to dissolve his marriage. Desertion of his wife is merely the indirect outcome of his decision to undertake the journey. At the time that this law was laid down it was sufficient for its purpose because a man was only absent owing to circumstances outside his control. Thus the situation was the same as if he became incurably sick which is no grounds for divorce.

446. It is a husband's duty to provide for his wife during his absence.

447. If he fails to do so he forfeits his right to claim compensation or divorce on the grounds of her adultery after he returns. (see para.432.)

448. Provision may be made as follows:

A man may send regular sums of money for his wife's upkeep.

449. A man may leave her in charge of his property with control over its assets.

450. The wife is then responsible to nobody with regard to the use of the money, but her husband's father, brother or blood-brother supervise her moral conduct. (see para.418.)

451. A husband may appoint a trustee for his property who also acts as guardian of his wife.

452. He may choose anyone to be trustee.

453. The trustee's remuneration must be agreed upon before the husband leaves, otherwise the former cannot claim anything.

454. Unless otherwise arranged the trustee does not have to render an account of his trusteeship.

455. Neither the trustee nor any one else except the husband can appoint a new trustee should the one chosen be incapable of carrying on the trusteeship.

456. The husband gives orders as to what proportion of the proceeds of the coffee harvest shall be devoted to his wife and family.

457. Cattle are left in charge of the wife subject to the control of the trustee who can take away the herd if he considers it necessary.

458. The wife's behaviour is the concern of the trustee. If she behaves badly he can reprimand her and inform her husband or his family.

NOTE: In Ihangiro the trustee can order the wife to leave the plantation and to return to her father.

459. If he is unable to control her he can resign from the trusteeship informing the woman before the village headman or elders that henceforward she alone is responsible to her husband for all his property.

III. NEGLECT OF DOMESTIC DUTIES.

460. Continued neglect of domestic duties such as cooking, carrying water and fuel and field work by the wife are acknowledged grounds for divorce.

IV. SYPHILIS: (Ebishona).

461. Syphilis of the wife is grounds for divorce.

462. If the husband knows who infected his wife he can also claim compensation from the man.

463. Syphilis of a husband is not grounds for a wife to claim a divorce.

NOTE: This uniliteral law is only understandable in view of the out-

look on adultery.   Syphilis is regarded as the outcome of adultery,
but only the adultery of the wife is grounds of divorce.

464. If she has been infected by her husband she can claim compensation.

QUOTATION: D.O's appeal No.30 of 1934.

Abdullah v. Makatunzi.
It was proved by a certificate from the Government Hospital that Abdullah
and his wife were both suffering from syphilis at the same time.   Abdullah
denied that he had lived at the time in question with his wife.   It was
held that he must be considered responsible for his wife's condition as
he could not, nor did he try, to prove that she had been infected by a
third person.   Abdullah was ordered to pay a Shs.10/= fine and Shs.15/=
compensation to his wife.

465. Other venereal diseases such as gonorrhoea are not acknowledged as
grounds for divorce.

V. IRREGULARITIES WITH REGARD TO BIRTH OF CHILDREN.

466. A.) Abortion (Kwiyamu enda)

467. B.) Causing mishap to a child during its birth (kwitila omumangi)
i.e. if a mother by reason of her fear or pain disobeys the orders of the
midwife and by so doing maims or kills the child during her labour.

468. C.) Mwana wa bisisi. If a man discovers that his first child will
be bisisi because his wife has had relations with another man at some time
before her marriage. (see para.187a.)

D.) Mwana wa luhoire. If a man can prove that his wife was pregnant
by another man when she married. (see para.172.)

E.) If a wife gives another man her husband's pipe, lance or arrow.

For a wife.

VI. CRUELTY. (Obuyebe).

NOTE: A wife has no legal protection against a husband who deliberately
maltreats her in order to achieve a divorce and to receive back his
brideprice, which he can use then to marry another woman.

At the time when Customary Law on this point originated it served the needs of the people because owing to bad communications and inter-district feuds most marriages took place within a circumscribed circle. There were few strangers and a man who maltreated his wife for such a reason would have little hope of marrying another since his character would be well known to parents who would refuse him as a suitor.

Under present day circumstances with internal peace and better communications chiefdoms have been brought into closer contact so that circles are widened and men can find wives in places where they are unknown. The law has not yet been altered to meet these modern condi-tions, but the first step has been taken in districts where restrictions on repayment of brideprice because of the birth of children have been introduced.

The rule that brideprice must under all circumstances be refunded is not offset by the granting of compensation to a wife in cases of cruelty. For instance if a man is ordered to pay Shs.60/= compensation to his wife and a divorce is granted on account of the severity of the injury, he claims Shs.100/= reimbursement of brideprice and is therefore still Shs.40/= in hand. Thus the intention of the Court which was to cause him a substantial loss is partially frustrated.

469. The following injuries are considered sufficiently severe to con-stitute cause for divorce:

Severe wounds inflicted intentionally;

Any wound inflicted by a spear, knife, bush knife or any sharp instrument;

Biting;

Fractures;

Permanent maiming;

Tying a wife to a post;

Causing defaecation by maltreatment.

QUOTATION: Gomb. Minazi No.58 from .1.1940

A man, according to the opinion of the Mwami, had divorced his wife and claimed the repayment of the brideprice solely in order to marry another woman with the money. The Mwami following the Customary Law could not refuse to grant the repayment of the brideprice, but he ordered that the father-in-law should repay the brideprice in instalments during

4 years. The husband's purpose was thus checked.

470. The court decides whether violence is **sufficiently** severe to constitute grounds for divorce. It is influenced in its decision by the circumstances in which the assault took place; for example provocation by the wife.

QUOTATION: D.O's appeal No.47 of 1938.

Kokwemage v. Kagaruki.
In a matrimonial quarrel Kagaruki caused severe bodily harm to his wife Kokwemage. Elders had tried previously to reconciliate the couple, telling the wife that she must obey her husband. It was held that the guilty party was the wife. She had refused to listen to the advice of the elders and wanted to rule in the house. The judgment was that she should return to her husband and mend her ways. Nothing was mentioned about the injury which was so severe that it necessitated the wife being kept in hospital for a month.

471. If an act of violence has caused severe bodily hurt a suit of divorce need not necessarily be filed. The wife may bring an action for compensation only.

472. The following acts of violence or their consequences are not looked upon as grounds for divorce:

> Minor blows,
>
> Beating with a stick (causing bruises or swellings),
>
> Pushing,
>
> Kicking.

NOTE: In such cases a wife usually goes to her father or a relative and complains. Elders are called and the husband is told to pay a trifling sum as compensation to his wife.

473. Minor hurts may be awarded compensation under certain circumstances: viz. Assault on an inherited wife who is legally the wife of the man who inherited her but often in fact merely under his protection.

QUOTATION: D.O's appeal No.41 of 1935.
Mbekomize v. bibi Kyozaile.

Kyozaile was the wife of Mbekomize's brother and after the death of his brother Mbekomize inherited her. He ordered her not to cut beer banana and she disobeyed his order. He beat her without causing a bodily hurt but was fined Shs.5/= in the Lower Court, of which Shs. 3/= were given to Kyozaile as compensation. It was held that he would have been justified in beating his proper wife for disobedience, but not an inherited wife.

VII. IMPOTENCE. (Mufa bushaija).

474. Impotence of husband at the time of marriage and after the marriage up to such a time as he could reasonably be expected to be potent is acknowledged as ground for divorce.

NOTE: The wife has the right of divorce, therefore impotence cannot be accepted as an excuse for adultery.

VIII. NEGLECT OF MAINTENANCE.

475. Gross neglect of maintenance by a husband is acknowledged as grounds for divorce.

NOTE: There can be no greater neglect than desertion without provision, which however is not acknowledged as grounds for divorce. (see para.445.)

476. Neglect, such as failure to provide clothing, is not considered as grounds for divorce unless it is obviously intentional neglect.

477. The husband may be held liable to pay compensation to his wife or her father, if the latter provided necessities for his daughter.

QUOTATION: D.O's appeal No.23 of 1935.

Bibi Mkabaikiliza v. Lugilahe.
Mkabaikiliza brought a suit for the dissolution of her marriage against her husband Lugilahe on the ground that he was not clothing her properly. The Lukiko Court ordered the husband to pay compensation of Shs. 15/= to his father-in-law, because he had not bought clothes for his wife for $1\frac{1}{2}$ years, and therefore the father had paid for them. All Courts agreed that this neglect did not constitute grounds for divorce.

QUOTATION: D.O's appeal No.60 of 1933.

Bibi Mailane v. Kavilyenda.
Kavilyenda, the owner of a plantation, refused to buy clothing for his wife. They went three times before elders who ordered that he should

buy clothes for his wife. The Court held that Kavilyenda should at once buy clothes to the value of Shs.24/= and give them to his wife. Further he should give his wife three cloths every year as is the custom for everybody.

IX. BREACH OF DOMESTIC CUSTOMS.

478. Neglect of a man to pay ihagiko to his first wife when he marries a second. (see para.409.)

479. If a man brings a concubine to his house without his wife's consent. (see para.410.)

479a. If a man commits adultery with a woman within the prohibited degrees of affinity. (see para.417.)

For either husband or wife.

X. NEGLECT OF CONJUGAL DUTIES.

480. Neglect of conjugal duties by husband or continued refusal for any reason by the wife are acknowledged grounds for divorce.

XI. MUTUAL ANTIPATHY

481. This if declared by both parties is acknowledged grounds for divorce. (Such a case is always settled out of Court.)

XII. ASSAULT OF EACH OTHER'S ELDERLY RELATIVES.

482. If a man hits his father-in-law or mother-in-law or any relatives of their generation.

483. If a woman hits her father-in-law or mother-in-law or any relatives of their generation.

484. If a man or his wife publicly abuses his or her parents-in-law.

XIII. WITCHCRAFT.

485. If one party believes the other to be a sorcerer, or if one party is suspected of sorcery by public opinion.

XIV. CRIME.

486. If either party commits certain crimes the other receives a divorce. Such crimes are:

Theft,

Arson.

(Homicide, justifiable or otherwise is not grounds for divorce.)

XV. LEPROSY AND EPILEPSY.

487. If either develops leprosy or epilepsy a divorce may be granted, because these diseases are considered to be hereditary and the fact that they were in the family should have been disclosed before marriage.

488. <u>No divorce is granted.</u> If the marriage is childless, if either becomes insane, if either becomes incurably sick.(exceptions being leprosy and epilepsy.)

LEGAL EFFECTS OF DIVORCE.

<u>Rules referring to property.</u>

489. Both male and female children belong in all circumstances to the father.

490. Small children may remain at first with the mother but when they are considered old enough they return to their father.

491. If at the time of divorce the woman pleads that the father is not fit to look after the children, the Court may at its discretion order that they stay with their mother or with a female relative.

492. If a father kidnaps his child while it is living with its mother he is liable to punishment.

QUOTATION: D.O's appeal No.3/P 1/5 of 1938.

Bibi Kobwijuka v. Salehe.
Salehe kidnapped his own child.   It was about 9 months old.   All three Courts agreed that a man should not take away the child from the mother

until it is weaned.   Salehe was fined Shs.10/= in the Lower Court   and Shs.15/= in the Appeal Court.

493. Permission to visit the mother must be asked from the father.   A mother can claim in Court her right to see the child.

494. If a divorced woman asks leave to return to live with her son after he has built his own house it is generally granted by her ex-husband.

495. A father from another tribe married to a Haya woman is not allowed to take his children so far away that the woman would be unable to see them.

   NOTE: This statement is open to contradiction but the majority view is that he cannot do so.

496. All seasonal crops, both in the fields or already stored in the house at the time of divorce are divided between husband and wife.

497. The wife has no right to share in coffee or banana crops.

498. Land even if it has been solely worked by the wife remains the property of the husband.

   QUOTATION: D.O's appeal No.1/P 1/19 of 1937.

   Nathanael v. Mafuruki.
   Mafuruki lived with the mother of Nathanael. After a time he
   found that his plantation was not big enough to sustain the whole family
   and he went to the chief to ask for a neighbouring field. It was granted
   him on payment of the usual fee. Nathanael's mother and sisters cultivated the land, planted banana and coffee trees.   After about 10 years
   the couple parted and Nathanael claimed the plantation.   It was held
   that he had no right to it, although it had always been cultivated ex-
   clusively by his mother and sisters.

499. A wife takes her private property including gifts from her husband with her.

500. The wife takes away with her such household goods as belong to her. Husband and wife have their separate household articles.

501. If a wife helped her husband with her private property to buy land, she is only entitled to ask for a payment of the borrowed sum and not for

a division of the land.

Rules referring to maintenance.

502. An ex-husband is responsible for the maintenance of his ex-wife only if:

a) she has no male relatives in the district and is not a wage earner herself.

b) she is a stranger and has followed her husband from another area. It is his duty to pay the expenses of her homeward journey. If she refuses to return home because her marriage with the man and her emigration with him makes it undesirable for her to return, he has to maintain her until she remarries or earns her living independently.

NOTE: It is seldom that an ex-husband is responsible for his ex-wife's maintenance, because a woman can easily earn her own living. If a man is not married to a woman with whom he is living, his duties under b are the same if he leaves her.

503. Once a legal obligation of maintenance has ceased to exist change of circumstances cannot revive it.

504. <u>Time from which a divorce takes effect.</u> A divorce becomes absolute when the husband receives repayment (in full or a first instalment) of the brideprice.

NOTE: Haya women often work to earn money to help with the repayment of their brideprice.

505. The actual receipt of a cheti cha talaka (divorce certificate) does not make the divorce legal.

NOTE: As a divorce is not legal until brideprice has been repaid, wholly or in part, logically if a husband refuses to receive it the money must still be paid. The Courts have found a way out of the difficulty by decreeing the setting aside of the rule in para.504, if a man is adamant in his refusal to accept repayment of brideprice. (see para. 301.)

506. It is the duty of the wife to ascertain whether her divorce is absolute, because until it is she is liable to be involved in a charge of adultery.

L A W   O F   P R O P E R T Y.

R E A L   P R O P E R T Y

GENERAL RULES.

507. Allocation fees (Kishembe) are paid on a plot as a unit, not on each separate division. If such a unit contains mwate the fee is Shs. 10/=; if it has no mwate the fee is Shs.5/=.

NOTE: Originally the word used for land allocation fees was buhaisa which means "something that is a case for giving". The word was not confined to the allocation of land but was used generally to denote a consideration which clinches a bargain between donor and recipient. The word Kishembe means a bribe and denotes the giving of a present to someone to induce him to intercede on behalf of the donor. Kishembe is now used generally, except in Kiziba, to denote the allocation fee. The original purpose of the dues paid for the allocation of land was that the acceptance of them by the Chief and his envoy was a recognition of the rights over the land in respect of which they were accepted. The amount paid varied; on the allocation of a nyarubanja the recipient usually paid a cow or a muzana (female slave) to the Chief. This was called kasha (that which produces). See Native Land Rules 1932. Letter No.20942/12 of 21-6-1932.

508. Should a man cultivate a plot for which he has not paid kishembe or transgress the boundaries of one on which he has paid, he is liable to a fine (exceptions, paras. 519, 519 note, 543, 595).

509. If he wishes to apply for the land he must then pay the allocation fee in addition to his fine.

510. If he does not apply for it, or if his application is not granted he may be required to uproot the crop.

511. Actual occupation of land confers no title, no matter how long it has been occupied.

512. Wherever the term ownership is used it implies "usufructory title nearly amounting to full ownership".

I PUBLIC TENURE.

Irungu.

513. This name is given to that part of the public land which is un-

114
occupied.

514. All allocations for which the fee (kishembe) of Shs.5/= is paid are taken from the irungu. The fee is payable to the Native Authority.

NOTE: The institution of the payment of kishembe is very old. In former times it was paid in kind.

QUOTATION: D.O's appeal No.73 of 1934.

Maschonko v. Rushakanza.
Maschonko claimed a piece of land from Rushankaza, stating that he had inherited it from his father; but Rushankaza could bring witnesses to prove that his father had paid an ox to the Chief on account of it. Maschonko lost his case because the payment could have only one interpretation, that the land passed into the ownership of Rushankaza's father.

515. There existed, and in some places still exists, a man known as the Muharambwa (or mwambansi or muhambansi or kusi) who has certain duties with regard to the irungu.

NOTE: The duties of a Muharambwa and his general position vary not only in the different chiefdoms but also sometimes in the villages of the same chiefdom. In many places the descendants of the Baharambwa have ceased to perform any of the duties of this office; in others they still perform duties of a religious character (see Appendix IV page 281). Where the office of Muharambwa is obsolete his duties are carried out by the Bakungu.

The Chiefs made the following statements as to the position in their respective areas :—

KARAGWE: No Baharambwa

IHANGIRO: The Muharambwa has no duties with regard to the irungu.

KIZIBA: The Muharambwa is the overseer of the irungu.

MARUKU: The Mukungu undertakes many of the former duties of the Muharambwa. The Mukungu is responsible for the boundaries of newly alloted plots in the Irungu. The Muharambwa is called as witness and assistant of the Mukungu.

516. The whole country was divided into districts each with its Muharambwa. The boundaries of these areas correspond with the village boundaries and therefore each village has its Muharambwa except where a village has been divided into two and no second Muharambwa has been appointed.

517. Where the Muharambwa still functions, his duties with regard to the irungu are that when land is allotted against the payment of kishembe, he is usually called to be present at the demarcation of the boundaries to ensure that they do not interfere with any existing land rights.

518. Before the new owner starts to cultivate it is customary for him to ask the Muharambwa to plant the first seed.

519. Should a clan find that its rweya rwa luganda (see para.590) has become insufficient for its needs it may temporally overstep its boundaries and cultivate in the irungu with the permission of its Muharambwa. In this case no kishembe is paid.

NOTE: There is a certain amount of cultivation done on free land; i.e. where there is free unoccupied land in a village no objection is made if the villagers use it for seasonal crops. That they do so confers on them no title to the land and no right to demand its use in future. They ask no permission and pay no kishembe, and should the land ever be required for allocation they have no rights in it. It was explained that the phrase used to denote such cultivation on land for which kishembe has not been paid is "Kulima rweya" while for land which is cultivated by an owner the correct phrase is "Kutumya rweya".

520. When this happens the Muharambwa may demarcate in the new area a plantation of his own, which is cultivated for him by the women who have plots in the rweya, for as long as the boundaries are overstepped.

521. Permission thus given to cultivate new land is merely temporary and confers no title.

522. It may happen that women from another village ask to cultivate irungu in the district of a Muharambwa not their own, in which case the Muharambwa concerned may give or withold permission as he sees fit.

523. The Muharambwa may enter any plot under seasonal cultivation to advise the women cultivating it on rotation and their work.

524. The Muharambwa is entitled by custom to small gifts in kind, which are called nsuka (except in Maruku where the name is maisho).

II INDIVIDUAL TENURE.

A. Kisi.

(In Karagwe: Enshambo; in Missenye: Itaka; in Kyamtwara: Kyeya.)

525. This is the name given to such arable land as is capable of bearing a perennial crop.

526. Kisi can be acquired only on payment of Shs.5/= to the Native Authority.

Proceedure for allocation.

527. A prospective settler who is a stranger has first to find a sponsor, called his Muhikya, who collects as much information as possible about the newcomer.   The Muhikya must be a man of standing in the village. The prospective settler may be introduced to his Muhikya by another villager to whom he is known.   While the Muhikya is collecting his information, which takes some time, the settler chooses the plot he will apply for. When the Muhikya is satisfied he introduces the newcomer to the village headman with a request that he will inform the Mwami (Sub-Chief) of the application for land.   If the Mwami approves he appoints an elder, who is known as a Mutaya, to go to the village. On the appointed day the Mukungu, the Mutaya, the applicant for the land and the neighbours assemble at the chosen plot.   It is customary also to call the clan-head of the leading clan and the Muharambwa as witnesses.   The Mutaya fixes the boundaries by planting a tree every twenty or twenty-five feet along them.   Mulinzi or murumba trees may be used but preferably mulamula (Kulamula means to decide').

528. All those present, particularly the Mutaya, are witnesses to the allocation and when the boundaries are fixed the applicant goes to the Gombolola to pay his kishembe.

529. Besides this form of boundary demarcation another method was used in former times where land was abundant.   The plot was allocated not by marking out definite boundaries, but by pointing out prominent landmarks;

thus a man was told that his plot extended "as far as the river," or "as far as the forest" and that the breadth of it was "between this hill and that hill" etc.   So common was this method that the Chiefs laid it down in their appeal case No.1 of 1935 that where definite boundaries are de- marcated it is proof that the land was not allocated unless it is of recent acquisition.

> ILLUSTRATION: A applied for a plot of land and B claimed that it could not be allocated to A since it belonged to him (**B**). A asked for proof, saying that there were no boundaries demarcated.   B replied that the fact that there were no boundaries was his proof of ownership coupled with proof that it had been in his family for many generations.

·530. Even for this form of allocation a Mutaya was appointed, and the Muharambwa and other witnesses above mentioned were called to the spot.

Owner's Rights and Duties.

531. The applicant becomes the owner so long as he complies with the rules of his tenure.

532. On applying for the allocation of arable land the applicant is asked what he intends to do with it.   If he states that he intends to cul- tivate it, he is bound to do so.

533. Should he not cultivate it within two years and if he has no reason- able excuse for not having done so he may be deprived of it.

> NOTE: The time limit mentioned here should not be taken too literally. See the following case:
>
> Chiefs' Appeal Court No.25 of 10—3—38.
>
> Fidele v. Mwami Antoni.
> Fidele was allocated a mbuga on payment of Shs.5/= kishembe. He went to the Congo without either planting it or building a house on it. After some time the Mukungu re-allocated it and a further Shs.5/= was paid, by the new owner.   After being away a year Fidele returned and claimed the plot.   It was held that since he had done nothing to the plot he had forfeited his right to it.

534. If he only crops it once with seasonal crops (ekirimo) and does

no more work on it he may also be deprived of it.

535. A man is not bound to plant any particular crop, even if he stated in his application that he intended to cultivate a certain one.

EXAMPLE: A man was allocated land suitable for bananas and coffee which he stated that he intended to plant. He then planted blue gums. No action could be taken against him though he probably intended from the beginning to plant trees and only stated coffee and bananas in order to acquire good soil.

536. A man need not build a hut on his land, unless this was a condition of the allocation.

QUOTATION: D.O's appeal No.93 of 1934.

Tibaganywa v. Mjuli.
Mujuli was allocated a mbuga for cultivation and for the building of a house. He did not do so and was deprived of his land.

NOTE: Most people do build a house on their land because there exists an idea that a homestead has some supernatural virtue in itself which makes the land productive. Though not for the reason given above, it is true that there are advantages in having a house on the land because of the manure from the cattle and goats housed in it, the household refuse of banana mulch and coffee husks for fertilizers and the constant attention which cultivation near a house receives. The owner of land cultivates it by law and lives on it by superstition, and therefore speculation in land is unknown. A parallel to this superstition is the idea which exists in the cocoanut plantations of the coast, that cocoanuts do best when they are within the sound of human voices.

537. A man is not allowed to sell his allocated plot either for cultivation or building until he has planted it with a perennial crop.

538. A man may allow other people to plant seasonal crops on his land, usually for payment in kind.

539. A man may with permission acquire land which he does not intend to cultivate immediately. In this case he must cultivate a small part of it yearly with seasonal crops, or allow others to do so, to show his interest in the land.

NOTE: Such permission may be given to a man who intends the land eventually for his sons, or who forsees that he will shortly require more land to replace coffee—trees which are going out of bearing.

Loss of Kisi.

540. 1. Obuchweke.

2. Failure to cultivate according to the above rules (see paras. 533 and 534).

3. Neglect of plantation, e.g., a man starts to cultivate bananas but later neglects his plantation so that the bananas will not bear. In this case the plantation reverts to the Chief after three years and the kishembe is forfeited.

NOTE: The assessors explained that if a banana plantation is left un-cleaned, in three years time the banana trees will be no higher than the grass and certainly will not bear.

541. If the owner of such a neglected plantation, which has reverted, wishes to lay claim to the land, he must do so within 6 months of the land being reallocated.

QUOTATION: D.O's appeal No.1/P1/11 of 1937.

Lwebogoro v Raphael.
Lwebogoro was allocated a kisi which he planted with coffee and bananas. After a time he left the plantation for reasons of superstition and took up virgin soil about 2 miles away. He was accused and convicted of neglect of the coffee—trees in the old plantation which he forfeited and which was reallocated to Raphael who put it in order. Four years after the reallocation Lwebogoro claimed the plantation as his property. It was held that he had no right to it, firstly, because he had un-doubtedly deserted it, and further because he had, probably purposely, delayed his claim beyond the time limit.

NOTE: In all questions regarding the neglect of plantations the law varies according to the form of tenure under which the land is held.

B. Rweya Rwa Nanka.

542. This is the name given to open land away from cultivated areas, which is unsuitable for perennial crops.

543. Rweya Rwa Nanka may be acquired:—

1. By allocation on payment of Shs.5/= to the Native Authority; the

boundaries are fixed in the same way as with Kisi.

2. By permission of the Mukungu (or in some places the Muharambwa) in which case no kishembe is paid and the land never becomes the individual property of the occupier. He has only been granted the right to cultivate it.

3. As part of the kisi in a case where the boundaries were not definitely demarcated.

NOTE: Where these vague boundaries are used it is possible that swamp land (lutatenga) may be included in the Rweya Rwa Nanka. A proof that a swamp is individually owned is the admission that the claimant has the right to dispose of any trees growing in it.

4. By inheritance, in which case it becomes the property of the heir and is subject to the rules of land under family tenure.

5. By purchase.

6. In satisfaction of a Court Judgment.

Owner's Rights and Duties.

544. No special rights and duties exist, as such land is either connected with the rest of a man's plantation or, if it has been allocated separately, the owner must fulfil the particular conditions under which he was given it.

545. Should Rweya Rwa Nanka be allocated for the planting of trees and after two years no tree has been planted it would revert to the Chief and the kishembe paid on it would be forfeited.

NOTE: As in cases of neglect of kisi, this time limit should not be taken too literally, see note to para. 534.

Loss of Rweya Rwa Nanka.

546. 1. According to the above rules.

2. If it is part of a plantation which is forfeited.

3. Obuchweke.

4. In satisfaction of a Court Judgment.

C. Kibanja.

547. A Kibanja holding may consist of

    a. Mwate, i.e. land planted with perennial crops (coffee or bananas).

    b. Kisi.

a. Mwate.

548. Mwate may be acquired:

    1. By allocation from the Chief on payment to the Native Authority of Shs.10/= for a plantation which is in bearing.

The new owner is shown his boundaries by a Mutaya (Muhaisa in Kiziba) who beats the bounds accompanied by the local village headman and a party of neighbours, for which work he receives a fee which is called obuhaisa. The new owner acquires all the water, fuel, road and grazing rights as held by his predecessor and also the latter's share in the rweya kyo luganda.

    2. By inheritance, in which case it becomes the property of the heir, restricted by the rules appertaining to land under family tenure (see paras.74-80). No ceremonial for beating the bounds exists.

    3. By purchase. Land thus acquired passes into the individual ownership of the buyer, i.e. during the owner's lifetime he may dispose of it to anyone he pleases, by sale, pledge, gift or disposition by will without restriction.

    4. In satisfaction of a Native Court judgment.

549. Mwate may be lost:

    1. By Obuchweke (see paras. 67-73).

    2. By neglect of plantation. If the plantation was acquired by allocation and the owner leaves it, and it can be proved that he intended

to abandon it, it reverts to the Chief for reallocation after three years. If the owner remains on the plantation but neglects it he cannot be expropriated.

NOTE: A plantation is usually abandoned for one of two reasons; either the owner dies obuchweke and so his holding reverts to the Chief, or an owner decides to leave because he believes that his plantation is bewitched. In the latter case no one else in the village or even in the same Gombolola is likely to take up the land. Everyone would be afraid of the evil spirits and even if a man were found who discounted them, he would be afraid that village opinion would be that he must be in league with the said spirits or at any rate have engineered a plot to get the owner to leave. Thus the only person likely to dare to take up the land would be a total stranger who could not have such an accusation levelled against him. If no such stranger appears it stands to reason that the plantation will remain neglected and such plantations are frequently to be seen in the middle of heavily cultivated areas.

NOTE: Kikamba. (Ku-kamba = ku-kanda).

This is the name given to a piece of land which has been under a perennial crop and allowed to go back to grass. There are many reasons why this should be, such as:-

1. Deserted plantation.

2. Superstition.

3. Coffee disease.

4. Failure to bear.

5. A holding is too big for the present owner.

NOTE: The Chief of Ihangiro states that according to Customary Law in his district such a plantation reverts to the Chief after 6 months. This change in the law is of a recent date.

For land under family tenure see para.576.

If the plantation was acquired by purchase, and the owner leaves and neglects it, he cannot be deprived of it.

NOTE: In Ihangiro, according to the statement of the Chief, a plantation even under these circumstances reverts to the Chief after 6 months.

3. In satisfaction of a Native Court judgment.

b. Kisi.

550. In a kibanja the plot capable of carrying a perennial crop and adjacent to the mwate is called kisi.   It is the remnant of the original kisi; its size varies from about 20 by 20 yards to one acre; it is left for the growing of seasonal crops such as sweet potatoes,millet for beer and cassava.

NOTE: In Maruku the term Kikamba is used to denote a piece of kisi
(land under seasonal crops adjacent to mwate) which is lying fallow.

551. It is acquired and lost together with the mwate.

D. Nyarubanja Tenure.

552. This is the name given to a group of plantations owned by one individual.   The landlord is known as Mtwazi,   the tenant   is known as Mtwarwa.

   In Karagwe this form of tenure does not exist.

History.

553. The Haya word for a banana plantation is kibanja and the word nyarubanja literally means "a large kibanja".

NOTE: See Mr. J.L. Fairclough's "Historical Notes" para.6 and see also
Mr. Griffith's "Land Tenure Notes" District Book.

   The following reasons for the creation of nyarubanja, which were advanced by the assessors, would seem to be the most likely:

   a. A clansman opened up new ground and in the course of time had many sons all of whom helped to extend the cultivation until it became big enough to be called a nyarubanja.   This clan community was ruled by its clan head, the father, so long as he was alive,and then by his heirs and descendants.   The clan head was the representative of his people in all dealings with the outside world.

   Naturally not all such nyarubanja continued in perpetuity.   For various reasons the plantation might revert to the Chief. It might hap-

pen that the whole clan decided to emigrate or that a clan head was convicted of witchcraft or that a clan showed cowardice or disloyalty in war
In either of the two latter cases the Chief had the right to dispossess
the clan head, either alone or with his whole clan, and reallocate their
land. Such a forfeited nyarubanja was usually given to a favourite or
a relative. The new landlord generally took possession of the house
and plot of the dispossessed clan head and either allowed the other members, if they had been not already been banished, to remain as his tenants or expelled them, according to how far he considered them to be personally concerned in the trouble which **had** led to the expulsion of their
leader. If allowed to stay, the holders of the plantations became his
tenants and were probably too glad to be allowed to retain their plantations to object to their change in status.

b. Another probable reason for the origin of some of the nyarubanja
holdings is that they were created by the Chiefs and given as a reward
of good service. Naturally there could not always be land which had
reverted available for this purpose and therefore the Chiefs, who had a
regular income from their subjects in the form of tribute, ceded some of
their economic privileges to a man whom they wished to reward and made
him landlord over a number of plantations, thus creating a nyarubanja,
and transferred some of their rights in the ceded area to him.

QUOTATION: D.O's appeal No.6 of 1930.

Tibalinda v. Muzamila.
Muzamila refused to admit that he was a nyarubanja tenant of Tibalinda,
basing his claim on the fact that his father was already living in the
plantation when Lwenduru was appointed landlord. It was held that the
Chief had the right to give a man an area as nyarubanja holding and to
divert the tribute from himself to the person appointed as landlord.

This appointment made little difference to the status of the kibanja
holders. It simply meant that in future they paid their trubute to the
landlord instead of to the Chief, and that the annual labour (nsika)
which they had had to render to the Chief was now given to the landlord.
In the case of obuchweke the land reverted to the landlord instead of to

the Chief.

NOTE: Tribute (ushuru) was due to the Chief annually in the form of beer, barkcloth, bananas, later, coffee and other commodities. Strict check was kept on each individual to ensure that he did not evade his obligations. Originally the clan heads were responsible for the collection of tribute and later the Bakungu were responsible to the Chief for it. When the Bakungu took over the responsibility they left the control of the individual shares to the clan heads.

Nsika: It was the duty of every able-bodied man to travel to the Chief's headquarters annually and to work there without payment for one month. The work consisted of cleaning plantations, erecting buildings, cutting firewood, herding cattle, etc.

553a. Whatever may have been the circumstances under which a landlord was appointed, he adopted a patriachal attitude towards his people, and his position was practically that of the head of a family. If a tenant's son wished to marry, the landlord assisted with the brideprice; he did not drink the tribute beer alone but shared it with his tenants. He was usually a Muhinda and as such a cattle owner and gave his cattle into the trusteeship of his tenants who thereby gained manure with which to enrich their land.

Perhaps the position is best illustrated by the custom that a landlord who was to be temporarily absent did not appoint an outsider to be his trustee but asked one of his tenants to look after his wives, children and property. Further that it was the custom for all tenants to build their houses with the doors facing the house of the landlord as a sign that they looked to him for everything.

553b. The fact that a tenant was at liberty at any time to leave his holding and go elsewhere indicates that the landlord had no hold over the individual unless the latter occupied the tenancy. He had a hold on the the land, as it reverted to him in the case of obuchweke and if a tenant left or was evicted for the transgression of certain rules; on the other hand the tenant acquired the ownership of his holding if the landlord behaved illegally. If a holding was vacated by a tenant the landlord was at liberty to occupy it with his family, but seldom did so as he needed labour which could only be provided by his tenants, outside labour being un-obtainable. Nowadays the situation has changed, since paid labour for cultivating the valuable coffee crop is available. The new rules acknowledge that the land is the restricted property of the landlord through the granting of a tribute to him. His ownership is restricted by the right of the tenant and his direct descendants to occupy the land so long as they comply with the rules of tenancy.

NOTE: While in former times the obligations of a tenant were not considered onerous and tenancy was even sought after, nowadays the introduction of money, trade and communications has altered the situation. Doubtless some landlords have abused their power under the new circumstances and have altered the old patriarchal system to one of serfdom, but the most important reason for the change lies with the tenants. When tax to the Government was introduced all tenants were included as tax payers; they still had to pay tribute to their landlords and therefore paid twice instead of once as before.

553c. The assessors gave the following account of the situation which brought about the compilation of the first nyarubanja register and, later, the framing of rules which ameliorated the lot of the tenant. They say that the attention of the authorities was drawn to the conditions of tenants by the fact that a tenant called Kalanga, who was expelled by his landlord for a petty offence, burned down his landlord's house and then ran amok and killed about 9 people. When the police arrived to arrest him he drowned himself in the river Kitema, near Kanazi.

553d. Originally there were fewer nyarubanja landlords and tenants than now appear in the register. (For explanation see the chapter "Squatters" para.608 Note).

553e. Rules for the acquisition, rights and loss of holdings and tenancies have been compiled by Mr. J.L. Fairclough in the following terms.

NOTE: The nyarubanja rules were first passed by the Bukoba Chiefs under Section 15 of the Native Authority Ordinance in 1930. They were revised by Mr. Fairclough in 1938 and it is the revised rules which are entered although they have yet not been approved by Government.

554. <u>Rents.</u>

I. A nyarubanja holder (hereinafter referred to as the holder), shall pay to Government through the Native Treasury, an annual rent in respect of his holdings, on the following scale:—

(a) A holder of less than five holdings shall pay an annual rent of Shs.2/50.

(b) A holder of not less than five and not more than 9 holdings, shall pay an annual rent of Shs.5/=.

(c) A holder of not less than ten and not more than 19 holdings, shall pay an annual rent of Shs.10/=.

(d) A holder of not less than 20 and not more than 29 holdings shall pay an annual rent of Shs.15/=.

(e) A holder of 30 or more holdings shall pay an annual rent of Shs.20/=.

QUOTATION: D.O's appeal No.21 of 1935.

Pesha v. Klementina.
Klementina claimed that Pesha was her tenant, which Pesha denied. Klementina lost her case because she had never paid any rent for her nyarubanja to the Native Authority.

II. These rents shall be collected by the Native Authorities and shall be paid into general revenue by the Native Treasury. Government will then refund to it half the sum so paid.

III. If a holder owns more than one nyarubanja in any one chiefdom, the rent to be paid shall be assessed on the total number of holdings in that chiefdom.

IV. If a holder owns nyarubanja in different chiefdoms such nyarubanja shall be assessed separately, chiefdom by chiefdom.

<u>Dues.</u>

V. A holder shall be entitled, in respect of each of his tenants' holdings, to the right to :—

(a) Reap annually in person, or by agent duly authorised in writing, the produce of one coffee-tree out of every fifty bearing trees or part thereof, with a maximum of five trees.

QUOTATION: D.O's appeal No.1. of 1938.

Baitani v. Chief Gabriel.
After the death of a tenant of the Chief's nyarubanja the brother of the deceased claimed that only a part of the estate belonged to the Chief's nyarubanja, the remainder being the property of the deceased's heir. In the disputed portion of the plantation trees marked with the nyarubanja tithe tree-marks were found. This was considered proof that the whole plantation was nyarubanja.

NOTE: In litigation as to whether a part or the whole of an estate is nyarubanja or not, it is helpful to know whether any of the coffee-trees within the area bear signs, called akabonera kubaija. Such a sign indicates that this tree has been chosen by the landlord for tribute.

(b) Select and cut annually in person, or by agent duly authorised in writing, four clusters of food bananas and four clusters of beer bananas.

QUOTATION: D.O's appeal No.1/01/37 of 1938.

Severian v. Tryphon.
Severian is the landlord of Tryphon. He marked 4 bananas as his, which Tryphon cut for himself. It was held that the tenant could do so, because the landlord has only the right to select and to cut four clusters of bananas, but he cannot mark them as he can coffee-trees.

(c) Remove annually in person, or by agent duly authorised in writing, the produce of one bark cloth tree of the types known as omushara or ekisibu or ky'enserere provided that any or all of these exist on the tenant's plantation.

(d) Enter a tenant's holding and cut two poles and such reeds as he may require for the express purpose of repairing or building his own or his child's house.

(e) Enter any thicket which may form part of a tenant's holding and cut such poles therein as he may require to repair or build the fence surrounding his house or the approach thereto, or to repair or build his own or his child's house.

VI. The holder may, if he so wishes, remit any or all of the dues to which he is entitled by these rules, and notice of such remission to be effective shall be registered before a Native Court. Mention shall be made in the agreement of the period for which the remission is granted, and each party shall pay a fee of Cts.50.

VII. The coffee and bark cloth trees mentioned in rules V (a) and (c) shall, when the necessity arises, be selected and marked by deputies chosen by the Sub-Chief and elders who shall also fix the fee to be paid to these deputies. Such fee, which will be paid from the Native Treasury, shall not exceed Shs.2/= per man, unless the Chief's permission has been first obtained. Trees selected under these or the old nyaru-banja rules shall not be changed from year to year; provided that, should any tree permanently cease to bear, another bearing tree shall be selected, marked and allotted to the holder; and further provided that, if all the trees permanently cease to bear, or if the price of coffee becomes negligible, the holder shall be entitled, in place of the produce of the trees, to up to 1/50th. portion of such other produce, if any, as shall be substituted for coffee by the tenant, who will in such cases harvest the crop himself, notwithstanding anything contained in rule V. The unit of weight to be used in any collection of dues under this rule shall be the kilogramme.

VIII. A holder shall not compel a tenant to perform free labour of any description.

Inheritance.

IX. If a tenant dies, leaving one or more sons, the holding shall pass to the latter and the tenant may decide, prior to his death, which of his sons shall inherit his holding. If, however, he leaves no will, either verbal or written, the inheritance of the holding shall be decided by members of the deceased's family, subject to an appeal to a Native Court, provided always that only sons of the deceased shall inherit his nyarub-anja holdings. **Any** necessary demarcation of new boundaries shall be carried out by the holder in accordance with the terms of rule XVIII.

X. If a tenant dies without male issue, his holding shall revert to the holder, who may dispose of it as he wishes, always provided that:—

(a) If the deceased leaves a widow and daughters they may continue to reside in the house on the holding until the widow's death; the native tax shall be a charge against the holder, who shall also provide her with food and clothing.

NOTE: The assessors unaminously interpret this paragraph to mean that a landlord cannot re-allocate the holding of a deceased tenant so long as the widow lives in it. If a widow decides that she will leave the tenancy permanently, she is not entitled to return to it later and claim maintenance from the landlord.

QUOTATION:

Agnes v. Mwami Lukambaiga.
A mtwarwa died leaving a widow. She claimed the inheritance of the tenancy. It was held that she is not entitled to it, but that it is the landlord's duty to maintain her until her death.

(b) Any daughters of a deceased tenant who leaves no male heir or widow, shall, at the discretion of the holder, either continue to reside on the holding, or shall evacuate it and live with other members of their family. The right to dispose of such daughters in marriage shall belong to the relatives of the deceased, and not to the holder.

XI. On the death of a holder, his son or sons, if any, shall inherit his holdings, any necessary division being arranged by the head of the family, in consultation with the family elders, in accordance with tribal law.

NOTE: The division of nyarubanja holdings on the death of a landlord is made in unequal proportions among his heirs. The Musika receives the greater share. If a landlord has 5 tenants, the Musika inherits 4 of them, the Maimuka one. Only the landlord's kibanja is under family tenure and not the tenant's holdings, because a tenant can at any time with the landlord's agreement purchase his holding; thus the landlord can agree to the sale without consulting his family (see also para.XXVIII).

XII. If a holder dies without male issue, the head of the family shall select another member of the family to be the holder, and such member shall be recognised as the holder of the nyarubanja provided that he abides by these rules. A landlord can under no circumstances disinherit his family; contrary to the rules laid down in para.48,49 and 50 for individual ownership.

XIII. In no case shall a woman become a holder, always excepting that a sister or daughter of a Chief may inherit a portion of her deceased brother's or father's holdings.

XIV. If a holder dies without male issue and no other male member of his family survives him, the tenants' holdings shall be declared free and shall pass into their ownership. They shall also pay the fee required by the Land Rules.

XV. No person shall be buried in a nyarubanja holding without the sanction of the holder. In any proceedings for an offence against this rule, no Native Court shall have power to order the exhumation of a body and its reburial elsewhere.

NOTE: Before the compilation of the rules by Mr.Fairclough, all Native Courts ordered the exhumation of corpses wrongly buried in a nyarubanja by the tenant. This order was given because sometimes a tenant claimed his holding as his property because he had buried a relative in it.

QUOTATION: D.O's appeal No.93 of 1936.

Lwekama v. Mustafa.
In a case as to whether a plantation belonged to the nyarubanja system or not, a man sought to prove that he was not a tenant because he had buried his child within the plot. From the register of nyarubanja holdings it was proved that he was a tenant and he was ordered by the Native Court to exhumate the corpse and bury it elsewhere within 7 days.

D.O's appeal No.62 of 1935.

D. Lwaitama v. Stanislaus.
Stanislaus buried his wife in his nyarubanja tenancy. He was fined

Shs.20/= in the Lower Court and ordered to exhume the corpse. The Appeal Court quashed the fine but confirmed the order for exhumation.

Maintenance of Holdings.

XVI. A nyarubanja tenant shall not sell, pledge or otherwise dispose of his holding or any part thereof, but he shall have the right to cut, either for personal use or for sale, any poles, wood, grass, reeds etc. growing within his holding, provided that he shall not sell produce taken from any forest land or thicket which may form part of his holding.

> QUOTATION: P.C's appeal No.8 of 1938.
> D.O's appeal L/P 1/3 of 1938.

Kamugisha v. Mwanika.
Mwanika stated that he mortgaged his nyarubanja tenancy to Kamugisha more than 20 years ago and now wished to redeem it. He lived for 20 years in Uganda. Both parties were agreed that the plantation is nyarubanja property. Kamugisha stated that he became a tenant after Mwanika had left. The Court held that a tenant is not allowed to pledge his holding and that therefore Mwanika's claim failed.

XVII. Further, a holder shall not pledge, sell or otherwise dispose of any of his tenant's holdings, except as provided in rule XXVIII. Any disposition of a holding in contravention of this or the previous rule shall not be recognised by any court.

QUOTATIONS:

D.O.'s appeal No.80 of 1934.

Rusharizi v. Sebastian.
Rusharizi was a tenant of Sebastian. Sebastian got into debt and his own holding was auctioned. He wanted to take a part of Rusharizi's holding, so that he had a place to live in. The Court held that the tenant cannot be deprived of the whole or a part of his holding for such a reason.

D.O's appeal No.2/P 2/21 of 1937.

Kagaruki v. Lugeyamba.
On the death of a landlord the executor decided that two nyarubanja tenants were to leave their holdings in order to give to the minor heir a plot big enough to keep a family. It was held that this was no reason to deprive the tenants of their holdings.

XVIII. A holder shall, when necessary, demarcate the boundaries of his tenants' holdings in the presence of two independent witnesses, one of whom shall be the village head man or his deputy. Any dispute arising out of a boundary shall be referred to a Native Court, whose decision shall be subject to appeal in the ordinary way.

XIX. Should a tenant for any reason fail to occupy his holding effectively and as a result it becomes neglected and overgrown, the holder may make an application to a Native Court, which shall fix a reasonable period during which the tenant shall be required to construct a house on the holding or to clean and cultivate the latter. Should the tenant fail to construct or to clean and cultivate he may be evicted. The Court fee for hearing a case of this nature shall be 1/=, payable to the holder.

NOTE: A tenant may not build a stone house or a house with a corrugated iron roof, nor may he allow another man to erect any kind of building on his holding without the permission of his landlord.

A tenant may not sell his house even if he has built it at his own expense.

A tenant may not dispose of his house by kularamu (See para. 981).

XX. When a tenant wishes to absent himself from his holding for a period of more than six months, and does not propose to leave some responsible person in charge, he shall enter into a written agreement with the holder before a Native Court in regard to the period for which he may absent himself. The fee in a case of this nature shall be Shs.1/=, payable by the tenant. Should the tenant absent himself, except for reasons outside his control, for a period in excess of that mentioned in the agreement, the holding may revert to the holder if he so desires, subject to confirmation by a Native Court.

XXI. Should a tenant leave his holding for a period of more than 6 months without entering into the agreement mentioned above, his holding may revert to the holder, if he so desires, subject to confirmation by a Native Court.

XXII.   A decision in any case in which surrender of a holding to the holder is claimed shall be subject to appeal in the ordinary way, and the tenant shall not be evicted until a final decision is reached.   If it is finally decided that he be evicted, he shall have the right to reap the crops sown prior to the application for eviction.

XXIII.   No holder shall evict a tenant or deprive him of part of his holding without the permission of a Native Court, whose decision shall be subject to appeal.

XXIV.   No tenant shall uproot or cut down any tree which has been marked in accordance with these rules. In any proceedings for a violation of this rule, a Native Court shall have the power, in addition to any other punishment which may be inflicted, to order the selection and marking of other trees in place of those so uprooted or cut down.

Penalties.

XXV.   Any person shall, subject to conviction by a competent court, render himself liable to the following punishments for an offence against these rules, in addition to the payment of any compensation which may be ordered:—

For a first offence, a fine not exceeding Shs.15/= or imprisonment in default of payment.

For a second offence, a fine not exceeding Shs.30/= or imprisonment in default of payment.

For a third offence, a fine not exceeding Shs.50/= or imprisonment in default of payment.

For a fourth offence, a tenant shall be liable to eviction from his holding, and a holder may be deprived of the holding of the tenant with whom he has been to law.   In such a case, the tenant shall pay the fee required by the Land Rules.

XXVI.   In addition, a tenant shall be liable to immediate eviction for the commission of any of the following offences, subject to conviction by a competent court :—

(a) Burning the holder's house.
(b) Committing adultery with the holder's wife.
(c) Rendering the holder's daughter pregnant.
(d) Slandering the holder to the Chief.

NOTE: A landlord may expel the female dependants of his deceased tenants for reasons a) and d) above.

QUOTATIONS:

D.O's appeal No.97 of 1934.

Mumbeija v. Bibi Bakakiyaa.
When Bakakiyaa's hut was burned down she said in her rage "I know who has done this -- Mumbeija (the landlord)". Mumbeija accused Bakakiyaa of slander and consequently wanted to evict her from her nyarubanja tenancy. It was held that rule XXVId could not be applied in this case as the woman did not make her remark to the Chief.

D.O's appeal No.2/P 1/13 of 1937.

Richard v. Kyebeleka.
Kyebeleka the tenant of Richard accused his landlord of arson and filed a suit against him in the Lukiko Court which was dismissed. The court held that under rule XXVId of the nyarubanja rules the tenant had made himself liable to expulsion by the landlord.

XXVII. A holder shall be liable to deprivation by the Chief of the holding of a tenant who is the complainant in a case in which the holder is convicted, by a competent court, of any of the following offences :—

(a) Burning a tenant's house.
(b) Committing adultery with a tenant's wife.
(c) Rendering a tenant's daughter pregnant.
(d) Slandering a tenant to the Chief.

In such a case, the tenant shall pay the fee required by the Land Rules; the Chief's decision shall be subject to appeal.

General.

XXVIII. Any holder may, if he so wishes, permit a tenant to pur-chase his holding, so that it becomes the latter's own property. Both parties shall appear before the Native Court, which shall confirm the proceeding in writing upon payment by each of a fee of cents 50. Fol-lowing on such a sale a holder may apply for and shall be granted any necessary reassessment of his nyarubanja tenants.

XXIX. It shall be the duty of a holder to bring immediately to the notice of a Native Court any change in the title to any of his holdings, and the Native Court shall then cause the necessary alterations to be made in its register, and bring the fact to the notice of its superiors.

QUOTATION:

Martha v. Kyayonka.
Kyayonka bought his tenancy for Shs.70/= which he paid to his landlord. The transaction was witnessed and appropriate documents exchanged. The landlord went away before the transaction could be entered in the nya-rubanja register, which is kept in the Lukiko. Mr. Fairclough con-sidered that in such a case the document about the transaction should be deemed valid as the nyarubanja register in the Lukiko is not always kept up to date.

III. FAMILY TENURE.

1. Kibanja kioruganda.

555. This name is given to a plantation under family tenure. Kibanja kioruganda can be acquired by inheritance only and every plantation which is inherited from a relative becomes Kibanja kioruganda.

Rights and Duties of the Owner.

556. The plantation is vested in one member of the family as owner whose disposition of it is restricted by the rules of family tenure only.

NOTE: If the family has been legally disinherited, the man who gets the plantation is the unrestricted owner but his children, when they inherit it, have to follow the rules of family tenure.

Sale.

557. The owner may not sell or give away the plantation without the consent of the members of his paternal family.

NOTE: A family consists of :—

1. Near Relatives. These relatives are called abakwatane (to possess property in common). All descendants of a common paternal ancestor in the male line may become near relations, because near relationship depends not on the closeness of blood relationship but on how many of the intermediate links are alive or dead. Thus the conception of near relationship is fluctuating; e.g. two men with a common great-grandfather would not consider themselves near relatives if intermediate links were alive, but if these were all dead they would become near relatives.

2. Distant relatives. All members of one clan.

3. Milango. All descendants of a common ancestor on the maternal side.

It is noteworthy that although the relatives of a man's wife have no legal rights, their influence is considerable. The relationship between a husband and his relations-in-law is as a rule very friendly and when necessary his children are frequently put in the care of their maternal relatives. A man often prefers a relative of his wife as his trustee to his own brother because he and his own relatives have too many common legal rights in family questions which may lead to dissension.

558. Paternal relatives have the right of pre-emption.

QUOTATION: P.C's appeal No.4 of 1938.
        D.O's appeal No.2/P1/ of 1937

Kaijage v. Lukiagabo.
Kaijage claimed that on the death of his uncle it was held in Court that the plantation of the deceased became the property of the Bahinda clan and that Lukiagabo should have the use of it. The latter sold the plantation and the relatives objected to the sale. It was held that the relatives must be given the first refusal but that if they did not wish to purchase the land the sale could stand.

QUOTATION: D.O's appeal No.23 of 1937.

Lubere v. Muganda.
Lubere and Muganda were brothers. Lubere sold a plantation which he

138

held under Kibanja kioruganda tenure and when Muganda wished to redeem it he refused to agree. The Chiefs' Appeal Court held that under the terms of the tenure the relatives must be given the right of pre-emption, and mentioned that it is important that a plantation under family tenure should remain in the family.

559. This right can only be exercised by the nearest relative available.

NOTE: The same applies to inheritance, guardianship and all matters in which family rights are concerned.

EXAMPLE: Should a man who lives in Ihangiro and has no relatives there sell his plantation, any member of his clan, even from another chiefdom, has the right to redeem the plantation by repaying the purchase price to the buyer. This clan member must first prove his right by proving his relationship which he does by naming all his ancestors back to the common one. Naturally such claims are seldom brought forward as it is unusual for a man to wish to buy land far away from his home.

560. A man must inform his nearest paternal relatives before he undertakes any transaction with an outsider with regard to his land.

If a sale is made without reference to the family.

561. Should the relatives concerned not have been informed that a transaction has taken place they have the right to invalidate the sale by bringing an action against the vendor, who must then return the purchase price he received, or allow the relatives to do so if he cannot find the money.

NOTE: The following procedure is sometimes adopted by people who, perhaps from a sense of personal grievance, wish to exclude their next-of-kin from exercising the right of pre-emption. The would-be seller arranges with a buyer a price for the sale of his plantation; at the same time he informs the buyer that officially he will say that the buyer has offered him a much higher price so that the relatives will forego their rights. Such negotiations may lead to litigation between buyer and seller.

562. The plantation is thus returned to the family and becomes the property of the man who repays the purchase price.

563. Should the vendor have died or cannot be found, the relatives may take action against the buyer, who must return the land on the payment

of the price he paid for it.

564. The buyer is entitled to compensation for any improvements he has made.

   QUOTATION: D.O's appeal No.1/P1/42 of 1938.

   Matayo v. Sospater.
   It was not quite clear whether Sospater, who objected to the sale of a plantation under family tenure, had had notice of the sale or not. The court ruled that in any case the sale was void and allowed Sospater to repay the buyer the purchase price plus compensation for wages paid by the buyer for the making of improvements to the plantation, after which Sospater was allowed to take possession of the plantation.

Rights of the Buyer.

565. The buyer has the right to harvest all seasonal crops which were planted by him.

566. The buyer has no right to the coffee harvest. Any coffee he has already harvested need not be returned but beans still on the trees are not his property.

Rights of the Original Owner.

567. At any time the original owner or his direct male descendants have the right to claim the return of the plantation from the relative, or the descendants of the relative who redeemed it, on payment of the redemption price. Any hardship to the present occupier incurred by his dispossession is not considered.

   NOTE: For this reason relatives who have only a vague right to interfere will not do so.

Time Limit for Relatives to declare a sale void.

568. The only time limit for the institution of proceedings to nullify a sale is that they must be instituted within 3 months of the date on which the relatives first heard of the sale.

569. An interested relative, who was absent at the time of the sale, is entitled to take action whenever he returns, provided he does not delay

doing so more than 3 months after his return.

NOTE: A relative who lives in the same village must take action within 3 months of the sale since it is assumed that he must have heard of it when it took place.

570. Should a man sell his plantation with the consent and in the presence of his relatives, and subsequently a nearer relation or one of the same degree who is not a party to the sale, demands its return he is entitled to do so, if he can pay the price received for the plantation.

NOTE: The practical consequence of this law is that a lawful buyer will insist on the presence of the vendor's nearest available relative as witness to the sale. Should a buyer have omitted this precaution the sale is probably suspicious and he can only expect any consequences that may arise from his omission.

571. Under no circumstances may an heir or a guardian sell a plantation so long as he has maintenance duties towards female dependants of the deceased.

Pledge.

572. A plantation under family tenure may be pledged, but any relative may at any time, even in the absence of the owner, redeem it.

573. If a relative does so, the payment of the money does not give him possession of the plantation. The redemption money is due to him as a common debt by the owner.

574. If the plantation has been pledged on the condition that it will become the property of the creditor failing the repayment of the debt within an agreed time, a relative has the right to redeem it, even after the time limit has expired, as in invalid sale (see para. 561); in which case it follows that the plantation becomes the property of the man who redeems it.

575. If a pledged plantation is auctioned to repay debts, no relative is entitled to take action for redemption against the buyer.

Loss of Kibanja Kioruganda.

576. A man cannot be dispossessed on account of neglect of his plantation.

(The Chief of Ihangiro states that a man can be dispossessed if he leaves a plantation and it is neglected.)

577. The presumptive heir to a plantation has no legal means of forcing the owner to keep it in good order.

Absentee Owner.

578. A man cannot be deprived of the ownership of a plantation if he leaves it and settles elsewhere in a known domicile.

579. If a man leaves his plantation and his new abode remains unknown for any length of time, the clan council has the power to appoint another clan member to look after the plantation.

NOTE: It seems that in former times, up to the war of 1914-1918, the plantation of a man could in these circumstances be re-allocated by the Chief.

QUOTATION: P.C's appeal No.15 of 1935.

Marko v. Mulaki.
It was stated by the court, "It seems that at that time(1914) a Chief could dispossess a man without giving a reason, but that it was rarely done".

580. If a man before he left appointed a trustee (musigire) who neglects the plantation, nothing can be done since he is responsible to no one but the owner; but if the trustee gives up his trusteeship then the clan council can exercise its rights and put in a caretaker.

581. When the absentee owner returns the plantation must be handed over to him; the man appointed by the clan council to care for it during his absence can claim no compensation and the owner can claim no account of the proceeds.

582. When the absentee owner returns he must make his claim for the return

of his plantation within a reasonable time of first hearing that another man is in occupation of it.

QUOTATION: D.O's appeal No.34 of 1935.
Judgment of Governor's Appeal Court, 11.9.35.

Marco v. Chief Lwaijumba.
Marco left the Bukoba district in 1912 and went to Zanzibar.   He left his plantation in the care of his aunt. When she died the predecessor of Chief Lwaijumba re-allocated the plantation.   Marco returned to Bukoba about 1925; he brought a case before the Lukiko Kabale for the return of his plantation, which he lost. He did not appeal to the District Officer, but Chief Lwaijumba is said to have promised to give him another plantation.   Marco did no more until 1934 when he revived his old claim, giving as his reason for doing so that he never received the other plantation which was promised him.   He lost his case in all courts.   It was held that he had delayed his claim without giving reasonable grounds for so doing.

NOTE: The Provincial Commissioner in the case quoted gives an explanation of what should be understood by "a reasonable time". He says "I can understand a man seeing another in what he considers to be wrongful occupation of his land not bringing an action for one season. He might say he would wait for the end of the agricultural season before doing so, so that he may enter before the begining of the next".

583. If no one can be found among the clan members who is willing to tend the plantation until the return of the owner it becomes the common property of all clan members as kisi kioruganda (see para.606).

584. Should a plantation under family tenure be re-allocated by the Chief to a man of another clan, the clan is entitled to object to the allocation provided that it puts forward its claim within 6 months of the new owner taking possession. This time limit does not prejudice the rights of the original owner who may make his claim on his return;   it refers only to the claim of the clan itself.

2. Rweya Rwa Luganda.

585. This name is given to a piece of open land under family tenure. It is vested in one member of the family who has disposition over it restricted by the rules regarding land under family tenure.

NOTE: The same name is given to open land communally owned by a clan. (See para.590).

586. Rweya Rwa Luganda of this kind can only be acquired by inheritance.

587. Every Rweya which is inherited becomes rweya rwa luganda.

Rights and Duties of an owner.

588. Rweya Rwa Luganda is usually part of the unit of a Kibanja Kioruganda and therefore is under the same rules.

3. Kisi kio Ruganda.

589. The kisi of a kibanja kioruganda is a kisi kio ruganda and is under the rules applying to kibanja kioruganda.

IV. COMMUNAL TENURE.

1. Rweya Rwa Luganda.

All Chiefdoms except Kiziba, Missenye and Ihangiro.

590. This name is given to the open land communally owned by a clan in which are planted the seasonal crops.

NOTE: Sometimes called rweya bananka to distinguish it from rweya rwo ruganda as described in para.585.

591. Rweya Rwa Luganda was acquired in the following way: In former times, when there was plenty of land, a settler was granted a large area of land as his rweya. The boundaries were often demarcated by the shooting of arrows; thus a man would be told that he might have four arrow shots in length and three in breadth; in other cases the rweya boundaries were indicated like those of kisi by means of some prominent landmark. On the owner's death his heirs did not take individual possession of the shares of the rweya, but inherited the whole as a body. Their descendants did the same and thus all this land remained in the hands of the first owner's clan and under communal tenure.

NOTE: Nowadays no rweya rwa luganda of this kind is created because a new settler is only granted a small piece of irungu sufficient for his own use as rweya. On his death his heirs inherit it as rweya rwa luganda according to the sense of the term in para. 585. The reasons for this procedure are not known but it seems probable that it is due to the small intrinsic value of the land and the necessity for a lengthy rotation.

Rights and Duties.

592. Rotation, which occupies from 5 to 7 years according to the particular location, made it necessary to divide the rweya into yearly plots. Each member of the clan living in the village has the right to cultivate a certain portion in each of the rotational divisions.

Rights of a new owner who possesses a plantation other than by inheritance.

593. If a man is allocated a plantation by the Chief on payment of Shs. 10/= kishembe his allocation carries the right to cultivate the plots in the rweya rwa luganda which go with his mwate.

NOTE: The heir to a kibanja automatically inherits the plots in the rweya rwa luganda which belong to the kibanja.

594. If a man buys a kibanja he has to ask permission of the clan-head to cultivate the plots in the rweya which go with his mwate.

595. If this permission is refused he may either ask for the allocation of a rweya nanka against a payment of Shs.5/= kishembe, or ask permission from the mukungu (or in some places the muharambwa) to cultivate a plot in the irungu; he pays no kishembe in the latter case and the plot never becomes his property, he is only given the right to cultivate it. For the sake of rotation he has to ask for a new plot every year.

596. It is also permissible for a newcomer to come to an arrangement with a clan member who has sufficient land in the rweya rwa luganda that he shall be allowed to share the plot, in which case rwinamo is usually paid.

597. A village usually has as many rweya rwa luganda as there are clans.

598. Among these clans there is always a leading clan; the clan of the first settler, the name of whom is often that of the village. The Muharambwa is invariably a member of the leading clan.

599. Should a clan in a village find that its rweya rwa luganda has become

insufficient for its needs it may overstep its boundaries and cultivate in the irungu with the permission of its Muharambwa, or where he no longer functions of the Mukungu. This overstepping involves no payment of kishembe since it is temporary and the land never becomes the property of the clan using it. (See also para.519).

600. The boundaries between the rweya rwa luganda of different clans in a village are under the supervision of the Mukungu. The boundaries of the rweya rwa luganda and the irungu are the responsibility either of the Muharambwa where he functions or of the Mukungu where he does not.

The boundaries of the plots within the rweya rwa luganda are the responsibility of the respective clan-heads.

601. No clan member may sell or pledge his plots, nor can they be distrained.

602. It is not forbidden to cultivate a plot which is not in the area being used for the year's rotation.

NOTE: This right is seldom exercised because the women, who do the cultivating of the seasonal crops, prefer to work together.

603. A man may cultivate more than one of his plots during the same year.

604. The same crop is planted in all plots in the same year.

KIZIBA AND MISSENYE.

605. No rweya rwa luganda of this kind exists in these Chiefdoms. Seasonal crops are planted either in kisi or in the irungu. No kishembe is paid if irungu is used, and the use of a particular place by one family for many years confers on them no title to it.

2. Kisi kio luganda.

606. A deserted kibanja kioruganda becomes a kisi kio luganda, which means that all clan members have the right to cultivate seasonal crops in it. (see also para.583.)

V. SQUATTER.

607. The definition of a squatter is a man who occupies land in the

plantation of a kibanja holder, either in the owner's personal plot or in another part of the holding.

NOTE: Squatter holdings probably originate for one of the following reasons: either a man inherits more land than he can use himself and therefore allows other people to occupy the extra parts as squatters, or a nyarubanja landlord prefers to replace the tenant of a vacant tenancy with a squatter instead of installing a new tenant.

Squatters are often minor heirs who found their share of the inheritance insufficient for their needs and appealed to the owner of a large plantation to let them have enough land from which to make a living, preferring to work in a plantation already under cultivation than to apply for an allocation of land and work it up from the beginning. The assessors emphasized that a squatter who has to leave his plantation usually prefers to become a squatter again rather than to start a plantation of his own.

608. The owner of the land is called mtwazi as in nyarubanja and the squatters are called his bapangi or bapangisa but the name batwarwa (the nyarubanja term for tenant) is sometimes used.

NOTE: When Mr. Fairclough's nyarubanja register was compiled all the Chiefs except the Chief of Ihangiro entered their squatters as nyarubanja tenants and most of the other nyarubanja landlords did the same. Some squatters tried to claim ownership of their plots after this, basing their claims on the fact that their names were not entered in the nyarubanja register.

QUOTATION: D.O's appeal No.79 of 1935.

Lwaitama v. Joseph.
Joseph installed Lwaitama as a squatter in one of his plantations after the compilation of the first nyarubanja register. Several years later Lwaitama claimed ownership of the plantation on the grounds that his name was not entered in the nyarubanja register. The Court found it proved that he had received the plot from Joseph as a squatter and dismissed his claim.

On this subject Mr. Fairclough writes, "In 1922 Mr. Baines directed the compilation of a nyarubanja register. Mr. Baines wished to stabilise the pure nyarubanja. All nyarubanja tenants were registered at that time as required, but in addition any native who had squatters on his land was allowed to register them as nyarubanja tenants although a chief had never given him or his ancestors a pure nyarubanja. This step was either taken in ignorance of the difference or through a misunderstanding of Mr. Baines' instructions."

At an earlier date, Mr. A.V.M. Griffith had written, "When the Bakama entered into preliminary discussions of the nyarubanja rules they pointed out that it was proposed that this set of rules should apply both to the recognised owners of nyarubanja and also to kibanja owners who had let out portions of their bibanja to tenants (alias squatters) upon terms which are purely personal and are not controlled by native custom as in the case of nyarubanja tenants and landlords".

Rights and Duties of Squatters.

609. In pre-European times the relationship between a squatter and his landlord was much the same as that between a nyarubanja tenant and his mtwazi with the exception that a squatter could be expelled by his landlord at the latter's wish.

> NOTE: On the other hand the position of a squatter was socially higher than that of a tenant. The landlord regarded, and today regards, his tenants as his people or underlings, whereas the owner of a kibanja who allocates a portion of his land to another man as his squatter looks upon the latter as his partner in a contract, his junior partner certainly, but nevertheless his social equal.

610. Nowadays a written contract is usually drawn up between the two parties which is signed by at least 4 witnesses.

611. Conditions of the contract vary, but generally include some of the original patriarchal clauses, such as the right of the landlord to use the squatter as a messenger etc.

612. The shares of the two parties in cash crops are defined.

613. No time limit is ever stipulated and it is mutually understood that either of the two has the right to terminate the contract at any time.

614. If a squatter is expelled, the landlord must allow him to harvest his current seasonal crops. The squatter may be given a few days' notice only to evacuate his house but if it is not yet harvest time he must be allowed to return to reap his crops.

615. A squatter who is expelled has no right to compensation for any improvements he may have made in house or land.

Installation of Squatter.

616. When a squatter is installed his landlord points out his boundaries to him but they are not demarcated nor are any witnesses called.

QUOTATION: D.O's appeal No.81 of 1934.

Herbert v. Mushumbusi.
In this case, which arose from a dispute as to whether a plantation had been presented to the claimant as a gift or whether he had merely been installed as a squatter, the Court laid it down that for a change in ownership of a plantation two conditions are essential :—

1. The payment of obuhaisa (kishembe), i.e. a gift must be made by the recipient to the donor as a token that the plantation has been given to him for his own property.

2. An Omuhaisa must be called, i.e. a witness who must be present at the time of the handing over of the plantation to the recipient to attest that obuhaisa has been duly paid. The omuhaisa points out the boundaries of the plantation to the new owner as he is instructed by the donor. The omuhaisa receives a share of the obuhaisa.

If these conditions are not fulfilled the plantation has not been given to the occupier who has only been granted an usufructory right in it at the pleasure of the owner. At any time the owner or his heirs may retract this usufructory right and demand the return of their property.

Finally it is extremely unusual for a man to make a gift of land to another and the only person who is at all likely to do so is a Chief.

Inheritance.

617. On the death of a squatter his heir either performs the ceremony of kwehonga (see para.24) or the landlord is invited to the ceremony of the installation of the heir, called kuzikiso (see para.14) during which he is asked by the relatives if he accepts the heir in the deceased's place.

618. The landlord has the right to chose an heir other than the Musika to inherit the deceased squatter's plot if he so wishes.

619. A squatter's plot is not divided among his heirs but falls to the

one chosen by the landlord, and, if the landlord refuses to have any of them he can obviously do so and the heirs have no claim.

620. On the death of a landlord, the squatters have to wait the decision of the heir who inherits the land on which they have their holdings as to whether they may continue to occupy them.

Traders as Squatters.

621. A man who is given by another, without an agreement, a piece of land in order that he may build a hut on it for trading purposes, is considered a squatter.

622. The owner of the plot has the right to evict him at any time.

623. The squatter who is evicted has the right to remove the building materials which he used in the construction of his hut.

QUOTATION: Chiefs' Appeal Court No.41 of 9.7.37.

Klementi v. Kengabo.
Kengabo allowed Klementi to build a hut on a part of his (Kengabo's) land and to use the hut for trading purposes. No contract of any kind was drawn up between them. After about a year they disagreed and Kengabo told Klementi to leave. Klementi refused. The Court held that Kengabo had the right to expel Klementi and ordered him to leave the place and remove his belongings, including the hut, within four days.

Biteme Squatters.

624. The origin of Biteme squatters is said to be as follows:- About 50 years ago when coffee became recognised as an economic crop the Chiefs took over large areas of land capable of coffee bearing, or deserted banana plantations, and put them under coffee. The work of preparing and planting these areas, was done as nzika (forced labour) by the Chiefs' subjects. Owing to the belief that a plantation must be inhabited to prosper, squatters were encouraged to live in these plantations which were known as biteme.

625. The terms for the squatters varied, but in the main followed the ordinary squatter rules. Thus the only real difference lies in the

origin of the holdings.

626. Biteme squatters originally had the use of bananas and seasonal crops in their holdings but received none or only a very small share in the coffee harvest.[*]

627. In Mr. Fairclough's "Introduction" to Nyarubanja Rules (File No. 619), a list of the Biteme squatters in Kiziba is given; to which may be added the following :—

BUGABO.

1 Kiteme in Bishaka, Gombolola Kagia.   This is planted with coffee only and has no bananas.   No squatters.

3 Biteme in Mwemage,   Gombolola Buhendangabo. Squatters are entered as tenants.

IHANGIRO.

In this chiefdom there are a large number of biteme.   The squatters have never been entered as tenants.

KIANJA.

1 Kiteme in Kaninya,   Gombolola Muhutwe.

1 Kiteme in Mulegeya, Gombolola Ibuga.

    The squatters are not entered as tenants.   There are no biteme in Maruku, Karagwe, Missenye or Kiamtwara.

FORESTS.

General.

628. The keeper of a forest is called Mukumu.

NOTE: Native forest guards are referred to by the people as "Bakumu wa Bwana Miti".

---

[*] There is an old saying "Amwiru akutunga engemu akwaka omumwani"— If a man gives you plantains he takes the coffee.

629. Each Chief has a head Mukumu, under whom serve sub-Bakumu for each royal and public forest   (except Karagwe, which has no royal forests, all Bukama forests are in the charge of the Mukungu of the village in which they are situated).

630. The clan head appoints a mukumu for a clan owned forest.

631. The owner of an individually owned forest may appoint a mukumu for his forest if he wishes.

Rights and Duties of a Mukumu.

632. A mukumu is responsible for ensuring that the trees are not stolen and that the collection of fuel is carried out according to the rules.

633. A mukumu must know the individual boundaries within the forest.

634. The mukumu can be dismissed by the owner of the forest.

635. The mukumu has the right to cut branches for fuel for his own use, and to use fallen wood for the same purpose.

636. The mukumu may not cut poles for building nor dispose of any timber.

637. A mukumu may file a suit against a transgressor of the forest laws if the owner of the forest is absent.

638. If the owner sells trees the mukumu points out the trees in question to the buyer and receives from him a fee called luhenda.

The following forms of forest tenure exist :-

1. Royal Forests.   (Kibira kio Bukama.)

639. These forests are claimed by the Chiefs as belonging to the office of Chief.

NOTE: Originally all forests which were not individually or clan owned were Kibira kio Bukama.   In 1938 the Chiefs were requested to state which forests they considered to belong to the office of Chief and which belonged to the public as communal forests. Therefore a distinction must now be made between Kibira kio Bukama and Kibira kio Irungu (public forests).   The latter is a new name and is created by analogy with irungu (public land).

640. They may not be sold or allocated.

641. Timber from them is granted free to subjects of the Chief who apply for it to the Chief.

642. They are cut from time to time by communal labour.

QUOTATION: D.O's appeal No.16 of 1935.

Leonhard v. Ntale.
Leonhard claimed part of a forest as his private property, but since this part was cut together with the rest at the time of the communal cuttings of the Chief's forest, it was held that it must be part of the Chief's forest, as if it had been privately owned it would have been left out of the cutting.

2. Public forests.   (Kibira kio Irungu).

643. From these forests are taken all the allocations for which the fee (kishembe) is paid to the Native Authority.

644. No person may cut or destroy the trees in the unallocated forest without the permission of the Chief, or his representative.

645. Any persons who have cut trees under a permit in public woodlands may be called upon to help to replant the same area. (see Native Forest Rules, July 1930).

3. Individually owned forests.   (Kibira kio Nanka).

646. A man can apply for an allocation of kibira in the same way as he can apply for an allocation of rweya or kisi.

647. Very small plots only are allocated, usually not exceeding 60 x 30 yards.

648. The boundaries are demarcated by the planting of mulamula trees, and all procedure is the same as in the allocation of kisi, with the exception that the duties of boundary demarcation are carried out by the Mukumu of the forest.

QUOTATION: D.O's appeal No.2/P1/24 of 1937.

Mukungu Michael v. Omukama wa Kiziba.
When the Chiefs were requested to make a list of all forests which were not individually owned, a forest was entered which was claimed by Michael as his private property. The Court dismissed his claim because he could not produce a mutaya and witnesses to the payment of kishembe (or obuhaisa).

Owners' Rights and Duties.

649. The owner has full rights of disposition over his forest. He can sell, pledge, bequeath it etc.

650. On his death the forest is inherited by his heirs under the rules of inheritance of land under family tenure.

651. The owner may if he wishes cut down all the trees and change the forest into a plantation.

4. Clan-owned Forests. (Kibira kio Luganda).

652. This name is given to a forest which is divided up into a number of individually owned plots under family tenure. All the plots are owned by members of the same family.

NOTE: There are no communally owned clan forests. The name kibira kio luganda is used both as a collective and an individual name. Each plot within a kibira kio luganda itself constitutes a kibira kio luganda and is known as such.

653. This form of tenure originated in a man being given a forest which, at his death, was divided into individual portions by his heirs and subsequently redivided by their heirs, each heir receiving his plot with strictly demarcated boundaries.

QUOTATION: D.O's appeal No.1/P1/4 of 1938.

Mondo v. Muganga.
Muganga, a clan-head, paid Shs.20/= to the Chief in order to get a forest which belonged to his clan as his private property; Mondo, a member of the clan, objected to the purchase. It was held that the sale was void since the forest was the property of the members of the clan and Muganga could not deprive them of their plots.

654. The individual plots are held under the rules of family tenure which are the same as those governing Kibanja kio Luganda (see para.555).

NOTE: The tenure of a kibira kio luganda lies between that of a plantation under family tenure and a rweya rwo ruganda under the communal ownership of a clan. It is the common forest of a clan, but each member owns a plot under family tenure which is his own individual property.

5. Native Authority Forest Plantations (Lukiko Plantations).

655. These plantations are the property of the Native Authority in whose area they lie and are planted and maintained with N.A. funds and the revenue accruing from them is the property of the Native Authority.

6. Communal Village Forest Plantations (Gombolola Plantations).

656. These plantations are planted and maintained by the communal efforts of the villagers.

657. The Bakama have ordered, under Section 8 of Native Authority Ordinance, which has been confirmed by Provincial Commissioner's letter No.876/210 of 6th July, 1939, that their subjects be compelled to maintain and increase the village communal tree plantations, but have exempted the following from such work:-

I. Any person who can prove to the satisfaction of the Native Authority that he is planting and maintaining annually a tree plantation which is 10 yards by 10 yards in area.

II. Any person who possesses and is maintaining in good order a tree plantation which is not less in area than 50 yards by 50 yards.

LAND HELD BY VIRTUE OF OFFICE.
Chief.

658. All property appertaining to the office of Chief is known as Ebinto byo Bukama — The property of the State.

NOTE: A Chief may possess private property like any other man. Either he buys it personally from his own private income or from the income he receives from the ebinto byo bukama, or he was possessed of it before he became Chief, or it was given to him as a gift by his subjects.

1. Irungu and Kibira Kio Irungu.

659. The titles under which the Chief today holds these lands have nothing to do with Customary Law and therefore there is nothing relevant to say about them here.

660. Originally the Chief and his subjects considered all land to be the property of the Chiefdom, since the Chief, in his capacity as Chief, had the unrestricted right of allocation and deprivation (see Appendix IV, "Tribal Structure", p.281).

NOTE: The Chiefs probably still hold this view and certainly certain institutions which are still in force would appear to uphold it e.g. that of obuchweke, which holds that the landed property of a man who dies without male paternal relatives and without sons reverts to the Chief. There is no law that the Chief must reallocate this land. Since there is a possibility that any plantation in the Chiefdom might revert to the Chief, he must consider that in principle all cultivated land is the property of the Chiefdom, though the rights over it are very severely restricted and can only be exercised in certain circumstances.

2. Kikale.

661. This is the name given to the large plantation which surrounds a Chief's residence.

662. In former times each new Chief on his installation built himself a new residence.

663. Every Mwami and Mukungu in the Chiefdom had a plot in the Kikale in which he lived during visits to the Court.

664. At least 5 men, sent by the respective officials from their own villages, lived permanently in each of these houses as caretakers.

NOTE: It was in the interests of the Chief to keep in his residence a number of his subjects who would form a protection to him in case of sudden attack and an extra bodyguard when necessary. The kikale was and still is heavily fenced.

665. Nowadays it is still the custom to allocate plots to the various officials of the Chiefdom, but not on such a large scale. Usually every Mwami has a plot in the Kikale, some of the Bakungu and a few of the

156
Baramata (see para.22).

666. The whole plantation is under the supervision of a man appointed by the Chief, called Mkuru-we-Kibuga.

667. The boundaries between individual plots are vague.

668. Bananas may be cut by the occupier of the holding and also by the Chief.

669. All coffee is the property of the Chief.

670. The occupier of the hut is responsible for the cleanliness of the plot.

671. The Chief has the right to disposses any occupier and deprive him of the use of the hut and the plot.

QUOTATION: D.O's appeal No.1/P2/27 of 1937.

Mutairulwa v. Mukungu Lutaiwa.
Lutaiwa had a hut ("nju ya okulisa" — the hut of the keeper of the royal drum) in the Kigando at Gera. The hut was in bad repair and Lutaiwa did not repair it. The Chief ordered Mutairulwa to demolish it which he did. Lutaiwa filed a suit against Mutairulwa for doing so. It was held that the Chief had the right to give the order and that further, the executor of a rightful order cannot be made responsible for it.

672. No part of the Kikale may be sold by a Chief.

QUOTATION: D.O's appeal No.1/P1/8 of 1938.

Mukama Nestor v. Herman Kambuga.
The predecessor of Chief Nestor sold a plot in the Kigando (Kåkale) of the Chiefs at Kiziba to Herman for the sum of Shs.150/=. Chief Nestor filed a suit against Herman as this sale was contrary to Law and Custom. It was held that Herman must return the land, and since he must have known that he was not allowed to buy land in the Kikale, his only redress was to claim the purchase price back from the Ex-Chief William who also knew that he had no right to sell it.

For a similar judgment see D.O's Appeal No.1/P1/6 of 1938.

3. Nyarubanja.

673. Such nyarubanja are the Kikale of former Chiefs.

NOTE: Nyarubanja which are the Kikale of former Chiefs of Kiziba, are known in Kiziba as Kigando.

674. When the new Chief built his new residence, he divided the abandoned residence which had been occupied by his predecessor into plots which were occupied by squatters.   These squatters were entered in the first nyarubanja register (see para.608 and note),and therefore these nyarubanja holdings are now under the same rules as those for ordinary nyarubanja except that a tenant cannot buy his holding.

675. These nyarubanja may not be sold by a Chief.

4. Kibanja Kio Omukama Mkuru.

676. This is the official residence of the mother of the Chief in the Kikale.

677. A Chief's mother always lives with him in the Kikale and should she die another woman of her clan is appointed to be official mother.

NOTE: The Chief's mother or official mother holds the position of 'go between' between the Chief and his people. Often, on the death of the real mother, quite a young girl will be chosen to take her place. She can say whatever she wishes to the Chief, and people who wish him to know something which they dare not mention to his face approach her and get her to tell him, often without saying whence the information has come.

678. When a Chief dies his mother leaves the Kikale and is usually given by the new Chief, a nyarubanja holding for her life, which reverts to the Chief on her death.

Officials.

679. In former times if a Chief appointed as Mwami or Mukungu a man from another village, he usually gave a plantation to the new official which became in his property,but in some cases the official was allocated a plantation, not as his property but for his use while he held the office. If he was dismissed his successor took over the plantation.

680. In both the above cases the usual procedure for allocation was

158

followed, the only difference being that on the death of the official in the first case the plantation was counted in his estate which it was not in the latter case.

NOTE: In Kiziba there is 1 such official holding.
" Bugabo " " 4 " " holdings.
" Maruku " " 2 " " "
" Missenye " " 1 " " holding.
" Ihangiro " " 2 " " holdings.
" Kianja " " 2 " " "
" Kiamtwara " " 8 " " "
" Karagwe " " 20 " " "

681. Nowadays a newly appointed official who takes over an official plantation pays no kishembe.

682. A Mwami today often receives a small plot near the Gombolola building, on which is a good house, as his official residence.

QUOTATION: D.O's appeal No.76 of 1936.

Daniel v. Chief Ruhinda.
Daniel the Ex-Mwami of Bumbire, claimed ownership of two houses and a eucalyptus plantation after his dismissal. It was held that the houses and plantation were not his property because the houses were built and the trees planted by communal labour and were therefore the property of the office of Mwami of Bumbire.

683. A deserted plantation for which there are no applicants may be placed by the Chief in the charge of the local Mukungu who usually allows the villagers to cultivate seasonal crops in it.

684. The proof that a Mukungu is the custodian only is that when he takes it over no mutaya is appointed to demarcate the boundaries.

QUOTATION: D.O's appeal No.5 of 1940.

Tibaimuka v. Chief Lweikiza.
Tibaimuka claimed as his property a piece of land which Chief Lweikiza stated had only been held by Tibaimuka's father in his official capacity. The Court held that Tibaimuka had no right to the land since when his father took it over no mutaya was appointed which proved that it was not allocated to him as his personal property.

Land held by priests.

685. This form of tenure came into being owing to the belief that ancestral spirits manifested themselves from time to time in certain places. When this happened the place in which they appeared became kibanja kio muzimu (the plantation of a spirit).

NOTE: It is unlikely that a new kibanja kio muzimu would be created nowadays though it is not impossible.

686. Should a spirit appear in uncultivated land, the Chief, on the advice of his soothsayers, decided to create a plantation on the spot in the hope that the spirit would thus be encouraged to take up a permanent abode there. A Mbandwa (priest) was appointed to look after the plantation and to pay respect to the spirit.

687. This plantation became the property of the Mbandwa and the Chief gave up all claim to the land or its products.

NOTE: It was strictly forbidden for a Chief to touch anything which came from a kibanja kio muzimu.

688. The post of mbandwa was hereditary; it was considered that the spirit owned the plantation and the Mbandwa was his squatter.

Manifestation of the spirit of a Chief's ancestor.

689. Should the spirit of a former Chief appear, his grave in his kikale became a holy place and a mbandwa was installed and allotted a plot surrounding the grave. The Mbandwa's duties were as in 686 above.

690. Since the plot lay in the nyarubanja of the reigning Chief which cannot be sold or alienated it did not become the property of the mbandwa.

691. The post of mbandwa was not hereditary but by appointment of the Chief (except in Kiziba).

NOTE: The Chief of Kiziba states that the Chief does not appoint the mbandwa but that a man who becomes mbandwa inherits the right to occupy the Shamba.
This would seem far more logical because the post of mbandwa is

held by a man in whom the spirit of the deceased Chief is believed to manifest itself and therefore he cannot be appointed by anyone.　See "Heirlooms of the Chiefdom of Kiziba"　re　Mbandwa of Kibi I, in Bukoba District Book.

If a man is believed to have become possessed of a spirit.

692.　If the claims of a man to have become　possessed by a　spirit　were recognised, his plantation became Kibanja kio muzimu　and he　the　Mbandwa of it.

693.　The post of mbandwa was hereditary and the plantation　remained the property of the first mbandwa and his　heirs.

QUOTATION:　D.O's appeal No.1/P1/2 of 1936.

Chief Kalemera v. Bitailongo.
Chief Kalemera claimed the ownership of a plantation inherited by Bitailongo on the grounds that it was the　kibanja　kio　muzimu　of Kimuli. Kimuli was the son of the ancestor of Chief Kalemera, Kalemera I. Kimuli was killed by his father and buried in the bush.　It is said that after a time Kimuli's spirit showed signs of dissatisfaction at　this　treatment and eventually a man claimed to have been possessed by it.　On the advice of his soothsayers, Kalemera I. built a new　house　in the man's plantation and sent 9 cattle, 9 hoes,　9 cooking pots to furnish it and installed the possessed man as mbandwa.　The Court held that Bilailongo, as the descendant of the original mbandwa, was the owner of the plantation and that Chief Kalemera had no claims on it.

TREES DEDICATED TO SPIRITS.　(Ekigabiro).

A. Trees dedicated to the spirits in general.

694.　In many villages there stand one or more　very old　trees which are known individually by name, one often bearing the name of the village. They are holy trees before which sacrifices may be offered to any spirit.

B. Trees dedicated to individual spirits.

695.　Such trees are dedicated to a particular deity or spirit.

696.　If they grow on private land, they are not the property of the owner of the land, but belong to such part of the community　as　uses them as a temple.

697. The owner of the land may neither fell, cut, nor sell, the tree.

QUOTATION: Lukiko Kabale Appeal Case No. 74 of 1935.

Roki v. Mukungu Mutalemwa.
Roki started to cut an old tree which was dedicated to the god Wamara. The Mukungu interfered and laid a case against Roki in Court. Roki was fined Shs.3/=. He pleaded that he had bought the tree from another man, but the Court held that this was no defence since he must have known that such a tree could not be sold nor had anyone the right to cut it.

WATER RIGHTS.

1. Natural Water. i.e. Rivers, Springs, Lakes, Ponds.

2. Artificial Supplies. i.e. Wells, Water-holes, Furrows.

1. Natural Water.

698. Natural water is free to everyone and may be used by individuals for their own purposes provided that the community makes no objection.

699. There is usually a ban on the use of a stream for washing, bathing, cleaning of hides or barkcloth, above where it is used for drinking purposes.

700. The owner of a plantation which contains temporary water may forbid its public use if it lies within his cultivated area, but not if it lies in an uncultivated part or in his forest.

2. Artificial Supplies.

a. Wells.

701. The water from a well dug in the cultivated part of a plantation is the exclusive property of the owner.

b. Water-holes.

702. No permission is necessary from anyone to dig a water-hole in uncultivated land.

703. The digging of a water-hole does not confer exclusive use of the water on those who have done the work. If the water-hole needs deepening anyone may be called upon to help and a man who refuses is excluded

in future from using it.

c. Furrows.

704. The water in a furrow made by an individual for his own use is his property; people who live on the route of the furrow may not tap the supply.

Water Supplies on Private Land.

705. The public cannot be deprived of the use of water on private land which they have been accustomed to use for a generation or more.

EXAMPLE: Should an owner put under cultivation land which was hitherto uncultivated he cannot forbid the public use of water in this land.

706. An owner cannot forbid the use of water in his cultivated land which the public were permitted to use by a previous owner.

707. An owner who himself first allowed the public use of water in his cultivated area can revoke his permission for its use.

708. Priority of use of water is as follows :—

       1. Drinking Purposes.

       2. Watering of Cattle.

       3. Domestic purposes other than drinking water.

For the rules for the watering of cattle see para. 849.

RIGHTS OF WAY.

709. The following terms are used:—

    1. Main footpaths between villages in a Gombolola: Kihanda Ngazi in Ihangiro, Karagwe and Missenyi; Kiongolero in Maruku, Kiamtwara, Bugabo, Kianja, and Kiziba.

    2. District roads and some public pathways: Omuhanda.

    3. Larger District Roads: Omuhanda Nyaihanda.

    4. Footpaths, usually hedged, connecting plantations with the nearest public road: Malembo.

5. Occasionally used paths through private land: Kihanda.

NOTE: The assessors stated that most roads were originally native tracks, and that many of them were broader in German times than they are now to prevent the danger of ambush; others have been more recently enlarged to carry motor traffic.

1. Kihanda ngazi or Kiongolero.

710. A footpath from village to village may be narrowed if the owners of the land on either side of it agree. The path may not be narrowed in any place to less than the average width of the whole path.

NOTE: This rule usually applies to mashaazi, i.e. the entrance to a village where the paths leading in usually widen out and leave a square on which cattle are collected to be take out to pasture. Nowadays owing to the decrease in the cattle population these squares are much bigger than is necessary.

2. Omuhanda.

711. These are paths which have long been in customary use for the fetching of water, to grazing grounds, as fisherman's paths to the Lake, or as subsidiary paths from village to village; they are all public rights of way.

712. Should such a path run through private property, the owner of the land may not close the path unless he makes another in its stead at his own expense.

3. Omuhanda Nyaihanda.

713. There is of course nothing relevant to say here about the P.W.D. and District Roads which are maintained by Government.

4. Malembo.

714. These paths are the exits of individual owners from their plantations and connect with the avenues leading from the houses.

715. These paths originate from:-

a. The sub-division of plantations by inheritance or sale.

      b.   The creation of nyarubanja.

      c.   The planting of kisi with perennial crops.

716. a. When a plantation was sub-divided by inheritance it might happen that one part had no outlet to a public road.   It was usual for the administrator of an estate to grant an exit for this part.

717. If the administrator's settlement was unsatisfactory, the owner of the plot took a goat to the Chief and asked him to grant a satisfactory right of way.   The Chief then sent a delegate to investigate and if the claim was upheld a right of way was granted, either through the plot of a co-heir or if more satisfactory through the plantation of a neighbour.

718. A hedge was planted on both sides of the new Ilembo.

719. No compensation for the path was paid to the owners of the land through which the new path ran.

720. Nowadays only a co-heir can be forced to grant a right of way through his plantation, unless a man inherits a plantation wherein he is surrounded on all sides by owners who are not his co-heirs, in which case the neighbours may be forced by the Chief to grant a right of way through their land on payment of compensation.

QUOTATION: D.O's appeal No.56 of 1935.

Ijugo v. Ikwataki.
Ikwataki sold a plantation to Ijugo 17 years before the case arose.
There was then a pathway running along the side of the plantation which gave them both access to the road.   After a petty quarrel in 1935 Ikwataki claimed that the path was not included in the area sold and tried to close it.   It was held that though the path was probably the property of Ikwataki it could not be closed, nor interferred with in any way, nor could the trees on either side of the boundaries be tampered with, and that both parties had equal rights to the use of it.

721. b. A newly appointed mtwazi usually took the central part of his nyarubanja for his own plantation, on which he built his house.   It was customary for all tenants (batwarwa) to arrange their houses in such a way that the doors faced towards the landlord's plot.   The landlord then

constructed a broad highway (ilembo) to the public road and all the malembo of his tenants led into it.

722. c. If an owner plants perennial crops up to his boundaries his neighbour may demand from the Chief that the boundaries shall be put back on either side to allow room for an ilembo if one is necessary.

723. Malembo cannot be closed by anyone.

724. An ilembo may be decreased in width if none of its regular users have any objection.

5. Kihanda.

725. Paths used occasionally, but not regularly, by the public may be closed by the owner at will where they pass through private land. Such paths are: a path leading to a part of a rweya which is only used when that part is under cultivation, or short cuts between two points of another path, or herdsmen's short cuts to grazing grounds.

726. Abandoned rights of way may be decreased in width to a minimum but may not be closed without the permission of the Chief.

PUBLIC FUEL RIGHTS.

727. All fallen wood, except that in a kibanja, whether on private or public land is free to all.

728. If an owner fells a tree no one else has any right to take wood from it.

729. Firewood is the property of the collector as soon as it is gathered.

NOTE: If a woman collects more than she can carry in one journey the bundle she leaves on the side of the road to carry home later may not be taken by anyone else.

PUBLIC RIGHT TO CUT GRASS.

730. Grass, except that in a kibanja, may be cut by anyone whether it is growing on private or public land (see also para.1068).

PUBLIC RIGHT TO COLLECT STONES.

731.   Stones, except those in kibanja, may be collected by anyone whether the land is public or private.

QUOTATION: D.O's appeal No. 79 of 1938.

Kagaruki v. Nshekanabo
Kagaruki brought a case against Nshekanabo for taking stones from his mbuga to build a house.   It was held in the Gombolola Court that Nshekanabo had the right to do so and the case was dismissed.

C A T T L E.

FORMS OF OWNERSHIP AND TRUSTEESHIP.

1. Ntekwa (Karagwe : Enshumbo or Enshokerano).

732. Ntekwa is reserved for the Chief.

NOTE: In former times the Chief alone disposed of cattle. From the spoils of war, from his own herds etc. he distributed beasts among his relatives, favourites and prominent soldiers. Although for the last 50 years everyone has been allowed to own cattle, the original descendants of these recipients are still the richest cattle owners.

The head herdsman of a chief is known as Kakiza (Karagwe: Mushumba).

733. The Chief chooses a certain number of his cattle, cows, bulls, and calves, and gives this herd into the charge of one man.

734. The usual size of the herds in the different chiefdoms is as follows:

a. MARUKU, KIAMTWARA, KIANJA, BUGABO and KIZIBA: from 50 to 60 beasts.

b. IHANGIRO: any number from 2 beasts upwards.

c. KARAGWE and MISSENYE: any number of beasts.

735. Rules regarding the birth of calves and the disposal of milk in the herd differ in the various chiefdoms :—

Chiefdoms under a. above.

736. Every calf, when it is nine days old, is taken with its mother to the Chief, and remains in the Kikale until another calf is born in its ntekwa; the first cow and calf are then exchanged for the newly-calved cow and calf, the former returning to the man in charge of the ntekwa (known as the Mutekerwa) who from then onwards has the profits of her milk, manure etc.

Chiefdoms under b. above.

737. If a mutekerwa originally received less than ten cows as ntekwa, he does not send a cow and calf to the Chief until this herd numbers ten

cows. The first cow to be sent to the Chief is called mpereza (Karagwe: Ezakashai) and remains in the kikale while in milk. After the sending of the mpereza the rules for the birth of future calves are as in a. above.

Chiefdoms under c. Above.

738. No rule exists. If the man in charge of the ntekwa herd, is told by the Chief's head herdsman (in these chiefdoms known as the mushumba) that there is not enough milk for the Chief's requirements, he takes one or more cows and calves to the kikale.

General Rules.

739. The cattle remain the property of the Chief and are at his disposal.

NOTE: Though the cattle remained the property of the Chief in the old days when he alone was entitled to be a cattle owner, his trustees had very important rights as to their own use of the herds in their care. In Karagwe if a trustee married he paid brideprice from the Chief's cattle; if he wished to slaughter an animal he did so; he could buy slaves who became his property and pay for them from the Chief's cattle.

The reason that these wide powers were allowed lies in the fact that the trustees were Bahima for whom to be without cattle is to lose interest in life and a cause for suicide; therefore the Chief could be certain that his trustees would devote all their energies to the increase of the herds under their charge and that he (the Chief) would be the eventual gainer.

QUOTATION: D.O's appeal No.1/P1/1 of 1938.

Chief Petro v. Mijungo.
The father of Chief Petro gave some cattle into the keeping of the father of Mijungo. It was held that the cattle were not the property of Mijungo, but belonged to the Chief.

740. All calves are the property of the Chief and the birth of a calf must be reported to him.

741. The hide and all the meat of a beast which dies must be taken to the Chief, who usually returns one leg to the mutekerwa.

742. The Chief has the right at any time to take away the ntekwa from a

man.   The most common reasons are :—

    a. Personal reasons.

    b. Dishonesty of the mutekerwa.

    c. Careless herding.

743. The mutekerwa does not have to pay tribute whatever his profits from the milk, ghee and manure may be.

744. The mutekerwa is responsible for the cattle in the ntekwa herd.

745. If an animal is lost and he cannot produce its carcase he has to pay the value of it or substitute another in its stead.

746. The mutekerwa is allowed to kuheleka (see para.765) without asking the permission of the Chief.

2. Ntungwa.

(In Ihangiro, Nyebugirwa; Missenye, Yanyabiro; Kiziba, Ntungwa yakaba).

a. Ntungwa of the Chief.

MARUKU, KIANJA, BUGABO, and KIAMTWARA.

747. The Chief gives one or more head of cattle to a man called Mutungwa; the beasts remain the property of the Chief.

748. All calves are the property of the Chief.

749. The milk is the property of the mutungwa.

750. The hide and all the meat of a beast which dies must be taken to the Chief, who usually returns one leg to the mutungwa.

IHANGIRO, KARAGWE, MISSENYE and KIZIBA.

751. The Chief gives one or more head of cattle to a man, which become his property.

752. All calves, milk, meat and hides are the property of the mutungwa.

753. Since in these chiefdoms the cattle thus given become an outright

gift, certain customs are observed to distinguish the handing over of them from a handing of cattle into trusteeship. These are as follows :—

Customary observances on the handing over of Ntungwa.

754. The Chief hands over the cattle to a middle-man, called Muhaisa; this man is the witness of the transaction and passes the gift to the recipient from whom he receives Shs.4/=. The cattle are then driven home by their new owner who continually exclaims "Yakoba, Yakoba," as he goes, thus acquiring a number of witnesses to the gift in case his right to the cattle is ever in question.

   NOTE: In Ihangiro the custom of Yakoba does not exist.

b. Ntungwa of the ordinary man.

MARUKU, KIANJA, BUGABO, KIAMTWARA and IHANGIRO.

755. Cattle given as ntungwa remain the property of the donor. Calves are the property of the donor.

756. The hide and meat of a beast which dies, with the exception of one leg, are the property of the donor.

757. The recipient (mutungwa) has to make annual gifts of senene, ghee, bananas or beer to the donor.

758. The mutungwa is responsible to the donor for the cattle.

749. If an animal is lost and he cannot produce its carcase the mutungwa must pay its value to the donor or substitute another in its stead.

KIZIBA, KARAGWE and MISSENYE.

760. The cattle become the property of the recipient.

761. Calves, milk, meat and hides are the property of the mutungwa.

762. Since the cattle become the property of the mutungwa he has no annual presents to make and is responsible to no one for the cattle.

3. Kuhela kimoi. (Karagwe: Engabirano — a complete gift.)

763. Such a present of cattle must be made before witnesses. The witnesses are the donor's children and other relatives. The handing over of the cattle is a very solemn occasion and is accompanied by a beer-drink, the participants in which are also witnesses to the gift.

NOTE: I witnessed the presentation of a cow in Ihangiro. A long time ago a cattle owner had given a cow to another as ntungwa; this cow had calved 13 times and the owner ordered the mutungwa to prepare beer on a certain day. On this day the owner arrived with his son, four near relatives and many neighbours. The owner and the witnesses went to the kraal, chose a cow (presumably one of the offspring of the ntungwa cow) and said "My mutungwa has looked well after my property; I now give him a cow for his own. He may do as he likes with it. If my son should become poor and the cow should have calved many times, I hope the mutungwa will remember this gift and help my son; but if the cow and her calves should have died and the mutungwa has become poor, then there will be two poor men." H.C.

A gift of cattle is very rare, though on the occasion of the ceremony of blood-brotherhood a cow may be given by one of the blood-brothers to the other; in this case the cow is called nte nshumikano.

764. In Maruku, Kianja, Bugabo or Kiamtwara, a Chief who gives a cow as an outright gift to a man does so before witnesses saying "I give you this cow, you can slaughter it. Do not inform me when it calves or dies."

NOTE: Cases arise in which there is a discussion as to whether cattle were given to a man as Ntungwa or Kuhela kimoi; the proofs of the latter are:—

That none of the calves of the cow or cows in question were sent to anyone else; that if the cow in question has died, her hide and meat were kept by the man who claims her; that when the cow in question calved the man who claims her did not go officially, taking a present of beer or bananas, to inform another man of the fact.

QUOTATIONS: D.O's appeal No.3/P1/28 of 1938

Jakobo v. Mpeka.
Jakoba claimed 5 head of cattle from Mpeka which he said he had given into his charge 20 years ago. Mpeka denied that the cattle were the property of Jakoba and claimed them as his own. It was proved that in 1924 Mpeka had written to Jakoba to inform him that one of the cows in question had calved. This was taken by the Court as proof that Mpeka

172

was the mutungwa of Jakoba.

4. Mpelekwa.

765. Cattle are sometimes secretly handed over by their owner to another man. This may be done for the following reasons:

    a. The fear that they will be commandeered by the Chief.

    b. The fear that they may be distrained on account of the owner's debts.

    c. An epidemic in the neighbourhood.

    d. Fear of witchcraft.

    e. The wish to conceal the birth of calves.

EXPLANATION: This may be done by a mutungwa who wishes to cheat an owner; he places the cow during several years in the care of different men and after it has calved several times he informs the owner, but does not give the correct number of calves.

    f. To effect the exchange of calves at birth.

EXPLANATION: A mutungwa who is also a cattle owner himself may be very anxious to ensure that he has a heifer calf; for this reason he may secretly send two cows-in-calf to be cared for by another man, one being his own and the other in his charge as ntungwa. His idea is that if his own cow produces a bull calf and that of the other owner a heifer, he will claim the heifer and inform the other man that his cow has a bull calf. It would be difficult to arrange this if the cows were not sent away as they might not calve on the same day and the mutungwa is bound to inform the owner immediately his cow has calved.

766. It is obvious that when Mpelekwa is performed there are seldom any witnesses; since the most usual reason is the fear of witchcraft not even the nearest relatives are informed. If there are witnesses they receive no fee.

767. The Muhelekwa (the receiver of the cattle) has to send annual gifts to the owner.

768. If the cow or calf dies the Muhelekwa has to send the meat to the owner.

NOTE: The proof that these rules (767, 768) have been carried out takes the place of the evidence of witnesses. The only other persons likely to have any knowledge of the affair are the two men's Bakondo (see para.869). The cattle owner must have informed his mukondo if he transferred cattle from his herd and the mukondo of the muhelekwa would know if the latter had added to his. (See note to para.888).

5. Kusigira.

769. A man who intends to be absent for a time may appoint a trustee (musigire) to look after his cattle.

770. The most frequent occasions on which this is done are:— If a man is going on a journey, or has to serve a term of imprisonment.

NOTE: See also para. 229, re powers of a guardian to remove cattle from the care of an absent man's wife.

771. The appointment of the trustee takes place before witnesses chosen by the owner and the trustee.

772. The cattle and all future calves are the property of the owner.

773. All milk, manure etc. is the property of the musigire.

774. If an animal dies the musigire must inform the wife or a relative of the owner.

775. If this is not possible the musigire must call other witnesses, preferably the Mukungu or the Mukondo (see para.888).

776. The musigire may not skin the animal before the arrival of the witnesses.

777. If the meat of a dead animal is sold, the musigire is responsible to the owner for the proceeds of the sale.

778. The musigire is responsible for any damage done by an animal in his care.

6. Kukwasa.

779. Cattle whose ownership is in dispute may be placed in the charge of an independent person until the dispute is settled.

174

a. By mutual agreement of the disputing parties.

780. The disputants, then known as bakwasa, agree to place the cattle in the care of an independent person known as a mukwasiba.

781. The mukwasiba takes all milk, manure etc. of the animals while they are in his care.

782. All calves born during this time are the property of the man who eventually establishes his claim to ownership.

783. The mukwasiba is responsible for any damage done by the cattle while they are in his care.

784. The cattle are handed over to the mukwasiba before witnesses.

785. If a beast dies the mukwasiba must inform both parties.

786. The mukwasiba sells the meat of a dead animal and keeps the proceeds of the sale until the dispute is settled, when he hands the money to the owner of the cattle together with the hide and horns of the dead beast.

787. The mukwasiba must call witnesses to the sale of the meat.

788. The money received from the sale of the meat is called bishambyo.

789. When the cattle are returned to the winner of the case, the latter must pay the mukwasiba a sum of money from Shs.2/= upwards, depending on how many beasts have been in his charge. This fee is called obuheruzi.

790. If a cow should calve shortly before the animals are due to be returned, the mukwasiba is entitled to keep the cow for two months and to take the milk. In this case no obuheruzi is payable.

791. The mukwasiba is responsible for the loss of an animal if he cannot produce its carcase.

792. The bakwasa have the right to change the mukwasiba by mutual agreement.

793. The mukwasiba may not return the cattle to one of the bakwasa unless the other or his representative is present.

794. In no circumstances is the mukwasiba allowed to slaughter an animal.

b. By order of the Court.

795. Any court may order this measure.

796. The beasts in question must be brought into court.

797. The president of the Court appoints a mukwasiba.

798. If the president of the Court appoints a mukwasiba arbitrarily without consulting the bakwasa he, and not the mukwasiba, is responsible for the cattle.

799. Should anything happen to them, the president of the Court must pay compensation and, if the loss is proved to have been the fault of the mukwasiba, must claim the amount from him afterwards.

800. If the president consults the bakwasa on the choice of mukwasiba and they agree to his appointment, the muk asiba, not the president, is then responsible to the bakwasa.

801. In case of the death of an animal a mukwasiba who has been arbitrarily appointed must inform the Court.

802. The Court sends two elders as witnesses to the sale of the meat and the proceeds of the sale are taken on deposit by the Court.

803. With the exception of para.792, all rules under a. above apply.

7. Kuchwererera.

804. An agreement may be made by which a calf whose mother is dead may be sent by its owner to another man who has a cow in milk.

> NOTE: The word kuchwererera means literally to cheat, i.e. the calf is cheated because it believes that its mother is feeding it. The calf usually remains for one year since it is considered dangerous for its health to allow a calf to eat grass or any other food but milk before it is a year old.

805. The two parties agree either :—

a. That a certain sum, usually Shs.30/= or Shs.40/=, shall be paid by its owner when the calf is returned to him. This represents one year's keep; if the calf is returned earlier a proportionate amount is payable.

or

b. That the calf shall become the common property of both parties.

or

c. That when the calf is full-grown and starts to bear, its first calf shall be the property of the owner of the cow which was its foster-mother.

806. The owner of the calf is not responsible for any payment if the calf dies during the first year.

807. If the calf dies in the first year, one leg is the property of the owner of the foster-mother.

808. If the calf is lost and its carcase cannot be produced, the man in whose charge it is is liable to its owner for its value.

809. If a calf, sent to a foster-mother by a muhelekwa, a mutungwa, or a mutwasiba, dies its meat is sent to the owner and not to the trustee.

8. Exchange of Cattle (Kuhinga n'te).

810. A bull, a barren cow or a cow which has ceased to bear, may be exchanged as a slaughter animal for a cow or a heifer.

811. Unless otherwise stated, the cow and her future offspring are the common property of both the parties (except Ihangiro, Karagwe and Kianja).

IHANGIRO, KARAGWE and KIANJA.

812. This arrangement of mutual ownership is unknown in these three chiefdoms.

813. The usual form of exchange of a slaughter beast is against an unborn calf (see paras. 1025 et seq. "busito") which becomes the sole property of the slaughter beast's owner.

814. If the cow is dead and its meat is to be exchanged, the exchange

is against an unborn bull calf.

815. If the selected cow does not bear a bull calf at her next calving any bull calf already in the herd may be given as payment instead.

9. Communal Ownership. (Enkwatane).

816. The communal owners form a kyama (chama).

817. The contract between the members of the kyama is made before outside witnesses.

818. The payment for the cattle is made before outside witnesses. Each member receives a tuft of hair from the beast as proof of his share in it.

819. This tuft of hair is shown to his wife and son and is henceforward kept in his bed. This custom is called kukuza n'te (to breed cattle).

820. There is always an even number of shares in a beast; if there are an odd number of owners, one man takes two shares.

821. All conditions of sale laid down in the contract must be fulfilled by all members in all circumstances.

822. Payment of an instalment cannot be delayed because one of the members is absent; nor can a member who was absent at a time when a decision was taken by the kyama refuse to abide by it.

823. No member may sell his share to an outsider without first offering it to his fellow members.

824. A member may sell his share to any of his fellow members.

825. The position of the nkuru ya n'te (see para. 1040) is not affected by changes in the ownership of the shares, even if by sale within the kyama his share is no longer the largest.

826. All matters affecting the kyama cattle must be decided unanimously (i.e. sale, kuheleka, kuchwererera etc. see paras. 765, 804).

827. If a cow is sold each member receives a share in the proceeds proportionate to his share in the beast.

828. The cow is kept in turn at the house of each of the members; the length of her stay with each depends upon the size of his share.

829. The member concerned has the exclusive use of her milk and manure as long as the cow is kept in his house.

830. Calves are shared by all members, each having rights proportionate to his share in the mother.

831. If in the course of time the number of calves equals the number of members, the calves may either remain as common property or may be distributed, one to each member who becomes its sole owner.

QUOTATION: Chiefs' Appeal Court No. 103 of 1938.

Bushange v. Mushumbo.
These two men bought a cow A between them. A calved and in time this calf B calved. A and B both died leaving only B's calf C. Bushange claimed that Mushumbo had no right to a share in C because its mother B died whilst in Mushumbo's care. The Court held that unless there had been a distribution of the calves they were held in joint ownership.

832. A member in whose house a kyama cow calves is allowed to keep the cow for a double period as compensation for his work during the calving.

833. If the cow dies the meat is distributed among the members in proportion to their shares.

834. If the cow dies the hide may not be sold, nor the meat distributed before all members have seen the carcase.

NOTE: There is a saying "ey' ababili ejunda (The meat of a kyama cow usually rots)".

835. If the hide is unsaleable it is given to the members owning the smallest share.

836. If a member is absent and has appointed a trustee, the trustee is admitted as his representative but no one else can represent him.

837. Matters affecting the kyama cattle, such as arrangements for kuheleka, kuchwererera (see paras. 765, 804), are arranged by one member of the kyama

as its representative.   This member is not necessarily the nkuru ya nte.

838. If the share of a member is distrained it cannot be sold to an outsider before the other members have had the option of purchasing it.

839. During an animal's stay in the herd of a member, the member is responsible for its herding and for any damage to property it may do.

840. If the cow dies or is lost, the member responsible for it at the time must inform his fellow members.

QUOTATION: D.O's appeal No.1/P1/25 of 1938.

Malingumu v. Mpisi.
These two men were joint owners in the leg of a cow. The cow was bitten by a snake and died while in the care of Mpisi, who informed Malingumu. Later Malingumu denied that he had been informed and claimed compensation.   The Court held that it was established by the evidence of witnesses that he had been informed and his claim was dismissed.

841. The above rules apply also to kyama ownership of sheep and goats. (For sale of cattle see paras.992 et seq; for loan of cattle see paras. 1145 et seq.).

GRAZING RIGHTS.

Public Grazing.

842. Throughout Uhaya all open grassland is free grazing. Open grassland on privately owned land is free to all for grazing.

843. A cattle owner may graze his herd where he wishes irrespective of whether he lives in the area or not.

844. There is no form of grazing reserve.

845. Free grazing is not confined to the members of the tribe;   non-Bahaya have equal rights to it.

Private grazing.

846. An owner who wishes to reserve grazing on his private land for his own use must fence it so strongly as to make it impossible for any animal to enter. To demarcate the boundaries with stones or with a thin line of

trees is not sufficient.

Land which may not be grazed.

847. Land under cultivation, either cropped, reafforested, or planted with matate, may not be grazed.

Land from which crops have been harvested.

848. After the conclusion of the harvest such land becomes available for grazing.

WATERING OF CATTLE.

849. Rules differ in different chiefdoms.

IHANGIRO, MARUKU, BUGABO, KIZIBA, KIAMTWARA and EAST KIANJA.

850. Rules for the watering of cattle apply only to running water.

851. Cattle may be watered anywhere.

  NOTE: Owing to adequate rainfall there is plenty of running water and no necessity to dig water-holes.

852. No claim by users lies if a stream has been fouled by cattle.

KARAGWE and WEST KIANJA.

853. Cattle may not be watered in running water.

  NOTE: Most of the herdsmen in these areas are Watussi, and the water law of the Watussi is followed.

854. Water must be tapped from an adjacent stream into a water-hole for the use of cattle.

855. If no running water is available separate water-holes must be allotted to men and cattle.

856. If one man or a group of men dig a water-hole for cattle they have the exclusive right to the use of it.

857. Natural water supplies are free to everyone whether the user belongs to the village or not.

MISSENYE.

858. All the above rules apply except para.856. In Missenye, if a man or a group of men dig a water-hole, the water is not their exclusive property but they have prior claim in it.

HERDING OF CATTLE.

859. All cattle owners in a village form themselves into a kyama (Chama), the leader of which is known as the Mukondo. (see also para.1251).

860. The position of mukondo is hereditary so long as the family continues to own cattle.

861. All members of the kyama act as herdsmen in turn.

862. The herdsman for the day is responsible for the cattle in his charge.

863. If the owner whose turn it is to herd changes his day with another member of the kyama, the responsibility lies with him who does the herding.

864. If an owner whose turn it is to herd delegates his duty to a herdsman outside the kyama, the owner himself is responsible for the safety of the cattle on that day.

The herdsman's responsibilities include the following:-

865. The herdsman is responsible for any damage to property done by the cattle.

866. The herdsman is responsible for harm done to a beast at which he has thrown a stick, spear, etc.

867. The herdsman is responsible if a beast is missing on the return of the herd from grazing and its carcase cannot be produced.

868. The herdsman is responsible for harm to cattle caused by snake-bite, falling, eating poisonous plants etc. if he is grazing them on ground which it is customary to avoid on account of these possibilities.

869. If a cow calves during the day the herdsman is responsible for bringing home the calf; if he does not do so he is liable to replace it

182

with a full-grown beast.

NOTE: If he was able to inform the owner of the cow during the day he is not responsible for bringing home the calf.

870. A still-born calf must be carried home to the owner.

871. If a herdsman burns grass, which is frequently done to destroy vermin, he is responsible for seeing that the fire does not spread and cause damage to property.

The herdsman is not responsible in the following cases:—

872. If harm is caused to an animal by falling, snakebite, or eating poisonous grass, unless he has disobeyed the rule in para.868 above.

873. If two herds meet and the bulls fight.

874. If bulls fight within the herd and injure each other.

875. If damage is done by cattle to a cultivated plot which has not been properly fenced by the owner with a fence called Katangante (to keep out cattle).

NOTE: This applies to all plots situated within 25 feet on any side of a grazing ground.

876. If an animal kills or wounds a man.

NOTE: If a man is killed by a bull, the bull is slaughtered and the family of the deceased receives one leg.

877. The responsibility of the herdsman begins when he takes over the cattle from their owners at the place in which they are assembled in the morning and ends when the owners or their delegates (bataya) take them back in the evening from the same place.

878. If the bataya are late in coming to fetch their cattle in the evening, the responsibility is theirs and the herdsman need not wait for them; therefore if the cattle find their own way home and do damage en route the owners are responsible and not the herdsman.

879. If the herdsman is late in the morning he is punished, but if the

cattle do any damage while awaiting the arrival of the herdsman the owners are responsible.

880. The herdsman may be ordered by the mukondo to graze the cattle in a certain ground during the day and be punished if he disobeys.

Herdsman's rights.

881. The herdsman may refuse to take out to graze a cow which is likely to calve during the day.

882. The herdsman may refuse to take out to graze a cow which is sick or lame.

883. If any of the members brew beer the herdsman for the day is entitled to share it.

884. A herdsman may not milk the cows, or ride upon an animal.

Duties of an owner.

885. An owner must keep his cattle clean and tick-free.

NOTE: An owner whose cattle are not tick-free can be brought before the Court of the Cattle Owner (Ntegeko ya Mukondo) by the herdsman.

886. An owner must take part in the communal work which is done in the interests of herding, e.g. building little bridges through muddy patches, improving paths on the slope leading to a watering place.

887. An owner of a dangerous bull must remove it from the herd.

888. An owner must report any change in the number of his cattle to his mukondo.

NOTE: So strictly is this rule observed that a man who has lost an animal and hears that it has been seen in another district goes directly to the mukondo of that area, knowing that he must have information if a strange beast has entered any herd in his kyama.

889. An owner cannot leave the kyama without a reason and hence cannot be expelled without a reason.

890. An owner can be expelled from his kyama for breaking the rules re-

garding cattle.

QUOTATION: Chief's Appeal Court No.9 of 1938.

Iruganyuma v. Kyetobo.
Iruganyuma was expelled from his kyama for refusing to obey the orders
of his mukondo, Kyetobo, and was told that in future his cattle must
be herded separately.   Iruganyuma appealed against this to the Gombolola Court which upheld the mukondo.   He then appealed to the Lukiko
and finally to the Chiefs' Court;   all courts held that the mukondo's
decision was right and Iruganyuma lost his appeal.

891. An owner cannot be expelled from his kyama for reasons which have
nothing to do with cattle.

Strayed animals.

892. It is the duty of any man who finds a stray beast to keep it in
his house and look after it until the owner claims it.   It is then returned and no compensation can be asked by the man who has looked after it

For procedure of the Court of the Cattle Owner see paras.1251 et seq; for
Cattle as Brideprice see paras.305 et seq.

SHEEP AND GOATS.

893. Customary Law takes little account of sheep and goats in comparison
with cattle.

894. Sheep and goats are put out to trusteeship under Mpelekwa (see
paras.765 et seq.); Kusigire (see paras.769 et seq.); Kukwasa (see
paras. 779 et seq.).

895. Since the milk and manure of sheep and goats is considered useless
to the trustee, it is usually arranged that the trustee receives the third
lamb or kid born.

896. Where sheep and goats form ritual presents, mention is made in the
section dealing with the customary observance.

For Goats as Brideprice see paras.327 et seq.

RULES FOR FISHING IN LAKE VICTORIA

The Guilds of the Lake Fishermen. (Makokoro ba Bajubi).

897. Fishermen in Lake Victoria form themselves into guilds (kyama) called ikokoro.

898. All Lake fishermen within the Bukoba District follow the same rules.

899. All the waters of the Lake on the Uhaya coast are free, and no ikokoro claims particular rights over any part.

900. The members of an ikokoro form an economic unit and all the fishing is done by the various makokoro, no fisherman fishes on his own.

901. The number of members varies from about 6 – 12.

902. Each member owns a share.

The fishing outfit.

903. The fishing outfit, consisting of boat, net, rope, and baskets is owned communally by all the members of the ikokoro.

904. The outfit costs about Shs.150/= and each member contributes towards the cost.

905. This contribution entitles the member to a share and on the size of it depends the size of his share.

Inheritance of shares.

906. A share is inherited according to the law of inheritance of the Bahaya.

907. Women may inherit a share.

908. If a shareholder nominates, as the inheritor of his share, a man whom the other members of the ikokoro dislike they may, if they have knowledge of his choice, inform the testator that they refuse to accept the nominee; or if they do not know of the nomination until the testator

is dead, they may refuse to accept the heir and buy him out by repaying him the original amount paid for the share.

Sale of shares.

909. A member who wishes to sell his share must first offer it to his fellow-members for the price originally paid for it.

910. The above rule holds even if a higher offer should have been made by an outsider.

Pledge of shares.

911. A shareholder may not pledge his share to any person outside the ikokoro.

Repairs to the outfit.

912. The expenses for small repairs are divided among the members in proportion to the size of their shares.

913. A large expenditure, such as the purchase of a new boat or net, is also divided among the members in proportion to the size of their shares.

914. Should a member be unable to put down the money for his share of the cost, his membership expires and he is bought out of his share of remaining common property of the ikokoro by the other members.

Fishing.

915. All members are expected to take their part in the fishing.

916. A member who does not do so and has no good reason for his absence cannot claim his part of the day's proceeds.

917. A member may, with the consent of the others, appoint a substitute to do his work and take his share of the proceeds.

918. If a member does not take part in the work for some good reason such as old age, illness, family business, locusts etc. he is entitled to claim his share while absent.

NOTE: If, for one of these reasons, a member is unable to take his share of the work he will still receive his part of the proceeds, and if it is necessary for someone to be taken on to help in his absence, a man will be employed by the other members who will all contribute to pay his wages, which in this case are usually in kind.

919. Sometimes two or more makokoro go out together in order to cover a larger area, in which case each ikokoro claims the fish caught in its own net.

Proceeds.

920. The head (nkuru) of the ikokoro alone is allowed to take the money received from the sale of fish.

921. The daily takings are written down and distributed every two or three months by the nkuru.

922. The members receive amounts proportionate to the size and number of their shares.

923. A member who needs money before the time of distribution can be given it in advance.

924. The nkuru is responsible for the money and must refund it if he is short in his accounts.

925. The nkuru receives a small remuneration.

Expulsion from an Ikokoro.

926. A member may be expelled for one of the following reasons :

> Adultery with the wife of another member.
> Assault of another member.
> Theft of fish or fishing tackle.
> Embezzlement of money.

927. An expelled member is reimbursed the amount originally paid for his share.

For rules of the Court of the Fishermen (Ntegeka ya Bajubi) see paras. 1252 et seq.

S A L E.

I. IMMOVEABLE PROPERTY.

A. Land.

Forms of Sale.

928. A sale contract may be verbal or written.

NOTE: Sale of land was practically unknown until within the last forty years and therefore no rules were evolved by customary law to deal with it; even now the cases are comparatively few, so that no law adequate to social and economic life has come into being. Such rules as do exist have arisen to meet outstanding demands at one time or another and are in many instances illogical and contradictory and may easily fail to cover a particular situation.

In Karagwe the sale of land is most unusual and is said to have been forbidden by the late Chief.

QUOTATION: D.O's appeal No.35 of 1935.

Chief Edward Lwaijumba stated that no outright sale of land is, strictly speaking, allowed in his chiefdom without his permission. He admitted, however, that latterly this law has fallen into disuse and it is especially disregarded by persons who, while apparently pledging their land, actually, by agreement with the mortgagee, intend to allow it to fall in to him, and the contract is made on this basis. Difficulty has thus been experienced in maintaining a proper check on the sale of land, and the Chief has consequently ceased to make any real attempt to use his right to control it. In effect the lack of observance of the old law has reached such a pitch that most of those in Court held that the Chief had no right to be consulted about the sale of land and even Chief Lwaijumba himself confessed that he was doubtful as to whether he could still claim these powers.

929. All conditions of a sale must be stipulated before about 6 witnesses, an equal number representing each side (confirmed by D.O.'s appeal No.1/ P1/6 of 1938).

930. A sale without witnesses is void, even should both parties agree that it has taken place.

931. The witnesses are entitled to a small fee called endamu or kichwaiguzi (in Ihangiro: eichumu ly'eibanja).

932. A contract is not binding on either side before any payment has been made.

   NOTE: Option to purchase or first refusal is unknown.

933. Payment must be made in the presence of (about) 6 witnesses.

934. At the start of the negotiations, the boundaries of the plot are pointed out to the prospective buyer by the owner. If the buyer wishes to continue the negotiations another date is arranged on which the boundaries are again pointed out to him, with the neighbours as witnesses that they are correct.

935. After payment the boundaries are again approved and new boundary marks are placed in position where necessary.

936. The placing of the boundary marks is the duty of the witnesses after they have received their endamu.

937. The parties to the sale each pay half the endamu.

938. The buildings on a plot are not included in the sale, whether it takes place privately or by public auction, unless specifically mentioned.

   NOTE: Some of the assessors disagreed on this point and their opinion is upheld by the following:-

D.O's appeal No.4/Pl/3 of 1939.

Shabani v. Plucikila.
Shabani's plantation was auctioned to pay his debts and bought by two men who re-sold it to Plucikila. She demolished a house in the plantation and was sued by Shabani for compensation for it and for furniture and tools which he stated were in it, on the grounds that the sale of the plantation did not include the house. The Chiefs' Appeal Court refused to grant compensation, holding that a house is included in the sale of a plantation unless otherwise stated and that with regard to the furniture and tools, they should have been removed by the owner before the auction. The D.O's judgment on appeal upheld the Chiefs' finding.

QUOTATION: P.C's judgment in D.O's appeal Case No.3/Pl/23 of 1938.

Rajabu v. Ibrahim.

Rajabu's plantation was sold to pay his debts. In the order of sale it was stated that the plantation and the crops on it were included. The P.C. in his judgment remarks:— "I am informed by the Chiefs and Elders that if the house was to have been sold it should have been mentioned in the order for sale, and if it was not mentioned it means that it was not to be sold and was not sold."

939. Unless otherwise stated the sale of a plantation includes all perennial crops and excludes all seasonal crops.

940. Unless otherwise stated a vendor who includes fields cropped with seasonal crops in his boundary statement is understood to sell the ground but not the standing crops. He is entitled to harvest these crops.

941. Should it be arranged that a vendor remains in the plantation after the conclusion of the sale he is entitled to cut one bunch of bananas on the day of sale and after that may cut no more.

942. Verbal Contract. All above rules apply to verbal contract.

Written Contract. (Most transactions relating to land are nowadays contracted in writing).

943. All the above rules apply to written contract with the addition of the following:—

944. These documents follow no fixed formula.

945. Vendor and buyer each receive a copy of the conditions of sale, signed by the witnesses.

946. A clerk who writes out such a document must sign it.

947. If the document is lost it is admissible for the witnesses to declare its contents as proof of the contract (compare para.53).

Payment in Cash.

948. The whole purchase price may be paid on the day of the conclusion of the sale or payment may be by instalments.

949. The first instalment is called mukwato (a token).

950. Dates for the payment of instalments are agreed upon. The European calendar is generally used.

951. The property passes into the possession of the buyer on payment of the first instalment.

952. In the event of further instalments falling into arrears the vendor can   a) claim them as a common debt;

b) return the instalments already received and declare the sale void.

953. In the case of (b), the liabilities of the buyer are as follows:

1. If the buyer has erected new buildings he may either sell them to the vendor or demolish them if the vendor refuses to buy them.

2. The buyer must leave a new house, if he has built it, in place of one which he has demolished.

3. The buyer can claim no compensation for any improvements he may have made to the old buildings.

4. The buyer cannot claim a refund of house-tax paid by him if the plantation reverts to the original owner.

5. The buyer is not responsible for losses due to natural causes incurred during his occupancy (plant diseases, fire etc.).

954. Any change made in the sale contract after payments have commenced, must be stipulated in the presence of the witnesses for both parties, preferably those who witnessed the original contract.

955. The vendor cannot interfere with the work of the buyer on the plantation during the payment of instalments.

956. A buyer who has paid the first instalment of his purchase price is at liberty to re-sell the plantation at any time.

957. Should the original buyer, after he has re-sold the plantation, fail in the payment of the instalments, the original owner can take possession of the plantation under rule 952 (b) and expel the present

occupier, whose claim to compensation must be made to the man from whom he bought the land.

> EXAMPLE: A sold his plantation to B and it was arranged that payment should be made in instalments. B re-sold the plantation to C before completing the payments. B then fell in arrears with his instalments and A returned to him the amount which B had paid in instalments and expelled C. C claimed the amount of his purchase price from B.

958. If a buyer wishes to make an instalment payment on a date earlier than that on which it falls due, the vendor must accept it.

959. The payment of instalments must be made before about 6 witnesses preferably those who witnessed the sale contract.

960. If the contract was a written one, the payment of each instalment must be entered on the document and endorsed by about 6 witnesses preferably those who witnessed the drawing up of it.

Payment in Cattle.

961. The full purchase price may be handed over on the day of the sale or one beast may be handed over on the day of sale as an instalment and further payments arranged.

962. A vendor who has received cattle in payment has no claims on the buyer if they prove defective (barren cows, diseased animals etc.) even if it is proved that the buyer knew of the defect.

963. The vendor must fetch the cattle from the purchaser's kraal.

964. If a beast refuses to leave the herd or, if taken by force, returns to the buyer's kraal the vendor may ask for another in its stead.

965. If it is agreed that a cow-in-calf shall be the payment the calf is the property of the man to whom the payment has been made unless otherwise stated at the time of transfer.

966. All the rules regarding witnesses are applicable to payment in kind (see paras. 954, 959, 960).

967. If payment is made in instalments at least one beast is paid on

the day of sale.

968. The **size and age** of the beasts to be paid in future instalments is decided and included in the terms of the contract of sale.

969. It is usual to arrange that payment shall be made in heifers but other beasts may be used.

> NOTE: The reason given for the choice of heifers is that since neither party can tell how a heifer will turn out the risk is equally divided between them.

The following **types** of beasts often appear in sale contracts:—

Erusi	= Heifer shortly before first bulling.
Enkilaiziba	= Heifer one year before first bulling.
Echukile	= Heifer calf just weaned.
Nesiga ebyondo	= Bull aged 3 years.
Ekulasilwe	= " " 2 "
Echukile	= Bull calf just weaned.
Ezigija	= Cow which has calved 1 — 4 times.
Ezigija nkuru	= Cow which has calved more than 4 times.
Ehoile amazara	= Cow which will not calve again.
Eshanjwa) Kifaka)	= Barren cow.

970. The vendor cannot claim any particular beast but only one which fulfils the conditions of age and size laid down in the contract.

971. Beasts must be handed over in a condition considered satisfactory according to their age.

972. If a buyer is in arrears with his payments the contract cannot be declared void (contrary to para 952 above); in this case the vendor must sue for arrears.

Payment in goats.

973. Full payment may be made on the day of sale or a certain number may be handed over as a first instalment and further payments arranged.

> NOTE: The following types of beasts often appear in sale contracts:—
>
> | | | |
> |---|---|---|
> | Ebiguma | = | A goat which has already borne. |
> | Emiagazi | = | A goat which has not yet borne. |
> | Empaya | = | A he-goat. |

974. The sex and age of the goats to be paid in future instalments is laid down in the contract of sale.

975. Kids born to goats subsequent to their transfer as payment are the the property of the man to whom they have been transferred and do not count towards the purchase price.

B. Buildings.

1. Sale of buildings for demolition. (Ndara or Omushaka).

976. The object of such a sale is to procure materials for re-building. The contract may be written or verbal.

977. 2 witnesses are necessary.

978. Demolition must start within a reasonable time.

979. The buyer may not use the building for any purpose except that of demolition.

980. The payment of the purchase price, or an instalment of it, gives full possession to the buyer who has no claims on the vendor for damage to it by fire, theft etc.

2. Sale of buildings, exclusive of the ground on which they stand. (Kularamu).

981. The buyer may repair the house but may not demolish it and rebuild.

  NOTE: The sale contract is usually worded thus:— "I have sold my house to so-and-so for trading purposes." or "I have sold my house to so-and-so that he may live in it."

982. Repairs must be carried out in the same materials as are already in in the house, e.g. thatched roofs may not be repaired with corrugated iron, nor corrugated iron replaced with thatch.

983. The buyer may not rent nor re-sell the house, nor instal a new occupant without the consent of the man from whom he bought it.

984. If the buyer instals another man without such consent, the vendor

can expel this occupant and the buyer of the house has no claim for any loss which he may have suffered owing to the fact that his caretaker has been turned out.

985. The buyer may sell the house for demolition, but if he does so he has no right to build a new house on the site.

986. The buyer cannot bequeath the house except as ndara (for demolition) nor is it counted as part of his estate except in this way.

987. The vendor has no rights over the house even if the buyer should abandon it, and it fall into ruins.

3. Sale of buildings inclusive of the ground on which they stand (Kugula).

988. All rules which apply to the sale of a plantation, such as restrictions by the terms of the tenure, witnesses, boundary demarcation, etc. apply to sales of this nature.

989. If the buyer is expelled owing to failure to pay his instalments, he may not remove any materials he has used in the repair of buildings, new thatching, poles etc.

990. If the buyer has erected a new building on the site in addition to that which he bought (kitchen, store etc.) he may demolish it and take away the materials.

991. If the buyer has in any way lowered the value of the buildings by demolition and failure to rebuild etc. he must pay compensation to the vendor.

II MOVEABLE PROPERTY.

A. Cattle.

992. The beast to be sold must be produced when the contract of sale is being drawn up.

NOTE: If this is not done the contract is not binding on either party, even if an instalment of the purchase price has been paid. There is a saying "Kugula mugongo gwa 'nte (To buy the back of a cow)".

meaning being that if a man asks an owner "How big is your cow?" the latter describes its size by holding up his arm to show the height of its back. A sale conducted on these lines is not binding.

993. About 6 witnesses are necessary.

994. The fees of the witnesses are not paid until the whole of the purchase price has been paid.

995. Vendor and buyer each pay half of the fees of the witnesses.

996. Once the transfer of the beast from vendor to buyer has taken place it cannot be returned and the sale declared void.

997. If a beast awaiting transfer dies or becomes sick the vendor must return the money paid by the buyer.

NOTE: Customary Law makes no provision for cases of neglect of cattle. Asked about this point the assessors replied "It is impossible".

998. Should a cow calve, the calf is under all circumstances the property of the owner of the cow.

QUOTATION: D.O's appeal No.32 of 1935.

Ishebayondo v. F.Machumu for the Chief.
Ishebayondo bought a cow from Kitabe, herdsman of the Chief; the cow calved 5 times before it was discovered that Kitabe had stolen this cow from the Chief's herd. The Chief therefore ordered Ishebayondo to return the cow and her five calves to him; Ishebayondo brought an action against the Chief for unlawfully depriving him of six head of cattle. The Court held:— "Even if the cow was purchased by Ishebayondo in good faith, as it obviously was, it must be returned with its progeny to its rightful owner as it was stolen property."

999. The purchase price may be paid outright in full or may be paid in instalments.

Full purchase price is paid outright.

1000. A beast is the property of a buyer who has paid full purchase price as soon as the payment has been made whether it has been transferred or not.

Payment by instalments (In all chiefdoms except Ihangiro and Karagwe; see para.1019.)

1001. A man who pays for a beast in instalments is known as Muhampya.

1002. The ownership of a beast transfers from vendor to buyer when the transfer of the beast takes place and not when an instalment is paid.

1003. Unless specifically stated in the contract there is no time limit for the transference of the beast after the payment of the purchase price or an instalment of it.

a. A beast remains with the vendor until all instalments are paid.

1004. Milk is the property of the vendor.

1005. Calves are the property of the vendor.

1006. If the beast dies the vendor must return all the instalments he has received.

1007. All meat and the hide are the property of the vendor.

1008. The buyer can at any time before the final payment demand the return of the instalments and revoke the contract.

1009. The vendor can at any time before the final payment return the instalments he had received and revoke the contract.

1010. The vendor may not sell the beast elsewhere unless he has returned the instalments received.

1011. Should the beast be included in a distraint on the vendor's estate the buyer has no claims on it and must claim the return of his instalments as a debt on the estate.

b. A beast is transferred to the buyer on payment of the first instalment.

1012. Milk is the property of the buyer.

1013. Calves are the property of the buyer.

1014. If the beast dies or falls sick before the final payment has been made the buyer cannot repudiate the debt and the outstanding instalments must be paid as they fall due.

1015. All meat and the hide are the property of the buyer.

1016. Neither vendor nor buyer can revoke the contract of sale under any conditions.

1017. The buyer is at liberty to sell the beast at any time.

1018. A beast cannot be included in a distraint on the vendors property but can be included in one on the buyer's property.

IHANGIRO and KARAGWE.

1019. The main difference between Ihangiro and Karagwe and the other Chiefdoms is that a beast becomes the property of the buyer who is paying by instalments, only when the final payment has been made and not on the transfer of the animal as in other places.

During the payment of instalments, when a beast has been transferred to the buyer.

a. Milk is divided equally between buyer and vendor.

b. If the beast dies the vendor must either replace it with another or return the instalments received.

c. Neither buyer nor vendor may sell the beast to another person.

d. If a distraint is placed on the property of the vendor, cattle for which he is receiving payments by instalments, is counted among his assets.

e. Calves born during the payment of instalments are the property of the vendor.

f. If the cow does not calve during the payment of instalments the buyer is entitled to demand another beast in her place.

   NOTE: Since a man who buys a cow naturally intends to purchase a fertile animal the contract has not been fulfilled if it proves to be
   barren; equally, the vendor is selling a fertile cow, and if he does

not receive his price according to the conditions of sale the contract has not been fulfilled. The payment of instalments is usually spread over a long period so that the fertility or otherwise of the animal may be practically demonstrated.

g. If the vendor in these circumstances has no other beast, he has to return the instalments he has received and the contract is dissolved.

Alteration in contract owing to the instalments being in arrears.

h. If a buyer is in arrears with his instalments and the cow bears a heifer calf, the buyer, on completion of his payments, receives the heifer and not the cow which he had originally contracted to buy.

i. If in the above circumstances, the cow bears only bull calves, the vendor may refuse to accept any further payments until she has borne a heifer. When she has done so the payments will be continued and the buyer will receive this heifer calf at the completion of his instalments and not the cow herself.

j. The final payment is celebrated by the payment of bichungu by the buyer to the vendor. Bichungu consists of the following:-

>   1 he-goat.
>   1 calabash of beer.
>   1 hoe.
>   1 load of mtama.
>   1 bunch of bananas.
>   1 house pole (nguso)
>   Cowries (nowadays cents 10.)
>   Sh.1/= for the tail
>   Shs.1/= kitindire (which sum is received by the wife of the vendor.)

NOTE: This custom is vanishing and a celebration in the form of a beer-drink attended by witnesses is taking its place.

Sale of a cow-in-calf.

1020. About 6 witnesses are necessary.

1021. In such a sale the purchase price is in two parts:—

      a. The price of the cow.

      b. The price of the unborn calf, called kigaliro or matundu.

1022. Kigaliro must be paid before the birth of the calf, otherwise it is the property of the vendor.

1023. If it proves that the cow was not in calf when sold the kigaliro must be returned.

1024. If the cow slips the calf the buyer cannot claim the repayment of the kigaliro.

Sale of an unborn calf (Buto or Buzito).

1025. About six witnesses are necessary.

1026. The cow whose unborn calf is sold need not necessarily be in calf at the time of the contract.

1027. It is agreed that the next heifer calf of a certain cow is sold to the buyer.

1028. The usual price is about Shs.60/=.

1029. If the payment is to be made by instalments the dates on which these fall due are stated in the contract.

1030. The cow remains with her owner (All districts except Ihangiro and Karagwe see para.1039).

1031. The owner informs the buyer when the calf is born.

1032. The calf becomes the property of the buyer on its birth.

1033. If a bull calf or calves are born prior to the birth of the heifer they are the property of the cow's owner.

1034. The calf remains about one year with the cow.

1035. The milk is the property of the cow's owner (except in Kianja where it is divided between owner and buyer).

1036. Should the calf die during its first year the buyer is entitled to the next heifer calf of the same cow.

1037. When the calf is transferred to the buyer all obligations on the part of the cow's owner are at an end.

1038. The buyer can claim no repayment of purchase price unless the cow dies or becomes barren before the heifer calf is born.

IHANGIRO and KARAGWE.

1039. a. The cow is kept by the buyer of the calf (For confirmation see D.O's appeal No.137 of 1940).

b. The buyer informs the owner of the cow when the calf is born.

c. The calf remains for about one year with its mother.

d. The milk is divided between the two parties.

e. If the parties live within reasonable distance of each other the cow and calf stay in turn in each herd.

f. If, owing to distance, this is impossible, the owner of the calf makes butter from the milk throughout the time that the cow should be in her owner's herd and sends the butter to the owner.

NOTE: At the beginning of milking the amount of butter should be 7 pieces of butter the size of a fist (entome) and at the end of milking 4 similar sized pieces per month.

Sometimes another arrangement is made whereby instead of sending butter the owner of the cow appoints as his representative a man who lives in the vicinity and the cow is sent to him during the owner's turn.

g. If a bull calf or calves are born prior to the birth of the heifer calf they are the property of the cow's owner.

h. The cow's owner must fulfil the contract that the buyer shall receive a heifer calf and cannot return the money and demand the return of the cow.

i. The milk is distributed between both parties as above if the calf is a bull.

j. If kuchwererera is necessary (i.e. the sending of the calf to a foster mother) the owner of the cow must pay for it.

k. If the calf is sent to a foster mother because its own mother is dry, the cow remains with the owner of the calf until the calf returns from the foster mother.

l. If the cow dies from natural causes the buyer is not responsible unless he cannot produce the carcase.

Cattle bought and owned by more than one person. (Enkwatane).

1040. The owner of the largest share in a beast belonging to several people is known as the nkuru ya n'te. (see also para.816 et seq. Communal ownership of cattle).

1041. If all the shares are equal the man who chose the beast for communal purchase is the nkuru ya n'te.

1042. The negotiations for the purchase of the animal are conducted between the vendor and the nkuru ya n'te who represents the joint buyers.

1043. Any questions which may arise after the purchase are also conducted by the two parties as above.

Sale of Shares.

1044. About 6 witnesses outside the kyama are necessary.

1045. If a share is sold for a higher price than that originally paid, the buyer is not entitled to a larger share in the beast.

1046. The names denoting the size of the shares are as follows:-

       Olubaju = Half the beast.
       Okugulu = A quarter of the beast.
       Ekyara = One-eighth of the beast.
       Eigembe = One-sixteenth of the beast.

B. Sale of the Coffee Harvest.

1. Advance sale of the coffee harvest of a specified plot.

1047. The following types of sale are made:—

    a. The complete harvest of a plantation.

    b. The harvest of a certain part of a plantation.

    c. The harvest of certain trees.

    d. The nyamwaka harvest (the crop ripening between April and the end of August).

    e. The ndagashe harvest (the crop ripening between September and March).

    f. Both Nyamwaka and Ndagashe harvests.

    g. The crop of a certain year, in which case the European calendar is used, i.e. the crop for 1940 beginning January 1st and ending December 31st.

1048. The owner of the plantation is responsible for cleaning the plantation.

1049. At least 2 witnesses are necessary.

1050. The money is always paid at once in full.

1051. The buyer harvests the coffee.

1052. The owner of the plantation can claim no compensation for accidental damage done to a tree during picking.

1053. The crop is dried at the house of the buyer.

2. Advance sale of a specified quantity of coffee.

1054. a. A sum of money is paid in advance against the delivery of a fixed amount of coffee to be delivered at harvest time.

    b. A sum of money is paid in advance in respect of an agreement that the entire crop of the man who received the cash will be sold to the money lender.

NOTE: Crops other than coffee are not usually sold in advance.

a.

1055. At least 2 witnesses are necessary.

1056. The owner of the plantation harvests the coffee.

1057. The amount of coffee is usually stated in terms of debis or baskets full.

NOTE: Most growers prefer the basket measure because of the danger that the buyer may enlarge a debi by soldering on a false piece.

The measure basket (kiibo) full: In every village there are one or more baskets, belonging to individuals, each of which is known to all the villagers as the kiibo of so-and-so. The amount which each basket holds is well-known. Every villager, at the time of the coffee harvest, measures his crop in one of these baskets before taking it for sale to the coffee buyer. Though he may not understand the weights kilo and frasila and cannot read the scales, everyone knows that so many baskets-full should bring him so much money and can argue with a buyer, who, trading on his inability to read, tries to give him less than his due.

These baskets are also used in many transactions between the inhabitants of a village; the fact that they are owned by a third person forms a check on the amount transferred in case of future questions.

1058. No definite date is as a rule fixed for the delivery of the coffee, but it is understood that it must be taken from the current year's crop.

1059. If the debtor cannot deliver the coffee he may arrange with the money-lender to pay him an amount equivalent to that which the coffee would have fetched according to the price prevailing on the day that he hands over the cash.

1060. The money-lender cannot sue for the delivery of the coffee until the harvest is over.

1061. If, after the harvest is over, the debtor cannot deliver the coffee the debt is changed into money (as in the preceding para. 1059) but the amount is reckoned on the highest price of the season.

b.

1062. At least 2 witnesses are necessary and the conditions of the loan are usually supported by a document signed by both parties and by the witnesses.

1063. The money-lender deducts from the proceeds of the crop the amount which he has advanced and hands over the remainder to the owner of the crop.

1064. The money-lender harvests the coffee.

1065. If the crop of the borrower fails, the money-lender can sue for the return of his money after the harvest.

1066. The money-lender can claim no interest.

1067. If a man who has borrowed money on these terms does not sell his crop to the money-lender and instead returns the amount which he borrowed, the money-lender cannot insist that the crop be sold to him.

NOTE: Despite the fact that it is obviously ridiculous all assessors insist that this is so. It can only be assumed that they hold this opinion because they are growers and not lenders.

C. Sale of grass for household use.

1068. In all districts except Ihangiro grass, whether growing on public or private land, except in a kibanja, is free and may be cut by anyone.

IHANGIRO.

1069. All grass is free unless :—

a. The owner encloses a grass patch, usually with reeds, to indicate that he will not allow free cutting.

b. A man plants a certain kind of grass called Nkinchwe (erogrostis blepharogrumis) in an enclosed plot.

1070. The rules for the sale of matete apply to the sale of privately owned grass.

Sale of Matete (Elephant grass).

1071. At least 2 witnesses are necessary who receive no payment.

1072. The sale may be either:—

  a. Matete not yet ready for cutting.

  b. Matete ready for cutting.

In the case of (a) the buyer must cut the matete when it comes into flower even if, owing to the season, it should bloom while it is still thin and short.

In the case of (b) the buyer must cut the matete immediately.

The matete must be cut by the buyer.

Until the matete is cut the vendor is responsible for it.

A buyer may not sell uncut matete for which he is paying in instalments.

Sale of Timber.

1073. At least 2 witnesses are necessary; they receive no payment.

1074. A tree must be felled by the buyer.

1075. The buyer must fell the tree within a reasonable time.

 NOTE: This rule safeguards the vendor; for example, a man sells fito (long, thin switches), and if they are cut, within a year the parent trees will have sprouted again and another crop of fito will be ready.

  In the contract of sale the purpose for which the buyer requires the timber is usually stated; e.g. large posts (nguso) for building material, small posts (fito) for building material, bwato to make a dug out beer boat. A man may not buy fito and leave the trees un-felled until the fito have grown into nguso.

1076. The vendor can make no claim for compensation for any damage done to his property during felling.

1077. The buyer is liable if damage is done to a neighbour's property during felling.

1078. Unless otherwise stated, all wood which cannot be used by the buyer for the purpose for which he bought the timber remains the property of the vendor, e.g. brushwood which has been chopped off the poles.

Private sale of weapons, tools, household articles, clothing etc.

1079. The number of witnesses necessary depends on the value of the article for sale.

1080. If no witnesses are called the sale may be declared void.

QUOTATION: Chiefs' Appeal Court No.49 of 1937.

Stephano v. Kagaruki.
Kagaruki sold firewood to Stephano for Shs.12/=. No witnesses were called and later Stephano claimed that the price agreed upon was only Shs.5/=. The Court held that since there were no witnesses to the sale it could not stand and therefore Stephano must return the firewood to Kagaruki, or if it had been already used, an equivalent amount. The exact quantity to be returned was to be ascertained from the men who were employed to carry the firewood from Kagaruki's house to that of Stephano.

1081. An article which is taken away by a buyer on payment of an instalment of the purchase price is the buyer's property.

1082. An article on which an instalment of the purchase price has been paid but which has not been taken away by the buyer remains the property of the vendor.

1083. If the vendor re-sells the article he must return the instalments he has received to the payer of them.

1084. An article becomes the property of a buyer as soon as he takes delivery of it.

QUOTATION: Chiefs' Appeal Court No.92 of 1938.

Kaharabi v. Bibi Kalikwenda.
Kalikwenda sent two men to Kaharabi to buy 2 calabashes of beer; she gave them Shs.2/80 with which they paid for the beer. When Kalikwenda tasted the beer she considered it bad and sent it back to Kaharabi and demanded the return of her money. Kaharabi refused and Kalikwenda sued him for it. The Court held that he was within his rights to refuse re-payment since once a thing has been bought and taken away by the purchaser it cannot be returned and repayment demanded.

SPECIFIC PERFORMANCE.

Contract with a workman to make an article.

1085. a. If no advance payment is made when the order is given: The customer cannot be forced to take delivery of an article he has ordered.

1086. b. If an advance payment (mukwato) is made when the order is given:

Repayment of the instalment (mukwato) can be claimed by the customer if the completed article does not come up to standard or if delivery is unduly delayed.

NOTE: When the order is given the date of delivery is only vaguely stated; if after what seems to the customer a reasonable time the fundi is not ready, a more definite date is fixed; if, after this, delivery is still delayed the customer may claim the return of his advance payment in Court.

1087. The customer cannot be forced to take delivery, but if he refuses to do so on any grounds except that the article is below standard he forfeits his mukwato unless the maker can sell the goods elsewhere.

1088. When the customer takes delivery he is liable for the immediate payment of the remainder of the purchase price if not otherwise stated.

1089. If the customer provides the material for his order and it is destroyed through no fault of the workman (fire etc.) the workman is not responsible for its loss.

1090. If the material is stolen from the workman's house he is responsible.

1091. If a workman spoils raw material or an article given him for repair he is responsible.

Building Contract.

1092. The following rules apply only to the building of native huts (msonge).

NOTE: There are no rules under customary law for contracts for any other type of building.

1093. At least 4 witnesses to the contract are necessary.

1094. The witnesses receive no payment.

1095. The contract may be written or verbal.

1096. Materials are always supplied by the customer.

1097. The contractor is always responsible for supplying all ordinary labour necessary but in the case of certain heavy jobs, lifting the roof, setting up the main poles etc., which need temporary extra labour the customer must supply the necessary men.

1098. The payment usually consists of two parts:—

 a. An advance payment of part of the price, called nyimukia, or lwiyo or rubuturo.

 b. Payment of the remainder on completion of the work.

1099. Usually no time limit for the completion of the work is specified in the contract.

1100. If the contractor is unable to complete the work, he must return the money which was advanced to him, keeping such an amount as is adequate payment for the work already done.

1101. If the work cannot proceed because the customer has not provided sufficient material, the contractor may refuse to complete the contract and demand payment for the work he has done.

1102. In this case the amount due to the contractor is settled by agreement between the representatives of both parties.

Contract for Medical Treatment.

1103. The fees of a doctor (mganga) who prescribes for a patient he has not seen are called kutera kishaka and are always paid in full at the time of consultation.

1104. The fees of a doctor who examines and prescribes for a patient are called rubuturo and are paid before the mganga leaves his house to visit the patient.

Contract for cure.

1105. At least 1 witness is necessary.

1106. The fee of the mganga, called mukimba, is usually fixed and is payable after the invalid has recovered.

1107. If the patient recovers the fee may be claimed in Court.

   NOTE: The recovery need not necessarily be a permanent one. If the mganga can claim that he found his patient bedridden and that after treatment he was able to walk, his claim for fees is justified even if the patient relapses again before long.

1108. If the patient does not recover the doctor has no claim to his fee.

   NOTE: A mganga will often undertake a case which has little chance of recovery because during the treatment he has many opportunities to take payment in kind and thus is covered even if he loses his final payment.

1109. If a patient wishes to change his mganga during treatment, he must inform him of his intention, in which case he is not liable to pay the discarded mganga's mukimba.

1110. If a patient changes his mganga and does not inform his original adviser, he must pay his mukimba even if he recovers under the treatment of another.

Witchcraft.

1111. No Courts, not even those of the village and clan elders, recognise claims arising out of contracts involving witchcraft or anti-witchcraft measures.

   NOTE: Nor is compensation granted to sufferers from witchcraft. The assessors explained that the victims have the remedy in their own hands, they can either employ anti-witchcraft measures or get their adversaries ostracised in their villages.

Labour Contracts.

There are 3 usual forms of contract:—

1112.   1. Labour engaged for a wage computed by work-days.

a). The work-days are either written down or knots to represent them are made in a string.

b). If the employee has to sue for his wages he claims them as a common debt.

1113.   2. An employer engages labour to undertake certain work at a fixed wage.

a). Should these labourers fail to complete the work for which they were engaged for any reason, within or outside their control, they are entitled to a proportionate amount of their wages for the work done.

b). If the employees have to sue for their wages they claim them in Court as a common debt.

1114.   3. An employee is engaged without any stated terms.

a). He lives in the house of his employer as one of the family; he does no specified work but is expected to carry out any orders given by his master.

b). He receives no regular wages but is paid by receiving his food, clothes, and occasional gifts of money (often his tax is paid for him).

QUOTATION: D.O's appeal No.3/Pl/5 of 1937.

Nyema v. Mwami Mlaki.
Nyema worked for 18 years as the servant of Mlaki with whom he had no
contract for regular wages.   He claimed in Court that Mlaki owed him
Shs.12/= per month for 18 years = 2592/=.   It was held that he had no
claim since Mlaki proved that on various occasions he had given Nyema
remuneration in cash with which he had been satisfied at the time.

c). If an employee is dissatisfied with the remuneration he receives he can go to Court and ask that it may be decided whether his claims are justified according to the work he has performed.

NOTE: In former times paid labour was unknown.   It was   the   custom
for fathers to give their sons from the age of about 12 years into the
charge of a friend or relation who kept them in exchange for the boy's
work.   This system was called kulera. The boys usually remained until
they married;   they helped the master of the house   in all branches of
his work and learnt manners, tribal traditions etc.

L O A N (Kwehora).

MONEY.

1115. At least two witnesses are necessary for a loan involving more than a few shillings.

NOTE: The following were the conditions of loan in former times: Loans, either in kind or money, lent for a particular purpose over a certain period were made without interest. If the loan was monetary and was not repaid at the time arranged, the lender was entitled to claim an additional sum, usually 100%, over and above the loan.

Money might be lent to be repaid when the specified purpose, for which it was loaned, was completed irrespective of time, or it might be lent for a certain period of time. Examples: 1. A lent B Shs.20/= to be used on a trading expedition. B returned from this expedition and set off on another without repaying the loan. On his second return A was entitled to claim Shs.40/= because he had lent the money for the first safari only.

2. A. lent B Shs.20/= to be repaid within one month. B failed to repay and at the end of two months, when he was ready to repay, A was entitled to claim Shs.40/=.

If a debtor was unable to pay, his nearest relative was responsible for the debt. A debtor could be fettered (on the same principle as being put in the stocks) by order of the Court, or if he could not be caught his brother was fettered in his stead.

If the debtor died his heirs were responsible for the debt.

1116. The witnesses receive no payment.

1117. The contract may be written or verbal.

QUOTATION: Chiefs' appeal Court No.26 of 1937.

Irkanani v. Bamwandika.
In their judgment the Chiefs state "In these days it is better to write down transactions in money than to state them before witnesses, but a debt must be acknowledged if reputable witnesses can be produced".

1118. A debtor should go to his creditor and pay where his creditor is, unless to do so will cost the debtor money.

NOTE: The Indian Contract Act. Art IX states "Where no place of payment is specified either expressly or by implication the debtor must follow his creditor and pay where his creditor is."

1119. If the debtor dies, his heirs are responsible in all circumstances for the repayment of the debt (see para.130).

1120. A creditor may not cede a debt to another man without the consent of the debtor.

> NOTE: "Eibanja tilimara lindi" (A debt cannot be ceded in payment of a debt).

Repayment of Loan.

1121. Repayment of a loan must be made before at least 2 witnesses, preferably those who witnessed the loan.

1122. If a loan is repaid in instalments, each payment must be made before at least 2 witnesses; and if the agreement was written, each payment must be entered on the document and initialled by the witnesses.

> NOTE: Most loans are said to be repaid in instalments even if this was not in the original agreement.

Delayed repayment of loan.

1123. If a debt is not repaid on the date arranged, the creditor must ask the debtor for payment before filing a suit against him for it.

> NOTE: "Rutonga tamalirwa e'ibanja" (A man does not pay debts which are not claimed).

1124. There is no time limit for claiming the repayment of a debt, if it has not been paid on the date agreed upon.

> NOTE: The saying is "E'ibanja tilijunda (Debts do not rot)".

Absent debtor.

1125. If the creditor finds that the debtor is out when he goes to demand payment, it is sufficient if he leaves word with the wife, family or neighbours of the debtor that he has called to collect the debt.

1126. If the debtor is away from the village when the creditor calls to collect his debt, a suit cannot be filed against him until he returns.

> NOTE: The principle is that no one can be prosecuted for a debt in his absence.

1127. If the debtor is absent from the village, but the creditor knows his present address and that he is likely to remain there for some time (as in the case of a man who has two plantations and lives sometimes at one and sometimes at the other), the creditor may file a suit against him, provided that he is not living outside the Bukoba District.

Absent creditor.

1128. A creditor may nominate a representative to collect his debt, provided that he does so in the presence of at least 2 witnesses.

NOTE:"Atwara akahu obuhazi niwe akaiyayo" (A man who takes a hide to be dressed must return to fetch it himself.)

1129. It is not necessary to inform the debtor of this nomination, but the representative, when he goes to collect the debt, must be able to show proof that he is accredited, by taking with him either a written statement or the witnesses to the transaction.

Lost document.

1130. If a document admitting the debt was drawn up and this paper is lost or destroyed, a statement by the witnesses as to its contents is sufficient to justify the claim for the debt.

1131. In this case, after payment the debtor must be given a document, witnessed by at least 2 people, to say that the debt has been paid and that the creditor has no further claims; or payment must be made in the presence of at least 2 witnesses.

1132. If the document is lost and the creditor informs the debtor that he intends to draw up another in its place, he must call the debtor and at least 2 witnesses to be present when it is written and the debtor must sign it.

Time limit.

1133 a). A time is fixed for repayment, either a date according to the European calendar or a time according to the season:

e. g.   Ekyanda   = the dry season (July to September).

Akanda   = the south monsoon (January to March).

Toigo   = the rainy season (April to June).

Omusenene = the grasshopper season (October to December).

b). A loan is made for a particular purpose and is to be repaid when that purpose is completed.

c). No time is fixed for repayment.

1134 a. If repayment is to be at a certain season, it is understood to mean the beginning of the season.

1135 b. The creditor cannot claim repayment until the purpose for which the loan was made has been completed.

EXAMPLE: A made a loan to B to be used on a trading expedition to Uganda. Until B returns from Uganda, A cannot claim repayment of his money whatever the length of time that B may be away.

1136 c. The creditor may at any time claim repayment of the debt.

Interest (Amagoba).

1137. If interest is to be paid on a loan, it always paid in a lump sum at the time of the repayment of the loan, an arrangement being made at the time of the loan that on repayment the sum paid shall be greater than that lent.

1138. The time for which the loan is granted is not taken into account in fixing the interest; a short or long term loan can carry the same amount of interest.

1139. If an original loan was made without interest, and is not repaid at the time arranged, a new arrangement may be made prolonging the time for repayment and including interest.

1140. At least 2 witnesses are necessary for this agreement, preferably those to the original agreement.

1141. If the original loan was made without interest, no further sum can be added if repayment is overdue except by a new agreement as above.

1142. If the loan carries interest and the debtor can prove that he could not use it for the purpose for which he borrowed the money, he is entitled, providing he does so within a reasonable time of finding that he cannot use it, to repay the original sum lent without the interest.

EXAMPLE: A man borrows money for the payment of brideprice and the marriage does not take place.

Guarantee of Loan.

1143. If a loan is guaranteed the creditor can claim against the guarantor if the debtor fails to repay.

1144. The heirs of a deceased guarantor are liable for his guarantee.

LOAN OF A COW-IN-MILK.

1145. No witnesses are necessary.

NOTE: The most usual reason for borrowing a cow in milk is that milk is needed for a child or an invalid.

1146. The borrower is responsible for the herding and for any damage to property that the cow may do.

NOTE: Should there be an argument after a man's death as to whether the cow belonged to him or was borrowed it is a proof of ownership if the cow remained in the house on the day of his death. All cattle owned by the deceased remain in the house on the day of his death to observe the mourning with the rest of the household; cattle which are in his trusteeship or borrowed go out to graze as usual.

1147. The borrower is not responsible if the cow is stolen provided he has made all possible arrangements for her safety.

NOTE: This is contrary to the rules referring to custody, see para.759.

1148. The borrower is not responsible if the cow dies through no fault of his.

LOAN OF COFFEE.

1149. Whenever loans are made in kind they must be repaid in kind, unless the borrower's crops fail and he has none to give, in which case he can repay in money.

1150. Coffee is usually borrowed for very short period only. The measure used is mostly that of the kiibo (see para.1057).

1151. It is often arranged that the amount repaid shall be greater than that borrowed.

 NOTE: "Amwengu gumoi oguhile guhinda embisi ebili" (A cooked vegetable is better than two raw ones).

1152. If, owing to the inability of the borrower to repay in coffee, the debt is translated into money, the amount is reckoned on the price of coffee prevailing on the day of repayment; or, if the debt is repaid after the buying season is over, the amount is reckoned on the highest price obtained during the season.

LOAN OF FOOD STOCKS.

1153. Beans etc. are usually borrowed for long periods, generally until the next harvest.

1154. The amount repaid is usually greater than that borrowed.

1155. If, owing to the failure of the borrower's crops, foodstuffs cannot be returned, the monetary amount he must repay instead is fixed by the village elders.

LOAN OF BEER BANANAS (Mbire).

1156. The amount to be returned is not calculated on the number lent. The repayment must equal or exceed the total quantity lent, e.g. when small bananas are returned in place of large ones lent, two may be demanded for every one lent.

P L E D G E (Kukwatiliza).

I. LAND.

A. Land planted with Coffee and Bananas.

1157. Contracts may be written or verbal. In either case at least 6 witnesses are necessary.

NOTE: For proposals regarding the mortgage of land etc. made by the D.O. see File 278/149.

1158. No one but the owner may pledge a plantation.

NOTE: For rules for pledge of plantations under family tenure see para.572.

The plantation cannot be pledged in the owner's name by his trustee during the absence of the former.

1159. Unless otherwise stated, the house is not included in the mortgage.

1160. A repayment of the loan in instalments is possible, but none of the land is freed from the mortgage until the whole debt is repaid.

Rights and duties of owner.

1161. The owner is responsible for the upkeep of the plantation, except in Ihangiro and Karagwe where the mortgagee is responsible for the upkeep of the perennial crops.

1162. Unless otherwise stated the owner has the use of all seasonal crops, while the harvest of the perennial crops belongs to the mortgagee.

QUOTATION: D.O's appeal No.4/Pl/25 of 1938.

Dona v. Kyonaboine.
Dona pledged a part of his plantation to Kyonaboine for Shs. 40/=. Later he forbade Kyonaboine to cut bananas in the pledged part, saying that he had only pledged the coffee. It was proved that when the plantation was pledged nothing had been said about coffee only being mortgaged and the Court therefore held that all the perennial crops in the pledged area were mortgaged.

NOTE: The principle being that a mortgagee may harvest but may not plant.

In a discussion as to whether a plantation was sold or mortgaged, it is a proof that the latter was the case if the original owner has continued to plant seasonal crops in it.

1163. A mortgaged plantation cannot be included among its owner's assets.

NOTE: Therefore if the owner is sued for other debts and he and his mortgagee agree that the latter shall not foreclose, the plantation cannot be auctioned.

Rights and duties of mortgagee.

1164. The mortgagee harvests the crops to which he is entitled.

1165. Any damage done to the plantation during the mortgagee's harvesting is his responsibility. He is also responsible for clean harvesting: i.e. that coffee berries are not left on the ground, that banana trees are treated in the usual way after cutting bunches of fruit, etc.

1166. The mortgagee can make no claim for any improvements he has made in the pledged land, since he has only the right to harvest and no right to make any alterations.

QUOTATION: D.O's appeal No.40/1933.

Katiko lent Shs.120/= to Mushamba to be repaid in one year, on the security of part of Mushamba's plantation. Katiko uprooted coffee trees without permission, which damage was assessed at Shs.50/=. No money had been paid on either side after 4 years and both men were dead. The heir of Mushamba, Irungu, was ordered to pay to the heir of Katiko the sum of Shs.70/= in expiation of the debt, the amount being computed thus: Shs.70/=, being Shs.120/= less Shs.50/= damages. The payment to be made within one month failing which the heir of Katiko was at liberty to foreclose on his mortgage.

1167. A mortgagee may transfer his rights in the mortgage to another person provided that the mortgager's consent is obtained.

1168. A mortgagee may not pledge land which he holds on mortgage.

Absent Owner.

1169. If the owner of a mortgaged plantation is absent, his trustee (musigire) is responsible for its upkeep.

1170. No claim can be made against the debtor in his absence unless it can be proved that he deliberately went away to avoid Court proceedings.

QUOTATION: Chief's Appeal Court No.85/1938.

Beba v. Makenge.
Makenge held part of Beba's plantation as security for a debt of Shs. 80/=. After four years the debt had not been repaid and the parties agreed upon a date for its repayment and arranged that if payment was not made the pledged land should become the property of the mortgagee, Makenge. Repayment was not made on this date and Makenge brought an action against Beba.

The Gombolola Court allowed a further two months' grace to Beba and ordered that if after this date the debt was still unpaid, the pledged land should be put up for auction. In due course the auction was held, and since there were no bidders the pledged land was given to Makenge. Beba subsequently appealed to the Chiefs' Court on the grounds that the auction had been held during his absence. The Appeal Court ruled that though the Lower Court had no right to hold the auction in the absence of Beba, nevertheless he, Beba, had forfeited the right to appeal because he knew the date of the auction and had deliberately absented himself, hoping thereby to frustrate the proceedings. The appeal was therefore dismissed.

Absent mortgagee.

1171. If a mortgagee is absent, his trustee is in charge of his interests in the pledged land; if he has not appointed a trustee, his wife and sons are considered as his trustees.

1172. If the owner goes to redeem his pledged land and finds the mortgagee absent, he may call witnesses, preferably those to the mortgage, to prove that he came to repay the debt and was unable to hand over the money, and may state that in consequence he forbids the mortgagee from that day to harvest any crops in the pledged land.

1173. The owner who does this may not himself begin harvesting until he has paid the money, either to the mortgagee or his trustee.

Neglect of Pledged land.

1174. If the owner lives in the plantation and neglects it, the mortgagee may complain against him in Court.

1175. The Court usually orders that the plantation be cleaned within a specified time. Should this order be disregarded the Court may give the mortgagee the right to have the pledged land cleaned with paid labour and charge the cost to the owner.

1176. Under these conditions, should the work involve the planting of seasonal crops, the harvest from them will be the property of the mortgagee.

Interest on money loaned.

1177. It is unusual to charge interest on money loaned against a mortgage, because the mortgagee receives the usufruct of the land mortgaged.

Timber in pledged land.

1178. If not otherwise stated, timber in the pledged land is the property of the mortgagee who may cut the trees.

Time limit.

1179. Land is usually mortgaged for at least one year.

1180. If the owner wishes to redeem the plantation before the end of the time specified, the mortgagee is bound to allow him to do so.

NOTE: Even if this happens just before the coffee harvest is due to be gathered.

1181. A mortgage is sometimes made with the condition that if the loan is not repaid by a certain date the plantation becomes the property of the mortgagee.

NOTE: This cannot be done if the plantation is held under family tenure.

QUOTATION: Case No. 36 of 1933.

Juma v. Kyokubaza.
Kyokubaza mortgaged his plantation to Juma as security for a loan of 290/= with the condition that if he did not repay the loan the plantation would become the property of Juma. The Appeal Courts (Lukiko, Chiefs' and European) held the contract valid and allowed Juma to take possession of plantation.

Expiration of the time limit.

1182. If the time limit expires and the plantation is not redeemed the amount of money due can be claimed by the mortgagee as a common debt.

1183. In this case the plantation must be auctioned, and if the price realized is less than the amount due the remainder may be claimed as a debt.

   NOTE: Despite this rule the following case is recorded, No.74/1934.

   Asmani v. Tibaijuka.
   Asmani lent Shs.80/= to Tibaijuka who pledged part of his plantation as security. Tibaijuka failed to repay the loan and was sued in Court by Asmani. The Gombolola Court allowed Asmani the ownership of the pledged part, which was kisi, and added a part of the plantation as it was considered that the value of the kisi did not amount to Shs. 80/=. The Chiefs' Appeal Court held that the kisi was rightly given to Asmani, but that the addition of a part of the plantation was unjust. In the judgment it was stated "If Tibaijuka can obtain Shs.80/= he may pay it to Asmani and free his kisi. If he cannot obtain Shs.80/= the kisi must remain the property of Asmani."

Procedure for attachment and sale (rules laid down in District Book.)

1184.a. The drum shall be beaten in the village in which the property is situated and the people told that the property will be sold on a certain date, which must be at least 30 days after the drum is beaten.

   b. The person whose property is to be sold may pay the amount due at any time before the fall of the hammer.

   c. If he fails to do so the property shall go to the highest bidder, who must pay the purchase price before sundown on the day of sale. If he fails to do so the property can be re-auctioned.

   d. If the purchase price exceeds the amount of the debt the balance must be paid to the debtor.

   e. If no bids are received the creditor may be given a part of the plantation to the value of his debt.

1185. The owner may hand over the plantation in expiation of his debt, in which case the mortgage becomes a sale; but the Court may not dispose of the case in this way.

If no time limit is fixed.

1186. The mortgagee or his heirs can at any time demand repayment of the loan and the owner or his heirs can at any time redeem the plantation.

QUOTATION: D.O's appeal No.97 of 1935.

Wilfred v. Mashauri.
Mashauri's son wished to redeem a plantation pledged by his grand-father to Wilfred's father 33 years before against an advance of Shs. 100/=. Mashauri's son paid Shs.100/= to Wilfred, who accepted the money but declared that the debt was more than that amount. It trans-pired in evidence that contrary to the usual custom, the plantation had been inhabited by the mortgagee who had doubtless made many improve-ments. The Native Court held that there could be no claim on this and that the plantation was redeemed by the payment of Shs.100/=. On appeal the Court decided that owing to the length of time which had elapsed, the plantation was unredeemable.

Special rules regarding mortgage of part of plantation.

1187. A boundary is fixed between the mortgaged and the free part; the boundary line is demarcated either with stones or trees.

1188. The witnesses to the mortgage must be present at the demarcation of the boundaries and the wife of the owner is usually called.

B. Mortgage of land used for seasonal crops (kisi and rweya).

1189. The mortgagee is entitled to plant seasonal crops.

1190. The mortgagee is entitled to harvest the crops he has planted, even if the land has been redeemed before harvest time.

1191. A mortgagee may fell trees in the pledged plot but may not plant trees.

1192. A mortgagee may allow a third person to cultivate in the pledged land.

C. Mortgage of forest or land planted with reeds (matete)

1193. A mortgagee is entitled to fell any trees but may not uproot a tree.

1194. A mortgagee may not plant anything in a pledged forest.

1195. All above rules apply also to matete under mortgage.

2. PLEDGE OF MOVEABLE PROPERTY.

NOTE: The pledging of property is not a new institution. All kinds of property, including children, have always been considered pawnable. The pledged property was not usually handed over to the creditor but remained with the owner. Should the owner fail to repay the debt a case was brought against him and the Court decided whether the creditor should be given the security outright or whether the debtor should be allowed a further time in which to repay.

Cattle.

I. Pledge of a whole cow.

1196. At least 3 witnesses are necessary. The contract may be written or verbal.

1197. It is unusual for a time limit to be fixed.

1198. The pledge may be redeemed, or repayment demanded, at any time.

1199. The cow is kept by the creditor.

1200. The milk is the property of the creditor (except in Ihangiro where debtor and creditor share it).

1201. All calves are the property of the creditor.

1202. If the cow dies the creditor may claim the repayment of the debt immediately.

1203. The debtor must be informed if the cow dies. Meat and hide are his property.

1204. The creditor may make his own arrangements, without reference to the debtor, for the herding, kuheleka, kusigira, and kuchwererera (see paras. 765, 769 and 804).

1205. Otherwise the creditor may not move the cow without permission from the debtor.

1206. If the cow falls sick the creditor is not obliged to call for a native veterinary mganga and cannot be held responsible even if the cow dies.

> NOTE: The reason given for this is that no Muhaya would allow a beast to die of neglect; besides which, the creditor has every reason to wish for the well-being of the beast because he gets calves, milk, manure etc.

1207. The creditor may not do anything to the beast, such as cutting its horns, using it as bait in a trap etc.

1208. If a cow dies "by act of God", neither creditor nor debtor has any claim on the other.

II. Pledge of a share in a cow.

1209. The owner of a share in a cow is at liberty to pledge his share, provided he first offers to pledge it to the other owners of the beast.

1210. The creditor automatically becomes a member of the kyama (see para. 816) and takes over all rights and duties of the shareholder whose place he has taken, with the following exceptions:

   a) The beast cannot be sold until the shareholder has redeemed his pledge (compare para. 826).

   b) The creditor has no rights in any calves born to the cow.

   c) If the cow dies the creditor has no right to a share in the meat; the share is the property of the debtor.

Goats.

1211. A goat is usually pledged for a short and limited period.

1212. The goat is kept by the creditor and any kids she bears are his property.

NOTE: It is usually arranged that if the pledge is not redeemed at the expiration of the time fixed, the goat automatically becomes the property of the creditor. Goats are troublesome and produce nothing which is of value to the creditor.

Food-stores.

1213. One witness is necessary.

1214. Food stores are never pledged for more than a very short time and a time limit for the redemption of the pledge is fixed.

1215. In no circumstances can the creditor take possession of the goods pledged if the money is not returned. He must file a suit for the repayment of the money.

1216. The pledged stores are kept by the creditor.

1217. The creditor is not responsible for deterioration or loss of the stores occasioned by fire, insects, vermin or other causes outside his control.

1218. If the stores are lost by such means, though the creditor is not responsible, he cannot claim the debt from the debtor.

1219. Should the debt not be repaid on the date arranged the responsibility of the creditor for the pledged stores remains.

1220. The creditor is responsible for loss of the stores by theft.

Weapons, Tools, Cloth etc.

1221. The number of witnesses necessary depends on the value of the goods to be pledged. At least one witness is necessary.

1222. Time limits are usually fixed but a certain amount of elasticity about the date is generally allowed.

1223. It is very often a condition that if the pledge is not redeemed at the proper time the pawned article becomes the property of the creditor.

1224. The pawned article is always kept by the creditor.

228

1225. The creditor may use it and fair wear and tear is allowed.

1226. The creditor is responsible for a pawned article in his possession.

1227. If the debtor goes to redeem the pawned article either before or on the date arranged, and finds neither the creditor nor his representative at home, the debtor may call for the witnesses and hand the money to them; they may then take the pawned article from the house of the creditor and return it to its owner.

1228. Interest on the money loaned may be demanded. The extra amount is payable together with the loan on the date of repayment.

Pledge of female child.

1229. A female child may be pledged by her father or, if he is dead, by the relative entitled to receive her brideprice. The conditions are as follows:

1230. The loan is usually between Shs.20/= and Shs.60/=.

1231. The child goes to live in the creditor's house.

1232. It is arranged that when she marries the loan shall be repaid out of her brideprice.

1233. The creditor is usually a near relative, though he may be a man outside the family.

1234. All negotiations preceding the marriage of the girl are conducted by the debtor.

1235. If the girl dies or runs away the loan must be reclaimed as a common debt. In the latter case the creditor must be able to say when she ran away and where she now lives.

1236. If the creditor should have sexual intercourse with the girl he has to pay to the debtor the usual brideprice minus the amount of the debt.

Goods entrusted to a man for safe keeping.

1237. A man who undertakes to look after another's property takes full responsibility for the goods.

1238. Witnesses are not obligatory.

1239. The receiver is responsible until the depositor takes away his property, whether a time limit has been fixed or not.

> NOTE: According to the assessors no man could undertake the charge of another man's property unless he knew the man personally and was convinced of his good faith, otherwise the responsibility on the receiver is too great.   An honest man would not keep any goods in his house after the expiry of the time limit without trying to find the depositor to return them, and failing that, informing the N.A. that he has the goods.   They were unanimous that grave suspicion of theft or being an accomplice would lie on a man who claimed not to know who had deposited goods in his safe keeping.

1240. The receiver is not responsible for damage to or deterioration of the goods cause by circumstances outside his control.

C O U R T S.

1. Ntegeka ya Bagurusi or Baraza Mukurato (The Court of the Village Elders).

NOTE: During discussion on these village courts the assessors made the following statements regarding the relationship between them and the recognised courts :

A. Hardly any civil case is heard in the Gombolola Courts which has not first been before the Court of Elders.

B. When the grounds of appeal are that witnesses have not been called, it is probable either that they are not true witnesses or that they are witnesses who were refused by the bagurusi.

C. If new witnesses are produced in the appeal from Gombolola to Lukiko Court, their integrity is suspected by the people because the man who puts them forward may be playing on the lack of intimate local knowledge of the Lukiko. Therefore, unless there is some good reason for their non-appearance in the lower court, new witnesses should not be accredited. The arbitrators in the village courts are sometimes called before the Gombolola and interrogated on their judgments in an unofficial way; their evidence does not appear in the case record, but it has a very strong bearing on the finding. Perhaps this explains why at times the Gombolola judgments appear to take little or no account of the evidence given before them.

Constitution.

1241 a. Two parties in a dispute who agree to place their case before the ntegeka ya bagurusi each appoint a certain number of delegates, who assemble to hear the case.

b. These delegates (bagurusi) are chosen by the disputants; they need not be old men, nor need they be inhabitants of the village in which the case is to be heard.

c. It is necessary for both parties to agree to the hearing of the case by bagurusi; if one side objects the case is taken direct to the Gombolola.

d. The bagurusi choose one of their number to be their chairman.

e. The Chairman arranges the times of the meetings and calls the witnesses for both sides etc.

f. The meetings are usually held at the scene of dispute or in the house of the Chairman.

Procedure.

1242. a. The procedure is the same as in a Gombolola Court; both sides state their case, the witnesses are heard and judgment is given.

b. If a witness refuses to give evidence, he is not forced to do so but is dismissed. It is considered that since one of the parties has called him it is not the business of the Court if he does not wish to give evidence; for the same reason a witness who does not attend is not made to do so.

c. The whole proceedings are carried out in a dignified manner, and if a disputant is guilty of contempt of Court the bagurusi refuse to go on with the hearing and tell him that he may go elsewhere with his case, and that he is in future debarred from having the help of the elders. This has a great effect and a man who has been guilty of contempt usually tries to reconcile the elders.

Jurisdiction.

1243 a. There is no limit to the powers of these courts which sometimes settle criminal cases such as rape, theft, arson etc.

b. The most frequent cases heard are those of inheritance, boundary disputes, and quarrels between husband and wife, father-in-law and son-in-law, guardian and ward.

c. All the judgments of this court are arbitrary.

d. Compensation may be awarded but fines are never imposed.

e. The amount of compensation follows no set rules; it is awarded entirely at the discretion of the bagarusi.

f. The amount of compensation often varies, not only in different districts but often in different villages, for the same kind of case.

Judgment.

1244. a. After all the evidence has been heard, the elders each in turn express their opinion of the case. If they are not unanimous in their findings, the Chairman discusses the case with those who are not of his opinion and usually tries to persuade them to his way of thinking by citing law points and judgments in previous cases.

b. In any case the Chairman has the final say, for he pronounces judgment according to his decision, and not according to the majority view; thus the other elders are really assessors.

c. The acceptance of a judgment is considered to have formed a contract between the two parties, and if one does not fulfil his side of it the other can sue him in the Gombolola for failing to do so, quoting the judgement of the bagurusi as his claim to fulfilment.

QUOTATION: D.O's appeal No.23 of 1935.

Bibi Mailane v. Kavilyenda
The couple were man and wife who had been three times before the Court of the bagurusi because Kavilyenda refused to buy clothes for his wife. The bagurusi gave an order that he must do so and when he did not obey, his wife appealed to the Gombolola court, who ordered Kavilyenda to give his wife Shs.24/= with which to buy clothes, and in their judgment referred to the decision of the bagarusi.

d. It is not considered by the bagarusi to be an insult if a man appeals from their judgment.

e. Gombolola Courts acknowledge to a great extent the authority of the Court of Elders.

EXAMPLE: The Gombolola Court of Minazi fined a man Shs.5/= for refusing to attend before a Court of Elders.

f. If a case is brought before the Gombolola Court for nonfulfilment of the order of the Elders' Court (see para.1244c above), the Gombolola Court refuses to enter into a discussion as to whether the judgment was correct or not, but merely hears the evidence with regard to the fulfilment of the contract.

g. A Gombolola Court often refers to a judgment of the Elders' Court when trying a case.

QUOTATION: D.O's appeal No.47 of 1938.

Kokwemage v. Kagaruki.
Kagaruki assaulted and severely injured his wife Kokwemage. He was not fined because it was proved that the couple had already been before the Elders' Court who had told the wife that she must obey her husband; she refused to listen to their advice and wished to rule in the house.

Court Fees.

1245. Court fees are as follows:—

All districts except Ihangiro:
a. Cases of personal affront (e.g. abuse of elderly relatives and domestic quarrels between man and wife, etc.) Shs.1/=.

b. No fees are charged for the hearing of other cases.

Fees are divided among the bagurusi.

IHANGIRO.

No fees are charged for any case.

Appeal.

1246. The appeal from the Court of Elders lies to:—

a. The Chief, who nominates elders, other than those in the Ntegeka, as assessors, and himself acts as their Chairman.

b. To the Baraza ya Kikale (see para.1250).

c. A man wishing to appeal may refuse to bring his appeal before either a. or b. and can take it to the Gombolola Court.

Executive Power of the Elders' Court.

1247. The Court has no legal executive powers but its authority is up-held by the following considerations :

a. A man hesitates to refuse to accept the Elders' judgment, as to do so will debar him from their help on any future occasion.

b. The bagurusi have the power to impose on a man who defies them a form of village ostracism; this is not so strong as to make him an out-cast, but it means that his co-villagers will refuse him customary assistance in such matters as the building of a house, invitations to his neighbours to attend a wedding, funeral etc. will be refused and neither he nor his family will be invited to village social events.

2. <u>Kyama ya Bagurusi</u> (The Council of the Village Elders).

(This must not be confused with the Ntegeka ya Bagarusi).

1248 a. The Kyama ya Bagurusi is not a stable institution, but consists of an assembly of the leading men of the village who meet together, when they consider it necessary, to discuss any matter which affects village affairs.

b. The activities of the Mukungu, Mwami, and even the Chief are discussed at these meetings in so far as they affect the village.

c. Any man of standing in the village who considers it necessary can call a meeting.

3. <u>Ntegeka ya Abanya Luganda.</u> (The Court of the Clan Elders).

1249 a. This court hears disputes which arise between members of the same clan.

b. Should members of the same sub-clan (ihiga) have a dispute the ihiga head may be called upon to arbitrate, but if they are of different sub-clans the dispute is heard by the clan-head.

c. If a decision on an important matter is necessary, clan-heads of the same clan in neighbouring villages may be called in.

d. Sub-clan heads sit as assessors in the clan Courts. The proceedings are similar to those of the Court of Elders but fees are never paid.

Appeal.

e. The appeal can lie direct to the Gombolola Court but is usually laid before the Baraza ya Kikale.

4. **Baraza ya Kikale, or Baraza Nyaruju.** (The Chief's Private Court.)
1250 a. The Chief is assisted by elders whom he chooses himself.

b. Any of his subjects has the right to approach the Chief in this Court and ask him to examine a case.

c. Most of the cases concern inheritance, disinheritance, cattle etc.

d. There is seldom an appeal from the Chief's judgment.

5. **Ntegeka ya Mukondo.** (The Court of the Cattle Owner).
1251 a. The Chairman is the Mukondo (see para.859).

b. The assembly is called together by the Mukondo, notice being given by him on the previous day in the following manner: — He informs all the members of his kyama that on the following day they themselves must bring their cattle to the mashazi (see para.710) to be handed over to the herdsman for the day.

c. All questions regarding the herding of the kyama cattle, the duties of the owners etc. are dealt with by the assembly.

d. Fines are imposed by the assembly.

e. The fines are on the following lines :—

I. Slight transgressions, such as a herdsman being late in arriving at the mashazi, a herdsman leaving the herd, a herdsman omitting to water the cattle: one calabash of beer, or two days extra herding.

II. Serious transgressions, such as refusal to remove a dangerous bull from the herd, or repeated disobedience to any of the rules etc: expulsion from the kyama.

Appeal.

 f. The appeal is either to the Baraza ya Kikale or to the Gombolola Court.

6. Ntegeka ya Bajubi. (The Court of the Fishermen).

1252a. The constitution of this court is much the same as that of the Court of the Cattle Owners. The Nkuru wa Ikokoro (head of the kyama, see para.920) is the chairman of the court.

 b. All matters referring to fishing and to transgressions of the rules of the kyama are dealt with by the court.

 c. Fines are imposed and expulsions ordered when necessary.

 d. A member of the kyama may be expelled for the following reasons:

 I. Adultery of a member with the wife of a fellow-member.

 II. Assault of a fellow member.

 III. Theft of fish, embezzlement of kyama money.

 IV. Repeated disobedience of kyama rules.

Appeal.

 e. An expelled member may appeal to the chairman of another ikokoro who will discuss the case with his own and other makokoro.

 f. Appeals may be made to the Baraza ya Kikale or to the Gombolola Court.

Legal Procedure in pre-European times.

1253. A chiefdom had five types of courts, in order of importance, from lowest to highest as follows:

 1. Omubuga (In Kiziba known as "Mukungu Mulagirwa"): The Court of the Mukungu.

 2. Rushulo (In Kiziba known as "Kushula"): The Court of the Mukungu Muziba.

3. Omurukali. (Kiziba, "Mugorola"): The Court of the Chief presided over by a sub-chief (mwami) as his representative. The sub-chief presiding over the court was in residence at the Chief's headquarters during his presidency.

4. Nyakaju (Kiziba, "Lwensinga"): The Chief's Court presided over by the Chief himself.

5. The Court of the Ntumwa: From time to time a Chief sent a trustworthy man, called ntumwa out into the chiefdom with powers to try cases himself and also assist the local courts in their work.

NOTE: These were the Courts which came directly under the Hima administration. The village, clan, cattle, and fishermen's courts must also have existed; their connexion with the Chief's Courts is rather obscure, but presumably was much the same as the relationship which exists today between these unofficial village courts and those of Gombolola, Lukiko, etc. (See also appendix IV, Tribal Structure).

Constitution.

1254 a. The president of every court was assisted by court elders known as ishebairu (the father of the people), who were appointed by the Chief and could only be dismissed by the Chief. The office of ishebairu often went from father to son.

b. The appointment of experts, known as ntumwa or mubaka was in the hands of the president of the Court.

NOTE: Appointment of Assessors and Expert Witnesses today.
Gombolola Court Assessors (all districts except Ihangiro).

Assessors are appointed by and are under the control of the Mwami and can therefore be dismissed by him.

IHANGIRO. Assessors are appointed and dismissed by the Chief himself. They act as informants to the Chief on Gombolola affairs. In addition to the Court assessors, the Chief of Ihangiro appoints at least two elders in every village whose duty it is to keep him informed on all affairs of their villages.

Lukiko Court Assessors.

In all districts they are appointed by the Chief and are directly

238

under his control.

Expert Witnesses: Ntumwa or Mubaka (Kiganda).

They are deputed by the Chief to investigate details in civil cases. They are considered to hold an official position as the representatives of the Chief himself and an insult to them is considered to be an insult to the Chief. When on duty they are frequently addressed as "Mukama".

Women in Court.

1255. No woman was allowed to plead in Court, but had to be represented by her husband or a male relative.

Jurisdiction.

1256 a. Cases of murder, witchcraft, and high treason could only be tried by the Chief's Court, the Nyakaju.

b. With regard to other charges, it lay with the president of the Court before which they were brought to decide whether he should hear them himself or refer them direct to the higher Court.

c. A president had the right to appoint one of his ishebairu to hear a particular case.

Appeal.

1257 a. The appeal lay to the next higher Court.

b. If an appeal were laid, the president of the Court from which the appeal was made had to accompany the appellant to the Appeal Court and give a summing up of the proceedings.

Procedure.

1258 a. The hearing was conducted as at the present day.

b. An accused or defendant who refused to appear before the Court was taken by force, and some of his property was seized by the Court as a bond.

<u>Oath</u> (Kunahira).

1259a. The words of the oath were:—

"Obuso Bwomukama" (By the Chief's countenance),

or "Engoma Yomukama" (By the Chief's drum).

These words were considered to be of the greatest significance and might not be lightly used; for example, to use them in ordinary conversation was punishable by the fine of a goat.

NOTE: The assessors stated that this oath is still considered most deeply binding today and carries great weight in village courts. They were unanimous that very few Bahaya would dare to break it.

b. If in Court a man on oath were proved to have committed perjury, the penalty was much more severe, the lightest fine being a head of cattle. If the perjury were committed in the Chief's Court (Nyakaju) the sentence imposed was death, which could be commuted at the Chief's pleasure to the handing over of a daughter of the delinquent to the Chief as a slave (muzana).

c. The most solemn form of oath was to touch the Chief's forehead with the tongue (Kuramba obuso).

<u>False witnesses.</u>

1260. Witnesses who were suspected of being corrupt were dealt with by means of Kutegula (the appeal to Wamara).

This step was taken by a man who believed that he had lost his case owing to false witness given against him. The agrieved man went to the mbandwa (priest) of Wamara who allowed him to beat the sacred drum and call on the god thus: "Wamara, you know right and wrong, you know I have been cheated by so-and-so, I beg you for justice". The all-powerful Wamara was believed to be reconciled only when the false witness presented one of his daughters to the priest as muzana (slave girl).

The fear of Wamara's wrath was so great that it was often only necessary to threaten to appeal to him for a bribed witness to confess immediately.

The relatives of a dead man who believed the deceased to have been guilty of corrupt evidence and to have died without making amends, would join together to do so and would ostracise one of their number who refused to take part in the expiation.

Torture (Kuboha).

1261. Torture was commonly used to extract a confession of guilt. The most common forms were :—

a. To tie a string round the head and draw it tighter with a stick (as a tourniquet).

b. To bend the middle finger backwards.

c. To tie the hands behind the back and then pull them backwards.

A particular form of torture was reserved for a member of the Chiefs family, who was tied down on a piece of bark cloth and forced to drink large quantities of beer. This was a mental torture, for the man was not allowed to leave the spot and suffered in his dignity and self-respect

Ordeals.

1262. Ordeals were only used in the Chief's Court (Nyakaju), and at the direct instruction of the Chief himself. They were only used in cases of witchcraft and bisisi. The men who carried out the ordeals were known as Bafumu. Among the ordeals were the following:—

Ntondo.
All the people concerned sat in a semi-circle, each with a small stick stuck in the ground in front of him. The Mufumu brought a stick on which he had placed a ntondo (a kind of grasshopper), and ordered it to fly on to the stick of the guilty person.

Nteniu.
All the people concerned sat on the ground with their legs stretched out in front of them. The Mufumu passed a red hot spear over the shin bone

of each man and he who was burnt was guilty.

Kagwi (The magic scissors).

Lwezilingo.

The Mufumu prepared a medicine which all suspected persons had to drink.
He who first behaved like a madman was considered guilty.

Fees.

1263. In all Courts except that of the Chief (Nyakaju), fees were paid
by both parties in a case.

A P P E N D I X   I

DESCRIPTION OF BUSHWERE CEREMONIES.

COURTSHIP.

It is stated that it was originally the custom in Buhaya for a father, or his son or his brother, during a meeting with his friends, to offer a girl to one of them as a wife. The man who accepted threw himself on the ground and embraced the legs of the father as a sign of his gratitude. The girl's consent was never asked and no brideprice was paid.

Later the custom altered and the suitor took the initiative, he sent an arbitrator (musigire[*]) to the chosen girl's father to ask for her hand in marriage. The father and mother discussed the acceptability of the suitor. Usually the father delayed his consent by convention. The girl was not asked for her consent either by her parents or her suitor, but the latter was unlikely to be a stranger to her as wives were usually chosen from the man's home district.

If the answer of the father was in the affirmative the young man then went to his own father, whose consent had already been obtained before the girl's father was approached, and asked for a goat. This goat was called kiteme ilembo (to see the way). This goat was sent to the girl's parents, and the day of its delivery was considered the real day of betrothal. Relatives of bride and bridegroom, and the musigire, assembled but not the bridegroom himself as it was a strict rule that the couple should never meet during their betrothal time.

At the end of the meeting the musigire received the rutwa rw'cmwani, a small basket filled with coffee beans. This he kept until the wedding day as a sign of the consent of the bride's parents. All those present at the meeting had sexual intercourse on the night following it to bring

---

[*]The more usual name is musheiezi.

good luck to the wedding.   From the day of his betrothal the young man carefully avoided meeting his mother-in-law to be.   No day was fixed for the marriage.   The time of betrothal lasted several months.

BETROTHAL.

During his betrothal a man had to make certain ritual gifts to the girl's family, which were counted part of the brideprice. He had to send another goat to his future father-in-law called katanga in Kiamtwara or "mberere mpugura" (shining fate) in Karagwe. To his future mother-in-law he had to send a hoe, called nfuka.   The goat was eaten by the girl's family after a piece had been consecrated to the spirits of their clan. The hoe was made by a native blacksmith and used only by the girl's mother When it eventually became worn out she took it to her son-in-law who re-placed it with a new hoe.

It was also the duty of the betrothed man to send regular presents of beer to his future father-in-law.

When several months had elapsed the man sent word to the girl's father that he wished to arrange a day for his wedding. If the father agreed to the proposed date arrangements were made for the payment of brideprice which was always paid in full before marriage.

WEDDING.

The last nine days[*] before the wedding were called   nunyinga   i.e. kunyinga (to adorn oneself).   The nearest relatives of the couple were not allowed to have sexual intercourse during this time.   Both bride and bridegroom prepared themselves for the wedding in various ways, among which frequent anointings of their bodies and four meals a day were the the most important.   Instructions were given to the man by his father,

---

[*]Nine is the holy number of the Bahaya, as it is to many primitive peoples. The Luhaya word for nine is mwenda which is derived from the verb kwenda (to wish).

and to the girl by her mother.

The last night before the wedding was spent by the bridegroom with his friends. A big log was kept burning throughout the night. The log was called balinda akasiki and was not allowed to go out as this would have been a bad omen. The bride did not sleep either. She passed the night in the hut with relatives and friends whose duty it was to make sufficient noise to drown the cries of jackals, hyenas and owls which were bad omens.

Early in the morning the bride was carefully washed for the last time in her father's house; great care being taken that no cracked vessels were used. Shortly afterwards the bridegroom's party arrived. In some districts it was the custom for the musigire and friends to come alone, in others the bridegroom and his father went too. The party on arrival was offered coffee beans to chew. The bride was then led to the door of the inner house for the ceremony kutera omushango (to state the case). Her father addressed the musigire saying:

"You ask me for a wife for so and so, and I have given you one. Do not treat her badly. Rather than that bring her back and I will refund the brideprice. She can always live here with us. Her name is Kamundage!"

This name is an allusion to a well known story which runs as follows: Nyamuhima had an only daughter whom he kept like a boy in his house. He made her a skin dress which completely disguised her sex. The Chief heard that Nyamuhima had a very good-looking son and sent to ask him to send the boy to court to serve as a page. Nyamuhima agreed to let the child to but made one condition, saying "I give you my son Kamundage for the Chief, but if anything should happen to him and the Chief should order him to be killed I must be informed before the order is carried out." At the Court one of the wives of the Chief tried to seduce the boy and when he resisted she became angry, ran to the Chief and accused Kamundage of trying to seduce her by force. The Chief ordered that Kamundage was to be killed. The man who had brought him to Court remembered the condition made by the boy's father and informed him at once. The father went to the Chief and had no difficulty in proving that the wife's accusation was pure blackmail.

The moral is that the girl's father is the only true judge of her character because he knows her better than anyone else; therefore her husband should consult his father-in-law and ask his opinion in case of any difficulties with his wife.

KUBUKARA. (lit: "The rocking.")

The father sits down and takes his daughter on his lap. After which he hands her to her mother who is also seated and who takes her for a moment on her lap. Then everyone stands up and the father puts the bride's hand into that of her bridegroom, or his musigire, saying words to this effect:— "I give you to the family of so and so. Be a good mother. Respect your husband."

He then turns to the representative (musigire) of the bridegroom, saying:

"I give my daughter into your protection. She is healthy and not pregnant. Take care of her as we have done."

KUMUKWENZA AKATI K'EILEMBO.
(lit: To break a twig on the road to the house).

After the father's words the bride's brother carries her on his shoulders out of the house and down to the cattle kraal, or to the end of the broad road which leads to the house. The bride picks twigs of the mulinzi and mushambya trees which she, still carried by her brother, brings back to her mother. This ceremony is a symbol that the daughter is leaving her parent's house as an obedient child, and with their consent. She is following out her destiny as a woman, observing all the necessary ceremonies.

Every female child, when she is given her name a few days after her birth, is placed on the floor of the house with her face towards the door, as a sign that, many years later, she will have to leave her parents' home. A boy is placed on the floor likewise, but he faces the interior of the hut.

During all these ceremonies the bride must by convention cry continuously, regardless of her true sentiments.

BILAGIZO. (Dowry).

The bride is then given her dowry by her parents, which is her own personal property. It consists of the following articles :-

Bark cloth.
Milk vessels and their nets.
Cloth, other than bark cloth.
A vessel, such as is used by married women only for their daily ablutions.

Sometimes she is also given a cow; called in Ihangiro, Karagwe, Missenyi, and Kiziba nshagalilano and in Bugabo, Maruku, and Kianja ndagijanyo. It is given to the bride by her father for her personal use and remains her property, together with any calves it may bear. In case of divorce it cannot be included by the husband in his claim for the return of brideprice.

OMUTURUKO. (Departure).

The bride sets out on her journey to the house of her husband's parents. She is accompanied part of the way by her nearest relatives, and may not look back. When these relatives leave her she is accompanied by her friends and several persons nominated by her brother to attend her. It is the duty of the latter to wipe away the tears and perspiration from her face. The party stops several times en route, and at each halt a little hole is dug.

YATAHA O'MUNJU. (Arrival).

The mother and sisters of the bridegroom greet the bride when she arrives at the entrance to the road which leads to the house. The people present sing, mostly extempore songs referring to events in the lives of the bridal couple.

OKULEJURA.

Presently the bridegroom arrives followed by his friends in single file. He goes straight up to his bride and taking her by the chin, says:

"otarinchumbira bisoroire, mukazi wange" (You must never cook anything bad for me, my wife).

KUCHWERANA (To spit upon each other.)

The bride is then led into the house and a vessel of milk is presented to her, or, if no milk is available, a vessel of native beer. Bride and bridegroom each take a mouthful which they spit out on each other. This is to invoke the blessings of fertility and riches.

The ceremony of kubukara is then repeated. The bride is taken on the laps of both her parents-in-law in turn, and rocked while they say:— "Our little boy has borne a little girl". Thus indicating that they will treat their daughter-in-law as a child of the house. The bride is then led to the bed which stands in a separate part of the house.

OKWEBOHORA (To be touched).

The bed is surrounded by women who pretend to try to hold back the bridegroom when he approaches his bride. After a short mock fight the bridal pair are left alone. Presently the bridegroom leaves the room and going to his father, embraces his knees as a sign of his gratitude. He then addresses the wedding guests who are dancing and drinking outside the house, saying:— "Eichumu riit'entare, n'engoi nkariabwa tatana mawe." (A spear is used to kill; I received one from my mother and father). To which the guests reply, "Wakura" (You are grown up now).

The guests often stay feasting for as long as two days. Every guest brings a present when he comes to the wedding, either a pitcher of beer, some bananas, beans etc. The donors make grass rings for their heads on which they carry their gifts, however small. These rings are strung on a post which is driven into the ground near the door of the hut, where

they remain until they have rotted away. The newly married couple themselves do not join in the wedding festivities with the guests.

OKWOGA (The bath).

The bride's brother fetches water in the evening of the wedding day
for the bath which is prepared the next morning. The bridegroom's mother
performs this ritual washing, using certain plants. First the room is
darkened and the couple sit naked on banana leaves. The mother first
washes her son, saying: "May you have many children. Always be honest
and then you will be happy." To her daughter-in-law she says as she
washes her: "Respect your husband and obey him." She then takes a twig
of the coffee tree with which she beats first her son and then his wife.
There are other people present as assistants and they take twigs and do
the same, exclaiming: "Otanyima, otanyanya." (Do not refuse us, do not
forget us). In Karagwe the man beats himself and his wife, saying: "If
you say one word I will say two". In Kiziba the proceedings differ from
other districts.

AMAJUTA (The anointing).

The anointing is performed with butter prepared by the husband's
mother.

YAZIRA (The refusal).

After the ceremony of anointing food is served. Up till now the
mugole, the newly married girl, has only eaten in secret. Food is now
offered to her which she refuses until her husband presents it to her, and
both eat together for the first time.

AMAJUTA N'OBUTOLERE (Anointing and seed).

A second anointing takes place on the evening of the day after the
wedding. This time butter is prepared by the mother of the bride. Two
children, whose parents are alive and who have brothers and sisters, carry
the butter to the bride and bridegroom together with a basket containing

various kinds of seeds. The children set out from their own homes accompanied by several grown-ups and follow the route taken by the bride the day before on her way to her father-in-law's house. They stop at the same places and put some of the seed into the holes that they find there. When they arrive at their destination, the bride and bridegroom take some of the seed on a piece of bark cloth and each takes some of the butter with which they anoint each other. Whereupon the two children sit down on the same spot and give a detailed repetition of the actions of the couple. The children remain in the house for the night.

This concludes the wedding ceremonies.

The details of the ceremonies differ in the different chiefdoms, for instance in Karagwe the consummation of a marriage takes place after the guests have left. That is, it follows the ceremonies of Okwoga, the first Amajuta and Yazira instead of preceding them.

The above recorded ceremonies and proceedings are the traditional ones. Under present day circumstances they are undergoing many changes, and may be carried out in their entirety, in part, or those that are performed may be altered in all but essence to suit individual tastes as influenced by modern thought and conditions.

The following are the proceedings of a very up to date bushwere.

BETROTHAL.

Betrothal is a matter for the couple themselves. When they have agreed to marry, the man informs his father and asks for his help Thenceforward the proceedings follow the traditional custom, with the exception that there is now no ban on the meetings of the betrothed.

WEDDING.

Whatever other ceremonies are performed, whether Christian or customary, those of Kubukara and Akati keilembo are always included. After the latter the bride is led outside the house where she is received by the bridegroom attended by a party of his and her friends. They all go together to the bridegroom's father's house. Shortly before they reach the house the party divides into two, that of the bride and that of the bridegroom, to meet again shortly in a ceremonial manner. When they meet, the bridegroom ties a silk cloth round the head of the bride, and she passes her hand gently over his forehead. The bride sobs continuously.

The bridegroom then leaves her and takes his stand near by, whereupon all his friends line up in front of him, and one after another they step forward and shake hands with him; after which he distributes a few coins amongst them. The whole party then resumes its way to the bridegroom's house, where a small clearing has been made and partitioned off by screens of sticks and banana leaves. Inside this enclosure a table and two chairs have been placed to which the bride and bridegroom are led. The bridegroom seats the bride on one chair and takes the other himself. Food is brought and he feeds her as if she were a baby. The bride is then taken into the house for the second ceremony of Kubukara, while the bridegroom joins the guests with whom he stays feasting and dancing until evening.

The bride remains for about eight months in seclusion in her father-in-law's house during which time she does no work. At the end of this time she goes to stay with her parents for a few days, and then returns to her husband bringing a hoe, as a sign that she is now ready to work in her husband's fields.

APPENDIX II

DAMAGES.

With few exceptions most of the offences for which, in Customary Law, compensation was the penalty, nowadays come under the heading of "Criminal Offences" and are therefore outside the scope of this book.

It may be of interest, however, to mention what Customary Law had to say on the subject. A convicted person might be ordered to pay compensation to an injured party either as the sole, or in addition to other, punishment. The system of fines was unknown since, without a Court treasury a fine could only be paid personally to the judge of the case, and as he was not the injured party he was naturally not considered to be entitled to payment. On the other hand he usually received a share of of the compensation from the man to whom he awarded it.

The computing of damages in Criminal Cases was left almost wholly to the Chief who assessed them as and how he saw fit. In civil cases the law was stronger and more binding.

MURDER AND MANSLAUGHTER.

No difference was made between the two.

(a) <u>Murder of a Chief or Member of the ruling family.</u>

The murderer and all his family were executed, and their property reverted naturally to the Chief (see obuchweke).

(b) <u>Murder of a commoner.</u>

Two courses were open :—

(1) A blood feud arose and the nearest relatives of the murdered person avenged his death by killing the murderer or any member of his clan.

(2) (The more usual course) The murderer took sanctuary with the Chief (who was recognised as sanctuary). The Chief assessed the amount due in compensation to the murdered man's family, usually 2-5 head of cattle or an equivalent value in goats. After payment a solemn bond of

brotherhood was formed between the two families, in the presence of a representative of the Chief, which ended the feud.

In addition it was usual for the murderer to surrender his plantation to his victim's family and go to live in another part of the Chiefdom.

THEFT.

The thief was ordered to return the stolen property or its value and in addition to pay a goat or a cow as compensation. If the thief himself had no property he was fettered until his relatives had paid up.

ASSAULT, CRIMINAL AND COMMON.

The sole punishment was compensation, usually assessed according to the severity of the injury.

RAPE.

1. An unmarried woman or a widow was allowed compensation only if she received any hurt.

2. In the case of an unmarried girl, compensation was paid to her father.

3. In the case of a married woman, compensation was paid to her husband.

DAMAGE TO PROPERTY.

Arson. Compensation was awarded but no punishment. If the culprit could not be found, the whole village was obliged to help to build a new house.[*]

The following case shows that courts in computing damages for arson today may take into consideration neglect on the part of an owner to safeguard his property against fire.

---

[*] This custom had its merits, because it supplied the injured person with a new and probably a better house, which frustrated the intention of the man who burned it down. (See letter No.278/108 of 18.1.37).

QUOTATION: D.O's appeal No.7 of 1935.

Karuli v. Elizabeti.
A grass fire started by Karuli spread and burnt down Elizabeti's hut.
Karuli was ordered to rebuild the hut, but Elizabeti was awarded no
compensation for the furniture etc. which was destroyed within the hut,
since she had not kept the grass cut in the vicinity and therefore her
house was burnt out.

No compensation was payable in the following cases:

1. Witchcraft, because the sorcerer was executed or deported and
his property confiscated by the Chief.

2. Slander.

3. Insult.

The following causes for compensation are offences in Customary Law
only, and have no parallel in British Law. They are acknowledged to
carry compensation today:

1. Adultery (see para.439).

2. Seduction causing pregnancy (see para.368 II and 368 IV).

3. Infection (Syphilis only). A man cannot claim compensation from
a woman who has infected him; a husband can claim compensation from a
man who is proved to have infected his wife; a woman can only claim
compensation for infection from her husband.

QUOTATION: D.O's appeal No.42 of 1936.

Leokardia v. Simon.
Leokardia, a married woman, committed adultery with Simon and became
infected with syphilis. She claimed compensation from Simon, but the
Court held that she was not entitled to do so because her infection
was caused by a man who was not her husband.

QUOTATION: D.O's appeal No.30 of 1934.

Abdullah v. Bibi Makatunzi.
Makatunzi claimed compensation from her husband Abdullah who infected
her with syphilis. She was awarded Shs.15/= compensation and Abdullah
was fined Shs.10/=.

NOTE: These rules regarding infection are of comparatively recent date since the incidence of infection was not understood before the arrival of European doctors.

BREACH OF CUSTOM.

There is no legal claim for such compensation; its payment is dictated by superstition and social pressure only. Examples are: A goat must be paid for ritual cleansing by the father of a wife who:—

(a) has committed adultery in her husband's house,

(b) has bitten her husband,

(c) has kicked her husband,

(d) has been living with another man for any length of time and returns to her husband.

A P P E N D I X   III

TRIBAL STRUCTURE IN UHAYA.

Uhaya under clan rule before the coming of the Hinda.

Most clans claim that their origin lies in Bunyoro. Little is actually known of these immigrants, but traces of their history may be found in the legends of the indigenous clans who claim them as their ancestors.

The immigrants seem to have come in family bands under the leadership of one of their members; they entered a sparsely populated country, and met, apparently, with little opposition from the indigenous inhabitants. When they reached a place in which they decided to settle, the leader probably became the family or clan head, unless some of his family was already settled there, when he placed himself and his band under the existing clan head. In either case there was no further communication with the original home and the new settlers became independent units under their own clan heads.

It seems that throughout a long period a continual stream of newcomers poured into Uhaya, but local tradition gives no explanation of the reasons for this movement, or of the events which impelled the people to start their migration to the south.[1]   That the immigration was not an organised movement seems to be borne out by the fact that local clan heads were independent of each other. The descendants of the original settlement leaders are today the clan heads, and no one of them is considered superior to another.

As a settlement grew, the original leader, after several generations, became to his descendants a mythical figure. He became known as omugurusi or patriarch. His deeds and prowess during his life time were extolled and exaggerated, and if he had been a very outstanding character he might be promoted to the position of the spirit of the clan, because

---

[1] The civil wars in Bunyoro which caused extensive depopulation of the country may perhaps have some bearing on it.

of the belief that the more powerful a man was in life the more influential is his spirit on the lives of his descendants.

Apart from immigrants from the north, in the course of time new immigrants went out from among the now-settled areas and established for themselves yet new settlements of which, after several generations, the leaders became the bagurusi, and the home settlements they had left were considered as the places of clan origin.

Sometimes the first settler did not himself become the omugurusi; he presumably taught his family to look upon the clan head in his old home as their omugurusi, and this idea was handed down from generation to generation, for clans are to be found here today who claim ancestors in Bunyoro as bagurusi, and the first settlers in Uhaya as mahiga heads.

Clan sub-divisions, (Mahiga).

If, within an established clan settlement, sub-divisions were created, these were called mahiga. (The word mahiga means "hearthstones"— the connexion being that the originator of the family group separated from the main body and built a new house with a new hearthstone).

Mahiga arose for various reasons, such as the following:—

(I) If a clan member left his home and settled in a new area but kept in contact with his stay-at-home relatives, he, as founder of the new settlement, became after several generations its ihiga head, not a clan head as he would have been if all connexions with home had been severed.

(II) When a clan group grew too big it was found practicable to divide the members into smaller family units for easier dealing with such matters as inheritance, maintenance of female descendants, etc. The senior member of each of these new sub-divisions became the ihiga head.

(III) If quarrels broke out between clan members, and relatives took sides, each side constituted itself a sub-division with its senior member as its ihiga head.

As with the omugurusi of the clan, so the originator of the ihiga became in time omugurusi of the ihiga, and gave his name to it. All mahiga names are the plural form of the omugurusi's own name: for example, Kagwesa is the omugurusi of the Bagwesa ihiga of the Baihuzi clan.

Totemism.

Every clan has its totem, but it is surprising that in Uhaya there are many clans but a comparatively small number of different totems.

The following theory was brought forward by the elders and is given for what it is worth. They suggested that what is known here as a clan is probably in reality only a sub-clan, i.e. ihiga. Sometimes the real clan name is preserved, but in many cases the ihiga name replaces it. The totem however remains unchanged. A good example is the Bahinda clan who claim Ruhinda as their "omugurusi wa luganda" or clan patriarch, but he is obviously a "omugurusi wa ihiga", since it is known that his clan was Babito in Bunyoro; thus the local belief is that all clans with the same totem, even if they have different names, were once the same clan.

Secondary Totem.[1]

Clans holding the same primary totem often hold different secondary totems. The elders explain this by saying that an omugurusi often adopted a secondary totem on account of certain events on his journey or in his life. For example, the omugurusi of the Basimba clan is Mauwe. On the day of his birth a dog had puppies. The dog often washed the child by licking it. Mauwe later, out of gratitude, ordered his descendants to consider the dog as their friend, and the dog became the secondary totem of the clan.

---

[1] The use of the secondary totem is becoming obsolete. Many people when questioned either did not understand or said that they had forgotten; whereas this was never the case when they were asked for their primary totem.

Spirits.

Every clan has its particular spirit.[1]   Some of them have one of the local deities, but others have adopted one of their family members. A clan spirit was not necessarily an outstanding character in life. For example, the spirit of the clan Abansingo is Katondolerwa, the daughter of the omugurusi Myambi who died as a child during a famine; the spirit of the clan Barwani is Kashasira.   He was an old,sick stranger who fell into a swamp and died.   He was found and buried by a Murwani, and, for unknown reasons, became the spirit of the clan.

Exogamy.

It is forbidden for members of the same clan to marry, except in the Bahinda clan, but different clans holding the same totem may inter-marry. (See also Appendix V "Clans" re exogamy and exogamous groups.)

Indigenous clans.

Certain clans are recognised to be indigenous because they were the first comers among the immigrants (see page 255).

Among them are:—

> Batundu
>
> Bahunga
>
> Bagombe
>
> Banyuma
>
> Baihuzi
>
> Basimba
>
> Basaizi
>
> Bakuma

Tradition makes no mention of fighting between these immigrants and the people whom they found in Uhaya. For example, a tradition in Missenyi says that the Batundu who came from the north under a leader called Mulinda first settled in Missenyi about the same time as Kintu founded the king-dom of Uganda. Mulinda was an old man at the time of his immigration and when he reached the Kagera he decided not to cross the river, so he remained

---

[1]The same clan may acknowledge different spirits in the different Chief-doms.

in Missenyi without opposition and younger members of his family crossed
the river and went on into Uhaya.

Arrival of the Hinda.

The great landmark in the history of Uhaya is the arrival of the
Bahinda about three hundred and fifty years ago.   The Bahinda also came
from Bunyoro. They are of Hima stock whose history is briefly as follows:—

Some two thousand years ago it is believed that a series of invasions
by a pastoral Galla people from the north took place in East Africa. Traces
of these people are found in the countries of the Acholi, Lango, Unwiro,
etc., but they did not settle there, probably because of the warlike
nature of the inhabitants.   When they reached Bunyoro and Ankole they
found favourable conditions and settled in these countries where they
eventually founded a Hima dynasty, the Bachwezi, who turned out the existing Bantu rulers.   It is not known for how long the Bachwezi held sway
but they appear to have reached the zenith of their power during the reign
of one Wamara.   They were in time succeeded by another Hima clan, the
Babito, one of whose members was Igaba, whose son Ruhinda went south and
became the chief of Karagwe and Ihangiro, whence developed the other Buhaya
chiefdoms with the exception of Kiziba, which claims to have been founded
by another son of Igaba, Kibi.

The Bahinda did not come to Uhaya alone but with followers belonging
to other clans.[1]   Among these the most prominent clan is the Bayango,

---

[1] "Not the whole population of Bunyoro was pastoral. There existed clans
of herdsmen, of husbandmen and of a mixture of the two. The latter clans
consisted of husbandmen who had been admitted by marriage into some of the
pastoral clans. Therefore it may be concluded that not all migrating clans
from Bunyoro were cattle breeders." Johnson,"The Uganda Protectorate."
   In "Totemism and Exogamy" Frazer also mentions three types of clans in
Bunyoro, pastoral, agricultural and mixed. Among the pastoral and mixed
clans which he lists appear some names and many totems which are also to be
found in Uhaya.
   "On the north and west of Lake Victoria a series of people — the Ganda,
Nkole, Toro and Nyoro of Uganda, the eight Haya tribes of Bukoba district
in Tanganyika, and the Ruanda of the Belgian mandated area — have arisen
from the conquest of Bantu agricultural people by Hamitic pastoral invaders
from the North." Hailey, "An African Survey."

260

some of whom are said to have arrived here even before the Bahinda. There must have existed a certain connexion between the Bahinda and Bayango. For instance Ruhinda is the clan spirit of the Bayango, and they share the Bahinda totems.

The Hinda invasion, like that of the early immigrants, was in the main peaceful. Doubtless the majority of the indigenous clans, being in no way organised, acknowledged without resistance the supremacy of the Bahinda.[1] A few exceptional instances of resistance by Batundu, Bahunga and Bakuma clan heads are related.

The ready acknowledgement of the Bahinda as masters was probably due to the fact that they were a more advanced people, who had already reached the stage of having chiefs, while the people they found were still in the stage of clan organisation. It is evident that the clan system was developing towards this higher stage, from the tradition that the Batundu had already gained a superior position amongst the clans; and it is possible to imagine that had they been left alone, a Mutundu would in the course of time have founded a ruling dynasty. A Kiziba tradition relates that the Bakuma were the most powerful clan at the time of the arrival of Kibi, the Muhinda invader. At first the Bakuma refused to accept him but he reconciled them by promising that if they allowed him to reign they should keep their power. Kibi is quoted as saying, "You shall enthrone my son. You shall demarcate the boundaries of my residence. You shall say where my houses are to be built. You shall open up my plantations. I will give you half my beer and if I kill an ox you shall have half of it."

The Bahinda had two main ideas which they were determined to put in practice: the idea of chieftainship, and that of cattle breeding. Once

---

[1] "These people as a whole were peaceful and kept up no national life outside their little village communities, but tended more and more to particularism; consequently they were unable to withstand the shock of invasion". Werner, "Native Races of British Central Africa."

the Bahinda had established themselves as rulers, they allowed the clan organisation to continue and made use of it as a part of their political machinery.

The Bahinda were a pastoral people and brought with them the long horned Ankole cattle common in Uhaya today. As cattle-breeders they were not at first interested in land under cultivation. However, the introduction of cattle on a large scale produced an economic revolution in land tenure. Up to that time the Bahaya had lived only partly on bananas, but the usual practice of African cattle-breeders, which the Bahinda also followed, of farming out their cattle (para.732) made it possible to cultivate bananas on a far larger scale because manure, which is a necessity for successful banana cultivation, was now available.[1] Thus bananas gradually became the staple food of the tribe, as they are to-day.

It is natural that the cultivation of a perennial crop should give rise to the idea of individual land tenure. No one would plant a perennial crop without some security of tenure. A banana plantation will provide a livelihood for a family throughout the generations so long as they inhabit it; therefore the form of land tenure will be a perpetual tenure on a hereditary basis.

Land was plentiful and in itself of no value, but a newcomer wanted not only to provide for his own livelihood but also to ensure that his sons and their families and descendants would not be dispersed, but would be able to live as neighbours. Therefore a new settler tried to acquire as large an area as possible, and the original clan settlements thus became the origin of the villages of today (see para.529.).

The Bahinda needed food stores for their courts, soldiers, etc., and therefore, in exchange for the manure produced by their cattle, and the consequent increased fertility of the land, asked for a share in the

---

[1] The importance of cattle is shown in the language — the word for "a rich man" is Mutungi which derives from the word "kutunga" meaning "to give cattle."

262

harvests.   This may be the origin of tribute.   It was paid in kind and
did not enrich the Chief, as no market existed for the sale of agricultural
products; it was used by him for the upkeep of his Court.

The Bahinda as Rulers.

The Bahinda were not despots.   They recognised the existing clan
organisation and, far from destroying it, installed themselves at its head.
This was the natural thing for them to do, since this was the system in
the country of their origin.   Thus the introduction of Chiefs was not a
revolutionary movement, but a step forward from the old system, drawing
together the hitherto independent clan units who had no national (tribal)
consciousness.

The Chief, as ruler, united all clans in his chiefdom as his subjects,
and that this idea of union became general is shown by the fact that it
culminated in all his subjects admitting themselves to be an ihanga, which
means the national unit comprising all inhabitants of a chiefdom.

The ihanga of Kiamtwara is Bayoza
   "   "   " Ihangiro " Banyaihangiro
   "   "   " Kianja " Bahamba
   "   "   " Karagwe " Banyambo
   "   "   " Maruku " Bakala
   "   "   " Bugabo " Bahendangabo
   "   "   " Kiziba " Baziba
   "   "   " Missenyi " Babumbiro.

The origin of the boundaries of the chiefdoms is not known. That the
chiefdoms became internally cemented units is shown by the fact that they
developed dialects of their own and differences in law and custom.

This new tribal consciousness concentrated itself in the person of
the Chief. He was acknowledged to have the right to depose a clan head
at the request of his people.   More evidence of his influence as head of
all the clans is shown by the fact that there are instances of a chief

creating new clans or sub—clans. For example the Bamiro clan was originally an ihiga of the Bagabo clan; one of its female members married Mukama
Wanumi of Kiziba, who decreed that her near relatives should thenceforward
be considered as belonging to the Bahima group. Thus the ihiga split,
one part remaining in the Bagabo clan and the other becoming a new clan,
calling itself the Bamiro and following the taboos of the Bahima. The
object of Wanumi's action was to raise his marriage from one which might
be called morganatic to one between equals, a child of which would be
entitled to succeed to the chieftainship. Such acts by Bakama are however very much disliked by all the pure Hima clans.

A new ihiga was created when Rugomora Mahe succeeded to the chieftainship of Kianja; at the time of his accesion he was in Uganda, and
on his return, he was acclaimed by his people; certain members of the
Bakoba clan offered a gift of honey and the Chief called them bamuneni
(the sweet people). These people formed themselves into a new ihiga
called the Bamuneni. Some members of the Bazigu clan ran away instead
of joining in the acclamations, and these the Chief called bauge — the
lost ones — which was adopted as their new ihiga name.

Thus the Chief came to be regarded as the supreme ruler in whom the
recognised authority and prerogatives of the clan heads were vested. This
attitude of both Chiefs and people restricted the power of the Chief.
This situation was re-inforced by inherent superstition, which was fostered
by priests and elders who by this means acted as upholders of the people's
rights, and by the common tendency of Africans to delegate their work to
substitutes. No despot can delegate his powers, for substitutes are
bound to achieve before long a good deal of independence in carrying out
their work.

The position of the Chief with regard to land illustrates the strength
and the limits of his power. Though the Bahinda were not at first interested in any but grazing land, the Chiefs, by virtue of the acknowledgment of their supreme power as judges, were soon drawn into the manifold

litigations of their subjects regarding land arising from the customary form of land tenure. A Chief had powers of life and death and therefore those of dispossession and allocation of land; they became donors and thence also owners of land. The Chief could kill a man, or deprive him of his land and give it to another, but he could only exercise this power so long as his subjects and their representatives consented to it, because he himself was liable to deposition, or his people might emigrate to another chiefdom if he became too despotic.

"The common law principle that 'the King can do no wrong' is doubly true in the case of an African community. That which the Chief did the will of the community sanctioned; when the Chief did that which the will and power of the community did not sanction he was no longer Chief. Every thing which a Chief did was right so long as he could do it."[1]

The compromise between the two powers resulted in the principle that the community is the chiefdom which is represented by the Chief, not as a person but in virtue of his office. The land was held by the Chief as trustee for the tribe. He allocated it in compliance with the customary form of tenure.

The Hinda Chiefs and the Clans.

The Bakama assigned certain duties about their Court to every clan, sometimes even to mahiga. This meant that some members of a clan were always in attendance at the Court, since the clan sent men turn by turn to fulfil their special functions. Clans with important duties such as cooks, watchmen, keepers of the royal drums, etc. had permanent houses in the residence. This practice of granting privileges was of advantage both to the Chief and to the clans. To the Chief because he had a large body of his subjects living permanently at his court who could defend him in case of necessity. To the clans because these duties placed the well-being of the Chief to a great extent in their hands. The keepers of the

[1] See Griffiths on Land Tenure — Bukoba District Book.

royal drums, for example were keepers of the Chief's position because the drums were the necessary insignia of office and only the holder of them could be Chief. In addition the clan members in residence watched over the interests of their own clan and guarded the prerogatives of clans generally.

Differences in status existed among the clans, usually determined by historical events. For instance if some of the members of a clan showed cowardice in battle it might happen that the whole clan was degraded, or if a chief's wife committed some crime her clan became despised. A chief was often debarred from taking bazana (female slaves) from such a clan.

The Clan Courts (ntegeka ya banaya luganda, see para.1249) remained unchanged except that the Chief's Court became the Appeal Court for them. Only much later, by the creation of Gombolola Courts, was the extent of their jurisdiction curtailed.

The Chief might not execute a man without first calling for his clan head who had the right to redeem any criminal in the name of the clan. The clan heads were made responsible for the collection of the clan's tribute to the Chief. They in their turn made the sub-clan heads (mahiga heads) responsible for the collection from their people.

As has already been stated, the clans, in matters which did not hold much interest for the Chiefs, kept their independent authority or at least shared it with the Chief. The responsibility for decisions on boundary questions within the plots of rweya rwaruganda (clan-owned rweya) was left to the clan heads. All uninhabited land remained under the supervision of the clans, whose authority was vested in Baharambwa.[1] (see para.516 et seq.)

---

[1] This at first sight seems unexpected, if taken in conjunction with the statement that the Bahinda had no interest in cultivated land, implying that they had in open land; but it is explainable by the fact that all grazing land was free, and being cattle-owners, grazing rights were their only pre-occupation.

The office of Muharambwa was vested in the original clan in a village, and the post was held, as a hereditary right, by the living descendant of the Mainuka of its omugurusi. A Muharambwa wore as his official dress a woman's grass skirt, kishenshe, and returned greetings in the women's fashion. The origin of this custom lies in the old rule that the Mainuka inherited the nju nyaruju (the father's big house) and lived there with his mother while the Musika built a new house on his father's estate or perhaps opened new land. The reason may be that the Mainuka, being the youngest son, must often have been still a child at the time of his father's death. At his mother's death the Mainuka inherited her personal belongings, as the Musika inherited the father's personal effects. As the Musika is wrapped in his deceased father's cloth when he is installed as heir, so the Mainuka wore his mother's cloth for two days after her death.

The Musika and his heirs inherited the omugurusi's position as head of the family (nkuru wa luganda), having the charge of all cultivated land, while the Mainuka and his descendants, the Baharambwa, inherited the supervision of all land outside the mwate, which, if cultivated, is solely under the care of the women.

The Muharambwa's position was a highly important one in the village. When a Muharambwa's son was installed in place of his deceased father, he was initiated into his duties by the neighbouring Baharambwa. On this occasion all the women in his area brought their hoes to be blessed. The drum called Kyabalimi, which is used to assemble the women or for ancestor worship, was handed over to him.

Baharambwa and their wives were expected to maintain a high moral standard in their private lives. It was very unusual for them to fail in this by such acts as adultery, taking bribes. etc. Should a Muharambwa be found guilty of adultery, the husband of the woman in question invariably expelled her from his house. He could claim compensation as in any other such case, but the expulsion was obligatory.

A Muharambwa and his wife's father were excused payment of all forms of tribute. When a Muharambwa died, all the people in his area had to abstain from sexual intercourse for four days. In some districts the only man to be buried in his own plantation was a Muharambwa. Should a Muharambwa die before his son was old enough to inherit his position, his wife carried on his duties during the child's minority and taught her son what his work would be. A Muharambwa's wife was completely identified with her husband's work and was expected to be conversant with the most important of his duties, particularly the knowledge of boundaries.

Should two Baharambwa quarrel about their boundaries, the one who threw himself on the ground and exclaimed, "This is my soil," and said to his opponent, "Bring a snake here and bury it if you dare!" was considered to have made a solemn statement on oath.

Theoretically the sphere of influence of the Muharambwa lay in uninhabited land, but seeing that originally nearly the whole of his area was uninhabited, it can be understood that his sway was soon not confined to the irungu alone. For instance, certain religious rites connected with the worship of local spirits were performed by the Muharambwa on a traditional spot which was once irungu, but might have become the centre of a village.

The Muharambwa was believed to possess supernatural powers for the blessing of hoes, of women that they might bear children, etc. If a house was burnt down in a village, he performed a ceremony of placation of the spirits, so that they would not cause the fire to spread to other houses. If anyone was burnt to death in the fire he took the corpse (or the ashes) and buried it outside the village. If a dog or snake died in the village, the Muharambwa alone might take it away to bury it in the bush. From this duty his name is derived (kuhara = to pull, mbwa = a dog).

If beer bananas, which had been brought to the house to ripen, were allowed to rot, the owner might not touch them but must send for the Muharambwa who threw them away in the plantation. Should harvest prospects be poor the women took small offerings in kind to the Muharambwa and asked him to intercede for them with the god, Irungu.

A Muharambwa who broke the rules of his office could be deposed by his clan head, who installed another member of the same ihiga in his stead. Clan members who were dissatisfied with their Muharambwa had the right to demand his deposition by their clan head. Should the clan head take no steps in the matter, the clan members could lay their case before the Mukama and ask for his intervention.

A Muharambwa was paid when he performed any of his many duties by small gifts, usually in kind. The women who went to receive his blessings on their hoes each took a small basket of potatoes, or eleucine, etc. In addition to these gifts he received a few cents for each marriage which took place in his area. The bridegroom, when he fetched his bride took these cents (or cowries in Ihangiro) and handed them to his father-in-law to be given to the Muharambwa. From every head of cattle slaughtered in his district he received a share of the meat, even from the Chief's cattle. The Chief was not exempt from the payment of the customary dues to a Muharambwa.

The position of the Muharambwa today is still one of dignity and importance in many villages. All elders agree that he is invariably a man of high integrity, and that the whole village would pay his tax between them should he be unable to do so. Further, if he is a cattle-owner he is not expected to take his turn in herding. His authority in land matters within his sphere is acknowledged, and it is seldom that an appeal is made against his decision in land cases.

The Muharambwa's position is maintained solely by the will of the community, while the Chief and his officials, for whom it holds no interest, probably try to transfer the duties of his office to the Bami or Bakungu. Thus it happens that in some districts the shifting of power is already taking place, or has done so, while in others the Muharambwa's authority is still great. The execution of his religious duties and the belief in his supernatural powers naturally depends on whether his people still hold their old beliefs or not.

INTRODUCTION OF BAKUNGU AND BAMI.

With an increasing population living on a perennial crop, it became necessary to fix the boundaries, in the first place, of the spheres of influence of the clans. These boundaries are the origin of the village boundaries which remain unchanged today. In each village the clan of the first settler was acknowledged to be the leading clan and still holds its position today.

When new-comers from other clans settled within the village boundaries, naturally quarrels began to break out between the clans. This made it necessary for the Chief to send an impartial arbitrator to settle disputes. He chose for this office, either a relative or a favourite, who made his home in the village. This is the origin of the office of Mukungu. In course of time the Mukungu took over from the head of the leading clan the right to allot land in his village, because the Chief was interested in the growth of population in his chiefdom, whereas the clan head was interested in keeping his domain for himself and his clan. This is perhaps how it came about that the right to allot land was taken from the clans and appropriated by the Chiefs.

The increasing population made the vague form of boundary demarcation in the allocation of land no longer feasible. It was necessary that boundaries should be clearly defined and a responsible man had to carry out this work. So was created the position of Mutaiya.

It is possible that the new form of boundary demarcation of allocated land brought about the custom of the payment of kishembe as fees. This payment was made by an applicant in the first place to the Mukungu, and was taken to the Chief in order to obtain his final consent to the allocation. The payment was not looked upon as a purchase price for the land, but as a recognition by both sides that the land had been granted under the proper form of land tenure.

As the chiefdoms became consolidated as separate units, inter-chiefdom feuds became more frequent and therefore it became necessary that the internal administration of a Chiefdom should be strong enough to combat external interference. The Chief placed a number of villages and their Bakungu under a common administrative head called a Mwami. These Bami were always chosen from amongst the Chief's relatives. The boundaries of the village units were determined by three factors: —

1. The importance of the relative who became Mwami.

2. The topographical features of the area.

3. The original village boundaries. This is the origin of the Gombolola[1]

The Gombolola soon took its place as the centre for local military organisation. Each Gombolola had its regiment called mutwe which formed a unit of the Chiefdom's army. The names of these mutwe are still extant and are popularly used by the people to this day. For example in Ihangiro:

Gombolola		Mutwe		Meaning of Name.
1) Buleza	=	Ababeregera	=	The archers.
2) Kahengiro	=	Abatairuka	=	Those who never run away.
3) Ilemera	=	Abakaito	=	Those of the heavy step
4) Mubunda	=	Abatahiaibega	=	Those who use their shoulders to push home an attack.
5) Ngote	=	Abahenzangaro	=	Those who fight with bare fists.
6) Bulabo	=	Abashawo	=	?
7) Nshamba	=	Abashami	=	?
8) Kishanda	=	Abajugo	=	Those with a loud voice

---

[1] It is impossible to say whether any or all of these institutions were copied from those existing in the original homes of the Bahinda.

Gombolola		Mutwe		Meaning of Name.
9) Mbalama	=	Abaganguzi	=	The looters
10) Kashasha	=	Abachwaihembe abatuwa	=	Those who strike first.
11) Bumbire	=	Abajumba	=	The surprise attackers.

MUTEKO.

Military education began in the muteko which was an institution for tribal education. All able-bodied boys between the ages of 10 and 12 years were gathered together at the Court and divided into companies, remaining there in turn for two months at a time. During these periods the boys were instructed in various subjects, such as tribal customs and manners, agriculture, and especially military training. After finishing this syllabus, which lasted about three years, most of the boys returned to their homes, but a few selected ones who had shown particular ability remained at the Court for further instruction, after which they were either given captaincies, made regents for the children who held office as sub-chiefs but were too young to execute their duties, or were given the offices of Bami or Bakungu when these became vacant.

Each Muteko has its special name, such as:

Omuganguzi	=	the fighters
Omushegeshe	=	porcupine
Omujuelo	=	helpers
Omuchumiko	=	stalkers

The members of the muteko had a strong idea of "esprit de corps". Even nowadays an old man, when asked his age, may reply "My muteko was so and so".

The institution of the muteko is now almost obsolete. Sometimes on special occasions, such as the enthronement of a new Chief, a new muteko may be created, but it has lost all practical significance and all the interest of the Chiefs as a means of education, because of modern educational influences.   There is no doubt that the older generation deplores its disappearance.

THE BAKAMA AND RELIGION.

The Bahinda brought with them a religious system which easily fitted in with the religious ideas of the indigenous people. Before long Hinda deities superseded in power those of their subjects, because since the Bahinda were the mighty men of the land, their spirits were considered to be mightier than those of lesser men.   Besides this, owing to the similarity in the religious rites of Bahinda and indigenous people, no objection arose from the latter to whom the new gods merely meant a change in the names of the objects of veneration.

It is an interesting point that some of these superimposed Hinda deities were historical characters, members of the ruling clan of the Bachwezi dynasty, who ruled before the Hinda family in Bunyoro; whereas here they are not known to have been living men but are considered as purely supernatural beings.

The most powerful deities are:

Wamara, the ruler of the universe, supreme among all other deities and spirits, and the sovereign of the souls of the dead.

Mugasha, the spirit of the Lake, who has power over rivers, wind and weather and also over plants which have been planted by men.

Irungu, the spirit of the earth, the bush and the forest and also the patron of travellers.

Kazoba, the spirit of the sun, moon and stars.

Round all these deities is woven a complex mythology. They all have sons and daughters to whom they delegate some of their power; for instance, Nyakarembe, the wife of Mugasha, is the goddess of agriculture; Kaiyura, his son, is the spirit of the thunderstorm; other sons, Mushoke and Rwebembera, are the spirits of wind and rain.

Nowadays the explicit knowledge of this mythology is disappearing and can be found only among a few old people.

The old clan gods did not diasppear, as is shown by the fact that the name of the ancient, vague but supreme deity Ishwanga is still vene-rated (some of the elders call him a son of Irungu and thus connect the old with the new); the majority of the old deities have continued as clan spirits (mizuka), for example, the mizuka of the Bahungu is Luhoha, the god of hunters.

Certain gods and goddesses were worshipped chiefly by women. Among them are Mhaya, daughter of Ruhinda — Msula, son of the great Ruhinda. Mhaya was cast off by her father for her promiscuity with men. She left Ruhinda-Msula's Court and died of sorrow in the village of Ijumbe. She is also the spirit of the Bakombe clan. A woman who has been deserted by her lover offers sacrifices to Mhaya. The woman smears butter on a mshumshu (a giant thistle) leaf and after calling on the goddess to send back the lover, hides the leaf near the man's bed; this she believes will make it impossible for him to sleep with another woman. Mhaya is also invoked by women whose love is not reciprocated. Such a woman smears butter on a stick and, after calling on the goddess, places the stick in a potsherd where the man will pass.

Nyakarembe, wife of Mugasha, is the goddess of all field work. The women sacrifice to her thus:—

All sorts of seeds and a new knife are placed in a ntukuru (basket) which is kept in the house as a "table for Nyarkarembe. If a good harvest is reaped a small portion of the crop is cooked and put in the basket.

Spirits peculiar to Karagwe women are Nyauleza, Kwako, Isengowa. Nyauleza is the supreme judge who is interceded with in cases of theft.

Under German Rule.

A. Administration.

During the German Rule, the European administration of the Bukoba District (and Ruanda and Urundi) differed principally from that of all other districts of the colony.

D.L. Baines, the first British Political Officer after the military occupation of Bukoba, describes the German administration as follows:

"Except when German interests were concerned the administration inter-fered as little as possible in the internal affairs of the various Sultanates.   Implicit obedience was required and undoubtedly obtained to all orders issued by the Government or Sultans.   Complaints a-gainst the Sultans were discouraged presumably with the true Prussian spirit that authority must be maintained right or wrong. Authority was entirely concentrated in the Sultans who worked directly with rugaruga."

B. Jurisdiction.

See: Law Reports Volume 1. 1921-1928.

"Jurisdiction (Civil, Criminal and Non-Contentious) over natives was exercised mainly by District Officers, Officers in command of military stations, etc. but in the Residencies of Bukoba, Ruanda and Urundi mainly by Native Courts."

Mr. D. L. Baines says:

"Minor cases were tried by Chiefs or Sub-Chiefs in their houses over a gourd of beer."

C. Taxes.

D.L. Baines states.

"Poll tax was collected by clerks paid by the Sultan at the rate of Rs.5/= per month.   The clerks were apparently responsible to

the Government, the Sultan and senior Katikiro having little administrative and no financial responsibility in the collection.
The actual collecting was extraordinarily inefficiently carried out,
large numbers escaping year after year. The clerks were notoriously
corrupt, as it appears to have been customary for candidates for the
position to pay Rs.10/= up to 40/= or 50/= to their Sultan for a
recommendation to the Government. The profits must have been considerable."

D. Land.

German Ordinance No.144/4/1900 states that all claims to land dependent upon the sovereign rights of Chiefs are transferred to the German
Empire. It would appear however that this ordinance was never enforced
since fees payable for allocation of land remained the property of Chiefs
until 1925.

Under British Rule.

The changes which have taken place under the British regime are too
well known to be relevant to this chapter.

In spite of all these changes, some of which have strengthened and
some weakened the Chief's position, his authority is still basically grounded
on the original foundations. "The history of all these people has taught
us that no Chief or head man is an autocrat under native law and custom.
He and his advisers and the simple peasants know quite well the degree in
which his powers are circumscribed by native tradition and custom."

Cameron "My Tanganyika Service and Some Nigeria."

Position of Clans.

The relationship between clan head and ihiga head corresponds closely
to that between Mwami and Mukungu. They still hold an important position
in the community. Besides their duties as chairmen of ntegeka (see para.
1240) they are accredited witnesses for wills (para.42), contracts, etc.
and their advice is sought in matters dealing with inheritance, maintenance
and guardianship etc.

276

QUOTATION: Chief's Appeal Court case No.45 of 1938.

It was stated in the judgment of the above case that it is the custom of the country to call the elders of the clan, and especially the clan head for winding up the inheritance.

One son of a deceased had trouble with his father and the clan head ordered him after the death of his father to bring a goat for re-conciliation so that he could be acknowledged as Mainuka.   ater his brother, the Musika, refused to give him his share and brought various witnesses to prove that the father had nominated another relative as Mainuka.   The Court did not believe these witnesses, who were of different clans, but allowed the evidence of the clan head.

Should a clan head send for his people no one would disobey him For this reason his help is often asked for by a Mwami or Mukungu who has to carry out some communal labour (village road work, cleaning of forest, plantation etc.).   Since his office has no official standing today, naturally his authority depends more on his personality than on his position. The clan heads are not now regularly called to meet and to discuss tribal matters with the Chief, but they are invariably assembled at the installation of a new Chief.   All the clan heads hold the status of Baramata and by means of kwehonga (see para.23) the Chief has reserved his right to nominate the Musika.

The clan head has traditional religious duties. Sacrifices, either by the clan or by one or more of its members, to the omugurusi or mizuka (spirit) of the clan are offered by him.   His religious position is further emphasised by the fact that no one suffering from an infectious disease, particularly syphilis, may enter his house. Should an infected person become cured he takes beer and a few cents as an offering and makes an official entry.

The following which was drawn up by the District Officer (Mr.Flynn) in April 1937 gives an idea of some of the clan duties which are still extant in the present-day Court, and incidentally gives an idea of the monetary obligations of a present-day Chief.

CHIEFSHIP OF KIZIBA: Dependants and Holders of Hereditary Posts in the

Household.

Great grandmother			25/= p.m.
Grandmother			25/= "
Mother			50/= "
Guardians of Drum Mukuru 1	8/=		
Batarara 6	6/= ea.		44/= "
Retainers, Household, Barwensinga	2 @ 6/= ea.		12/= "
Door Keepers, Outer, Kasita	1 @ 6/=		6/= "
" " Inner, Bochwa	1 @ 6/=		6/= "
Spirit House, Keeper of, Mwahangi	1 @ 6/=		6/= "
Herders Bashumba	3 @ 6/= ea.		18/= "
Head Elder Katikiro	1 @ 10/=		10/= "
Elders Baishaabairu	3 @ 6/=		18/= "
Mother's chair, Keeper of, Mukesi	1 @ 6/=		6/= "
Chief's " " " "	1 @ 6/=		6/= "
Guards Balinzi	1 @ 8/=		
	4 @ 6/= ea.		32/= "
Cooks Bayondo	1 @ 8/=		
	1 @ 6/=		14/= "
Gardeners Bekigando	2 @ 6/= ea.		12/= "
Labourers Balinda	5 @ 8/= ea.		40/= "
Guests Bagenyi	about		15/= "
		Total	345/=

The above persons, apart from the female relations and guests, are the persons who, according to native custom, make up the household of the Chief of Kiziba.

Position of Native Authorities.

The importance of the position of Gombolola and their officials, Bami and Bakungu, has been much enhanced by European policy, with a consequent lessening of the authority of clan heads and elders in villages.

Economic revolution.

The establishment of European rule caused little political change from the point of view of the people, but brought about an economic revolution owing to the new status of coffee.

Coffee was introduced by the Bahinda, and the right to plant it was reserved to the Chiefs; it was used entirely for chewing on account of its sustaining properties.

[1] "In course of time as the yield from the early plantings increased and supplies in the hands of the Chiefs accumulated, coffee in a non-viable form began to be traded in the territories to the north, Ankole, Uganda, Bunyoro and the Sesse Islands, in exchange for cattle. Whatever may have been the original reason for the Chief's reservation on coffee, the fact that it was bartered for cattle must have fostered this rule because the Chiefs wished to remain the sole cattle owners and therefore the source of riches to their subjects."

It is related that coffee from Uhaya found an outside market because of the particular way in which it was prepared which the people had learnt from the Arabs. When the Chiefs allowed other people to cultivate coffee the right was considered as a mark of royal favour. No plantations were started from seed, a few cuttings were handed over to a favourite.

"It is recorded by the first arrivals at the White Fathers' Mission in 1892 that at that time coffee belonged to the Chiefs alone and that such coffee trees as were found in individual native gardens had been planted by the Chiefs' orders, were regarded as his property and were maintained by the occupier of the plot for the Chiefs' use. The crop was collected and treated by specially appointed men called Babona who took it to the royal presence. That coffee was regarded as a royal crop of which the common people were unable to partake except by royal favour is borne out by the absence of any considerable number of really

[1] See "A History of Rubusta Coffee in Bukoba" by T.S. Jervis.

old trees today. Here and there a tree may be found of an age well over 100 years but the bulk of the older coffee in the native gardens averages no more than 35 years, which corresponds with the first awakening to the economic possibilities of this crop and the measures for increased planting by the German administration in 1903."

The first effort towards increased production was made by Emin Pasha when he planted seed nurseries for general distribution. From then on coffee was no longer a Chiefs' prerogative but common to all men. It was no longer used for barter, but markets were opened and the crop disposed of for money. Thus the factors in the economic revolution were twofold: first the general planting of coffee and secondly its status as a cash crop.

After the war of 1914-18 the British Government took the greatest interest in the coffee production of the Bukoba District. At various times, but especially about 1922 and 1930, large coffee planting campaigns were inaugurated and most of the native coffee gardens date from this time. Great care was taken over the marketing of the native crop and through the high prices achieved the whole community attained a high degree of prosperity.

The results of the economic revolution.

The introduction of a perennial cash crop of high monetary value increased the intrinsic value of arable soil. Land which up till that time had not been cultivated, was planted with coffee wherever it would grow. The Chiefs opened new plantations under a new system of squatter holdings known as Biteme (see para.624).

Customary law adapted itself to the new conditions by the introduction of rules for land transactions such as sale and pledge of land and coffee.

The intensive cultivation of a cash crop caused a great increase in traffic, which affected the movement of people and therefore villages became more and more cosmopolitan, a mixture of various clans settled together, which tended to decrease the influence of village clans and clan heads.

Religious changes.

Islamic Influence.

The Mohammedan faith has never had much of a strong-hold in Uhaya, in spite of the fact that colonies of Arabs were established more than a century ago, especially in Karagwe, who at one time held all the trade in their hands.

Christian Influence.

Christian mission work has adversely affected the importance of tribal gods, relegating them to a position of obscurity. Naturally, though the rites of the old religion are vanishing fast (except among the older generation), superstition, and its attendant influences still hold sway over young and old.

APPENDIX IV.

CLANS IN UHAYA.

It is realized that this list of clans is incomplete, and probably in parts incorrect, since both the collectors were transferred from Uhaya before there had been time to check it in detail.

The information was collected in the following ways:—

a) During safaris in the various chiefdoms, clansmen were questioned and their answers recorded on the spot; wherever possible two or more members of the same clan were interrogated together or separately and the information of each checked with that of the others.

b) All the chiefs were asked to send in a list of the clans in their particular areas, drawn up with the help of clan elders, giving the information as listed in the twelve columns of the tables which follow.

When these lists (b) were received it was found that at times the information contained in them was at variance with the information collected as in (a) above; the differences were chiefly with regard to the names of the present-day clan and sub-clan heads. When this happened the chief's lists were followed, since they are believed to have been drawn up with the help of the clan elders, whereas clansmen interrogated at random on safari might or might not be well informed about their clans.

Special mention should be made of the assistance of Mwami Lwamugira in connexion with the work on clans.

Clan groups.

The clans are divided into three groups :—

   a) Pure Hima clans (known as 'enfuro').
   b) Bastard Hima clans.
   c) Peasant, or serf, clans (known as 'bairu').

With regard to group a), these clans claim direct descent from the pure pastoral clans of Galla stock.

The enfuro includes the following clans:—

Bahinda.	Banyaijwi.
Bashaga (or Baishekatwa).	Bankango (or Baishekatwa).
Bashoga.	Balanzi.
Baishanza.	Bashenza.
Bazita.	Bashambo
Bateneita.	Baitira (or Bahutu).
Banyangezi.	Babito
Balisa.	Batwa.
Babele.	Bashaigi.
Basingo.	Bachwezi.

With regard to group (b), these are clans which were not originally in the enfuro group but belonged to the bairu group, and were raised to the enfuro by a Chief as an honour. The Chiefs have always had this right, but it is deprecated by the enfuro clans, who consider that a Chief who exercises it is letting down his own blood.

This group includes the following clans:—

Bakoransi.	Banyaigana.
Bakyambe.	Bazigaba.
Bazira.	Babwongo.
Bagai.	Bambwi.
Bashengya.	Batundu.
Barungika.	Balondo.
Baami.	Bamiro.
Balenge.	Balanzi.
Basindi.	Batamwa.
Baafi.	Basita (or Basaizi).
Bahunga.	Bangula.
Baganda.	

With regard to group (c), these are the peasant or serf clans, either indigenous or the descendants of immigrants who were not members of enfuro clans.   They have usually no claim to Hima blood but it may happen that a Hima clan is degraded to the rank of mwiru.   Two examples   are   the Babango and Bashamulo clans whose history is given below.

<u>Exogamy.</u>

No one may marry into:-

a) His own clan.   The Bahinda do sometimes marry within the clan if the relationship is very distant, but such marriages are disliked by the other en- furo clans.

b) The clan of his mother.

c) A clan in his exogamous group.

<u>Exogamous groups.</u>

Certain clans form exogamous groups.   The reason for this   may be that they are of common origin, e.g. Bankango-Bashaga-Babango; or it may be the result of a clan feud, e.g. Babanga-Basimba.

Some of the exogamous groups are as follows:-

(The letter preceding the clan name indicates the group to which the clan belongs.   a = Pure Hima, b = Bastard Hima, c = Bairu.)

a) Bakongo)	known as		a) Babito.	c) Basigu.	
a) Bashaga)	Baishekatwa.		c) Bashamulo.	c) Bahugi.	
c) Babango)			c) Bale.		
c) Bagiri.		c) Baganga.)	known as		
a) Bashaigi.		c) Basimba.)	Tibanyarilana.		
c) Bagombe.		a) Bahinda.		c) Baihuzi.	
c) Bagesho.		c) Bayango.		c) Bajubu.	
b) Basaizi.		a) Bashambo.		c) Basimba.	
b) Basita.		b) Balenge.		c) Bashasha.	
c) Bagwe.		c) Bashasha.		c) Babende.(?)	
c) Bakulwa.		c) Bambwi.		c) Bashozi.	
c) Baziba.		c) Bazirambogo.		c) Basimba.	

a) Batwa.   b) Bajubu.   a) Batundu.
a) Babele.   c) Bakiyama.   c) Bahugi.

                    b) Bamiro.   a) Basingo.
                    c) Bagabo.   c) Bahembe.

Notes on the exogamous groups.

Babango — Bankango — Bashaga claim common origin and are really the same
clan, their common name being Baishekatwa.   The reason for the degrada-
tion of the Babango to the status of mwiru is that fish is taboo for
the Baishekatwa and long ago some members of the Bankango ate fish and
were expelled from the clan; they formed a new group calling themselves
Babango, their leader being a certain Kiiza. An interesting point arises
in connexion with this.   The members who were expelled were from the
senior group of the Baishekatwa and in spite of their expulsion and de-
gradation they hold that position today;   that is to say that a Munkango
or a Mushaga addresses a Mubango as 'father'; at the marriage of a Munkango or Mushaga the bride is given away by a Mubango; a newly-married
Munkango or Mushaga asks a Mubango to come and bless his house; yet the
Babango are a mwiru clan with whom neither Bankango nor Bashaga, as enfuro, may eat or drink.

Babito — Bashamulo are really all Babito.   The split occurred thus:-
Kibi 1, the first Hima chief of Kiziba, was worried by the spirit of
Ntumwa, who in life had been the leader of the powerful Bakuma clan whose
position as leaders in Kiziba had been usurped by the Babito.   Kibi's
soothsayers advised him that Ntumwa's spirit would only be quieted by
the dedication of one of Kibi's children to its service.   Kibi ordered
that a child of his son, Mushamulo, should be given and the spirit was
appeased.   Mushamulo and his children and descendants were for this
reason turned out of the clan and called themselves Bashamulo with the
status of a mwiru clan.

Basaizi — Basita — Bagwe are really the same clan, the name Basaizi being
an alternative for Basita and vice versa.   The name Bagwe dates from the

time of the arrival of Rugamora Male; during the acclamations at his coming, a Musita fell into a hole and was nick-named by Rugamora 'Kagwe', which means 'he who fell in the hole'; his descendants adopted the name, calling themselves the Bagwe.

Other clans which are exogamous because of relationship are:—

Bagombe-Bagesho: Bahinda-Bayango: Bahembe-Basingo: Balenge-Bashambo-Bashasha: Bambwi-Bazirambogo: Batwa-Babele: Bajubu-Bakiyama: Bamiro-Bagabo: Bazigu-Hahugi:

Babito-Bale are an example of exogamy being the result of a clan feud. The story is that many years ago a chief of Kiziba (Babito is the clan of the chiefs of Kiziba) had a great friend who was a member of the Bale clan and was also the chief's most prominent leader in war. This Mwule had only one son, whom the chief insisted on sending to the war where he was killed; the Mwule then swore an oath that thenceforward there should be a feud between Babito and Bale and that they should never intermarry.

Other clans which are exogamous because of clan feuds are:—

Baganga-Basimba. Batundu-Bahugi.

If the clans within an exogamous group have different totems each clan observes its own totems only.

Clan Names.

In the old days every enfuro clan had a set of individual names which no other clan might use. A son was never called after his father but was given the name of his grandfather or one of the other clan names. The clan names of the Bashaga were Tabara, Rutahigwa, Nyakakuba and Muj-wauzi. Nowadays this custom is obsolete and clan names are used by all and sundry.

Totems.

Primary and secondary totems are looked upon in entirely different lights. The primary totem is a real taboo; it may not be killed, eaten, touched, or in some cases, even looked upon;   but the secondary totem is a more friendly thing altogether;   it is often described by the people as the brother of the clan.   For example, the secondary totem of the Baruwani is lightning, and a Muruwani said "Lightning is our brother, it would never harm us, no Muruwani could be struck".   The Bayango clan has the sunga-sunga ant as its secondary totem, and it is said that children of the clan can play with sunga-sunga without being bitten.   The Bagabo clan's secondary totem is the full moon, and on the first day of the full moon the clan head fasts as a sign that the full moon is really the head of the clan.

APPENDIX V

LIST OF CLANS

Babango
Babogo
Babito
Babobi
Babini
Babike
Babele
Babenge
Babago
Babende
Bagwongu
Babuta

Bachwerera
Bachwezi

Baafi

Bagabo
Bagiri
Bagai
Bagala
Baganga
Bagombe
Bagara
Bagimu
Bagesho
Bagayia
Bagwe
Baganda
Bagobela
Bagaya

Bahangaza
Bahimba
Bahinda
Bahunga
Bahutu
Bahuge
Bahembe

Baisiri
Baishansa
Baihuzi
Baitira

Bajubu

Bajwala
Bajolwa

Bakalaza
Bakainage
Bakaija
Bakilembo
Bakimbili
Bakulwa
Bakoba
Bakiyaga
Bakoma
Bakombe
Bakongo
Bakurwa
Bakuma
Bakoransi
Bakyambe
Bakyama

Balisa
Balenge
Baligi
Balebeki
Balanzi
Balondo
Balungika
Balama
Bale

Bamanye
Baami (Bahami)
Bamiro
Bambwi
Bamwena

Banjoju
Bankango
Banyuma
Banjenje
Bananai
Banyaijwi
Banyaigana
Banyangezi
Bangula

Bolomo

Bapina

Barigi
Baruwani

Bashambo
Bashasha
Bashozi
Basingo
Basita
Basaizi
Bashoga
Bashonde
Basimba
Bashaigi
Bashengya
Bashenza
Bashamulo
Basigu
Bashaga
Basindi

Batongele
Batuku
Batundu
Batwa
Batarara
Batagarwa
Batabazi
Bateneita

Baungu (or Bahungu)

Bawende

Bayango
Bayeru
Bayumba
Bayenja
Bayeyego

Baziba
Bazigaba
Bazirambogo
Bazira
Bazita

TABLES

1	2	3	4	5	6	7	8	9	10	11	12
CLAN = LUGANDA	CHIEFDOM = BUKANA	TOTEM = MUZIRO	SECONDARY TOTEM =EBINTU EBILI KUGENDA-GENDA	FOUNDER (PATRIACH) = OMUGURUSI	PLACE OF CLAN ORIGIN = ENTABUKO	COURT DUTIES = MWANYA or MURUKA or MWAGA	CLAN SPIRIT = MUZUKA	CLAN VILLAGES = VIJIJI VYA ASILI	PRESENT CLAN HEAD = OMUKULU WA LUGANDA	SUB-CLAN = MAHIGA	PRESENT SUB-CLAN HEAD = OMUKULU WA IHIGA
Babobi	Missenye	Rain water from the porch of a msonge (Amaizige Kishasi).	Ntale (?)	Kigulusi	Kafo (Bunyoro)	Keepers of the Chief's arrows called Kyelamra abnaruzi F.l.	Lukowe	Rukaba G.Nzunga	Kijoma of Rukaba	-	-
Babini	Bugabo	Buffalo	Buffalo	Mutinagwe	Byonga (Bugabo)	Fisher-men	Byonga (a leopard)	Byonga	Ngambe of Byonga	Bashaga Beyola	Ngamba Byanuma of Byonga
	Kiantwara	"	Kikonai (a bird)	Rujugo	"	"	"	Igombe G.Nyakato	Perisien of Igombe	Batambi	Bangima " Byonga
F.1 & 2 Babango	Missenye	Intestines of animals	Hawk	Rajale	Bunyoro	Keepers of the Chief's pipe	Mugasha	Part of the village of Kiambogo	Muwambya of Kiambogo	Bakituma Basumbuso Bakatwire	Zaibale of ? Kutasa of ? Mpanya of ?
	Kianja			F.l. Kiiza	Kitakura						
	Bugabo	"	"	Waila	Isheshe (Uganda)	Makers of amulets (hirizi) for the Chief	Wamara & Kaushoni (a leopard)	1)Kyamarange G.Rubafu 2)Buzi G.Bushasha 3)Bhembe	Kente of Kyamarange	Banombo Bakilya Baharila	Kente Nkanzi of Kyamarange Kagarulu of Kyamarange
	Kiziba	"	"	Tabaro	"	Black-smiths	Wamara	Bugombe G.Kanyigo	Bigirwa of Bugombe	-	-

Babobi F.1.

Col.7. They did not follow the chief to war since these were ceremonial arrows (upinde wa ngome) and they stayed behind to guard them.

Babango. F.1.

Cols.1 & 5. This clan was originally part of the Bankango Clan some of whom ate fish (a taboo of the Bankango) and were expelled. The leader or of those expelled was Kiiza. They formed a new clan, calling themselves Babango. (See also notes on exogamy.)

F.2.

Col.1. All Babango in the Gombolola of Kanyigo are under the mother of the Chief of Kiziba because the mother of Chief Magembe II,
Nyakairu, herself went to war and captured a number of the clan in the village of Makongora, at the foot of the Kamachumu bluff.
These Babango had to agree to come under her suzerainty and to give her their village of Bukoko which is still the property of
the mother of the Chief of Kiziba.

1	2	3	4	5	6	7
CLAN = LUGANDA	CHIEFDOM = BUKAMA	TOTEM = MUZIRO	SECONDARY TOTEM = EBINTU EBILI KUGENDAGENDA	FOUNDER (PATRIACH) = OMUGURUSI	PLACE OF CLAN ORIGIN = ENTABUKO	COURT DUTIES = MWANYA or MURUKA or MWAGA
Babogo	Karagwe	Buffalo	Buffalo	Nziruhire	Ihangiro	Milk-vessel makers
"	Ihangiro	Dove (njiwa)	Sisimizi (small black ant)	Kalemba	Bumbire	Assessors
"	Kiziba	Intestines	Francolin	Bwaile	Karagwe	Watchmen of Chief's mother
Babito F.2	Kanyange-reko	Monkey (tumbili)	–	Kabiito (lived at Katoma) F.1.	Ngando (Missenyi)	Treasurers
"	Kiziba	"	Nuna (an insect)	Igaba Kibi I	Bunyoro	The Chief and his relatives
				Kibi II		

8	9	10	11	12
CLAN SPIRIT = MIZUKA	CLAN VILLAGES = VIJIJI VYA ASILI	PRESENT CLAN HEAD = OMUKULU WA LUGANDA	SUB-CLANS = MAHIGA	PRESENT SUB-CLAN HEAD = OMUKULU WA IHIGA
		Nziruhile of Ihembe		
Wamara	Kashambia Ihembe	Nziruhile of Ihembe (G.Nyaishozi)	Katolole Makamba	
Karuhogo	Buhyo	Teshabwa of Kabagonda	-	-
Wamara	Katoma	Tega Katoma	-	-
Wamara	Kigarama Bugandika. Buyango Kitobo Ishozi.	Mukama Nestor	**Kibi I.** Bashamura Kyaruzi of Kigarama (a deputy for Nestor) Babwanamba Mjemura of Kikukwe Bagaju s/o Kachuba of Kyelima Bagembe Katabengwa of Nyabikwe Bashumba Kanyandekwa of Ruwija Baigara Kaiza of Rutara Barungu Phillip Kato of Nyabutaizi Baboneka Bukwizi of Kishoju Bahangarazi Rukara of Bugandika Barungu II Gervase Mwangara of Bikonge. Bayobia ? s/o Bibili of Bukwari dep. Cleofas Ndamagilwa **Kibi II.** Banyombi Gaurwa of Bwera Bangarazi Ngere Lugaurura of Kishoju Batatembwa Rukambaiga of Kanyigo Batahangarwa Mukama Nestor Baboneko Mtakubwa of Nkole dep. Rutinwa of Ishozi	

N O T E S.

Babito.

F.1. Col. 5   Igaba, son of Ruhinda the Great was the father of Kibi I the first Hima Chief of Kiziba. Ruhinda the Great's clan was Babito. The other chiefs of Bukoba district claim descent from a brother of Igaba, Ruhinda and have dropped the clan name of Mubito, calling themselves, Bahinda.

F.2. Col. 1   Babito. This clan has some special connexion with snakes. The spirits of deceased male members become Nkorantima and of females become Mpiri snakes. The spirit escapes as a snake through the head of a dead Mubito. See Rehse on Kiziba.

1 CLAN = LUGANDA	2 CHIEFDOM = BUKAMA	3 TOTEM = MUZIRO	4 SECONDARY TOTEM = EBINTU EBILI KUGENDAGENDA	5 FOUNDER (PATRIARCH) = OMUGURUSI	6 PLACE OF CLAN ORIGIN = ENTABUKO	7 COURT DUTIES = MWANYA or MURUKA or MWAGA	8 CLAN SPIRIT = MIZUKA	9 CLAN VILLAGES = VIJIJI VYA ASILI	10 PRESENT CLAN HEAD = OMUKULU WALUGANDA	11 SUB-CLANS = MAHIGA	12 PRESENT SUB-CLAN HEAD = OMUKULU WA IHIGA.
Bagabo	Kiziba	Black Striped cow	1) Crested crane 2) Full red moon	Kayanja	Ankole	Spear makers	Kana	Luhano	Lwentaro of Luhano		Kashumbusi of Bukwali Kawamala of Kyelima
"	Kiamtwara	Butter of a cow which has been covered by a bull	Baboon	Igambanowa	Ankole	"	Igonya-nyoka	Buhembe Nyakato	Nbamanya of Buhembe	Bagabo	Mbamanya of Buhembe
"	Kanyange-reko	A cow in milk which has been covered by a bull	"	Kyaruboine of Kaina (Muhuha)	Buzinje (Biharami-lo)	"	F.2. Igonya	Kaina (Muhuha)	Igambanowa of Kaina	-	-
"	Karagwe	Fresh milk	F.1. Full red moon Bitter Tomato	Kaitanga	Karagwe	Farmers	Kibyamira	Katembe Kyabumba Bulemba	Kabiswa of Bulembo	Kyanika Rukole Bacheija	-
"	Bugabo	Tailless cow		Mutabazi	Bugabo	1)Priests of the Bugabo spirits 2)Blacksmiths	Bugabo	Kyamarange	Ndibalema of Kyama-range	Begungu Abami	Nyabalema ?
"	Missenye	Hearts of all animals	Crested crane	Hangi	Munjama (Bunyoro)	Receive the bride-price of the Chief's daughters	Bukala	Kayanja (Nsunga)	Lukanja of Kayanja	Katongole 4 Lukyamuzi 5 Dungu 6 Kilibugondo	A.Diro of Ruwama (Kasambia) 4 Zavuga. Kalagala (Minziro) 5 Kyewalyanaa of Kigasi (Minziro) 6 Kaizi of Gera (Minazi)

N O T E S.

Bagrabo.

Col. 8 F.2. Has been worshipped since the days of Kyaruboine.

" 4 F.1. On the first day of the full moon the clan head does not eat to show that the moon is really the clan head.

1	2	3	4	5	6
CLAN = LUGANDA	CHIEFDOM = BUKAMA	TOTEM = MUZIRO	SECONDARY TOTEM = EBINTU EBILI KUGENDAGENDA	FOUNDER (PATRIACH) = OMUGURUSI	PLACE OF CLAN ORIG. = ENTABUK.
Bagara	Ihangiro	Striped cow	Chicken	Ihagama	Bukiri (Egypt)
"	?	"	Baboon		
"	Karagwe	"	"		
"	Missenye	"	"		
"	Kiamtwara	"	Entuwa (a stork)	Tokwo	Uzinza
"	Kianja	Olulisa (= an animal)	"	Kyebambe	Ruanda
Bagai	Karagwe	Striped cow	Franco-lin		
Bagai F.1.	Kiziba	Thunder	Thunder	Lwejuna	Npololo

7	8	9	10	11	12
COURT DUTIES = MWANYA or MURUKA or MWAGA	CLAN SPIRIT = MIZUKA	CLAN VILLAGES = VIJIJI VYA ASILI	PRESENT CLAN HEAD = OMUKULU WALUGANDA	SUB-CLANS = MAHIGA	PRESENT SUB-CLAN HEAD = OMUKULU WA IHIGA.
1) Charge of Chief's grave (Bamena ihiga) 2) Milkers (Bashengya ihiga) 3) Soothsayers by chicken (Bagara ihiga)	Wamara enshengya	Ntunda	Mamleki	Bamena Bashengya Bagara	
Chief's door keepers	Wamara		Misingo of Kyerunga Karangi of Nyabiyonza	Abaluju-mba	Bulimwezi of Kitwe
			Kwezi s/o Kajali (Bunazi)	Ababunyata	Kazimoto of Bunazi
Iron workers & cooks	Wamara	Bulyam-puro	Lwerengera of Bulyampuro	Bakenai Bafumbo Bajumba	Lwerengera of Bulyampuro Kalimba of Bulyampuro Kashamba of Bulyampuro
Iron workers					
	Karera-nduuru	Kansenene (Kianja)	Ndukeki of Kansenene	Babwiga Bayonga	Bernardo Kanumuna of Kansenene Kajugira of Itawa (Kiamtwara)
Makers of charcoal for soothsaying	Mulengela	Lushasha	Kashekya of Lushasha	Barungu	Ishempo of Muziro

N O T E S.

Bagni F.1. Col. 1. This clan came from Missenyo where the descendants of Kawa Barungu are to be found to-day. Ilungu was born there.

1	2	3	4	5	6
CLAN = LUGANDA	CHIEFDOM = BUKAMA	TOTEM = MUZIRO	SECONDARY TOTEM = EBINTU EBILI KUGENDAGENDA	FOUNDER (PATRIACH) = OMUGURUSI	PLACE OF CLAN ORIGIN = ENTABUKO
Baganga	Bugabo	Otter	1) Dog 2) Charcoal	Mbibi	Muzirmoija
"	Kiamtwara	Bush- buck	1) Bees 2) Dog	Kibunga	Buganda
"	Kiziba	"	Dog	–	Bunyoro
"	Missenyi	Striped cow	Nkunya (bird)		
Bagiri	Kiamtwara	Heart of all animals	Wart- hog	F.1. Wanumi	Bunyoro

N O T E S.

Bagiri.

F.1. Col. 5. Wanumi was nicknamed Kagiri because he ate pig's meat.

F.2.   "   7. A new stool is made for each chief.

7	8	9	10	11	12
COURT DUTIES = MWANYA or MURUKA or MWAGA	CLAN SPIRIT =MIZUKA	CLAN VILLAGES = VIJIJI VYA ASILI	PRESENT CLAN HEAD = OMUKULU WA LUGANDA	SUB-CLANS = MAHIGA	PRESENT SUB-CLAN HEAD = OMUKULU WA IHIGA
1)Keepers of sooth-saying chickens (Bateneita ihiga)	?	Mwizi	Rutenta (Mwizi)	Bateneita	Rutenta
2)Hunters of small game (Bashamba ihiga)				Bashamba	Irungu of Kyalo
3)Drumkeepers	Wamara Wamara	Ijuganyondo G.Kitendaguro	Kanyankole of Muyaba	-	-
4)Builders of Chief's house	2) Matwi	Nyabiokwe (Bwanjai)	Mugisha of Nyabiokwe	?	Simeo of Bukabuye
				?	Abdula of Lwamashonga
				?	John of Buekela
				Bakika	Kagaruki of Bulembo
				Bairira	Baliyakata of Bulembo
			Kalangali of Kyambo-go (G.Nsunga)	Abasoke	Mikinga of Kasambia
				Abamageni	Mulekwa of Kongolo (Ibwera)
				Abakachu-lagano	Kato of Luyiyi (Nsunga)
1) Village headmen 2) Shield makers 3) Drum-keepers (only ihiga Bakorwa) 4) Carriers of the Royal stool (throne) F.2. (only ihiga Bayioyio)	Wamara	Kitwe	Kajuna of Kitwe	Bakara Bakorwa	Kajuna Patrice)
					))Kitwe))
				Bayioyio	Kaijage)

1 CLAN = LUGANDA	2 CHIEFDOM = BUKAMA	3 TOTEM = MUZIRO	4 SECONDARY TOTEM = EBINTU EBILI KUGENDAGENDA AMUZIRO	5 FOUNDER (PATRIACH) = OMUGURUSI	6 PLACE OF CLAN ORIGIN = ENTABUKO	7 COURT DUTIES = MWANYA or MURUKA or MWAGA	8 CLAN SPIRIT = MIZUKA	9 CLAN VILLAGES = VIJIJI VYA ASILI	10 PRESENT CLAN HEAD = OMUKULU WA LUGANDA	11 SUB-CLANS MAHIGA	12 PRESENT SUB-CLAN HEAD = OMUKULU WA IHIGA
Bagiri	Kanyange-reko	Heart of all animals	Warthog	Kagiri who lived at Kitwe F.3.	Kitwe	Village headmen (Bakungu)	Kimli	Kitwe	Domician of Kitwe	Bakorwa Bakahale Abayoyo	Domician Kitwe ? ?
"	Kiziba	"	"	Kachu-kikato	Bunyoro	The Chief's Priest of Irungu	Kagolo	Ilundu	Mulokozi of Ilundu	?	Kashoro of Ilundu
Bagombe	Kiziba	Bush-buck	Hawk	Tabaro & Mwambi	Ihangiro	Bahambansi F.1. & Batalala (body guard) F.2. 1)Witch-finders (Bakambo ihiga) 2)Drumkeepers (Bashengelo ihiga) 3)Firelighters (Bakiyamani ihiga) 4)Queen mother's watchmen. (Bachwabuta ihiga)	-	Bugombe	Kato of Bugombe	Bashenge-lo Bakambo Bakiyamani Bachwabuta	Lushalila } Bugombe Kalebe " Karokola " Kazinja
"	Bugabo		Bush-buck	Lumanzi	Bunyoro	Soothsayers	Kilo	Kyamarange Bugombe Luhano	Kamugisha of Luhano (Kiziba)	-	-
"	Kanyange-reko	"	Hawk	Hangi of Kanyigo	Kanyigo	Expellers of devils	Kiziba Kiantumwa	Kanyigo	Bebwa of Kanyigo	-	-
"	Kiantwara	"	-	Nyakairu	Bugombe (Kiziba)	-	Wamara	Rugoze (G.Kitwe)	Gobunga of Rugoze	-	-

N O T E S.

Bagiri.

F. 3. Col. 5. Evidently Wanumi see note F.1. above. (Kiamtwara)

Bagombe.

F.1. Col. 7. **Bahambansi** (= Baharambwa see "Tribal Structure")

F.2. Col. 7. **Batalala.** The word means those who cannot starve i.e. those who live closest to the Chief and whom he feeds under all circumstances.

1	2	3	4	5	6	7	8	9	10	11	12
CLAN = LUGANDA	CHIEFDOM = BUKAMA	TOTEM = MUZIRO	SECONDARY TOTEM = EBINTU EBILI KUGENDAGENDA	FOUNDER (PATRIARCH) = OMUGURUSI	PLACE OF ORIGIN (PATRIACH) CLAN = ENTABUKO	COURT DUTIES = MWANYA or MURUKA or MWAGA	CLAN SPIRIT = MIZUKA	CLAN VILLAGES = VIJIJI VYA ASILI	PRESENT CLAN HEAD = OMUKULU WA LUGANDA	SUB-CLANS MAHIGA	PRESENT SUB-CLAN HEAD = OMUKULU WA IHIGA
Bahimba	Kianja	Buffalo	-	Kiribondo of Kanyange-reko	Karagwe	Keepers of the Chief's grave			Mutema of Muhutwe		
"	Kanyange-reko	"	Stork	Kahimbe of Buhimba Buhimba (Karagwe)	Buhimba of (Karagwe)	1)Install the Chief 2)Grave-keepers of the Chief	Bwogi	Buhimba	Lutabingwa of Kitendaguro	Abesisha Abega	Lutabingwa "
"	Ihangiro	"	Ant	Mulenzi	Karagwe	Barbers	Kilo	Kasheshe	Mashatanwa of Kabagunda	Abatyo-koro Abalange Abalungi-ka Abaihuzi Abashoga	Kyomunaju of Irema Ishabalenge Ijabalilo G.Bureza. Mbabi of Kabare G.Bureza Mukulasi of Kaina G.Bureza Meza of Kabagunda G. Bureza
"	Kiamtwara	"	-	Kalende	Karagwe	-	Wamara	Kiniga G.Itawa	Magangara of Kiniga	Abagaju Abanagwa Bamoyio	Magangara Salim Kajuna of Ijuganyondo
Bahinda	Karagwe	Monkey (tumbili)	Lion or Sunga-sunga ants	Ntare	Bunyoro	Chiefs & Nobles	Ruhinda	Kashebe, Gera & Ngarama	Mukama Ruhinda F.l.	Bokia	Byabato of Kyamatange
"	Bugabo	"	Sunga-sunga ants	Ruhinda	Bunyoro	Perform ceremonies to ensure abundant serene (grass-hopper) (Bakikuba ihiga only)			Mukama Kalemera of Kianja	Bakikuba Balimera	Keijage of Mushozi Kalamero dep. in Bugabo Zawadi of Rwangono

N O T E S.

Bahinda.

F.1. Col. 10. One informant says Chief Ruhinda is deputy only, the real clan head being Rutazindwa.

1	2	3	4	5	6	7	8	9	10	11	12
CLAN = LUGANDA	CHIEFDOM = BUKAMA	TOTEM = MUZIRO	SECONDARY TOTEM = EBINTU EBILI KUGENDA-GENDA	FOUNDER (PATRIACH) = OMUGURUSI	PLACE OF CLAN ORIGIN = ENTABUKO	COURT DUTIES = MWANYA or MURUKA or MWAGA	CLAN SPIRIT = MIZUKA	CLAN VILLAGES = VIJIJA VYA ASILI	PRESENT CLAN HEAD = OMUKULU WALUGANDA	SUB-CLANS = MAHIGA	PRESENT SUB-CLAN HEAD = OMUKULU WA IHIGA
Bahinda	Kiziba F.2.	Monkey (tumbili)	Bushbuck	Kizindo	Ihangiro	Demarcate the Kikale boundaries	Muru	Kigarama (G.Kanyigo)	Lutaiwa of Kigarama	Abauru / Barungu / Atinwa	Malijo of Kigarama / Ntambe of Kigarama / ?
"	Ihangiro	"	Kaceche (?)	Ruhinda I	Egypt	Chiefs	Wamara	Mishure G.Mubunda	Chief Petro Mugunda	Balimila / Bajunga / Bazita / Bagalagwa / Balemela / Bakuba / Banyanzinga / Bateboa	Rutena of Muyenje G.Kahangere / Nyamkwela of Ndsha G.Kahangere / Kashaija of Ruhija G.Kashasha / Byorwango of Rubungo / Ndanguzi of Buhyo G.Bumbire / Mututa of Katare G.Mbatama / Kyongo of Kajule G.Bumbire / Kashegeshe of Bunyo G.Bumbire
"	Kanyange-reko	"	Kamunywa-munywa (a bird)	Ruhinda (Karagwe)	Bunyoro	Chiefs	Kimuli s/o Kalemera Bwanshoni F.3.	Bweranya-nge (Karagwe)	Chief Daudi Rugomora Kwesi	Atalemera / Abagomora / Abakuba	Ch.Rugomora Got s/o Musa of Maruku / Nkeile of Maruku

NOTES.

Bahinda.

F.2. Col.2. Said to be linked with Bakuma here. (See"Tribal Structure").

F.3. Col.8. Kimuli ate bad food and died.

1 CLAN = LUGANDA	2 CHIEFDOM = BUKAMA	3 TOTEM = MUZIRO	4 SECONDARY TOTEM = EBINTU EBILI KUGENDA-GENDA	5 FOUNDER (PATRIACH) = OMUGURUSI	6 PLACE OF CLAN ORIG IN = ENTABUKO	7 COURT DUTIES = MWANYA or MURUKA or MWAGA	8 CLAN SPIRIT = MIZUKA	9 CLAN VILLAGES = VIJIJI VYA ASILI	10 PRESENT CLAN HEAD = OMUKULU WA LUGANDA	11 SUB-CLANS = MAHIGA	12 PRESENT SUB-CLAN HEAD = OMUKULU WA IHIGA
Bahinda	Kiamtwara	Monkey (tumbili)	Sunga-sunga ants	Ruhinda Lwanjunaki	Bunyoro	Drumkeepers	Wamara	Nshambya G.Nyakato	Kagaruki of Nshambya (Some acknowledge Daudi Rugomora)	Bakuba, Baremela, Batongira, Bagasha, Bakuni, Baikenga	Kagaruki Muzanila of Nshambya, Lyamukama of Nshambya, Tiayilwa of Kibeta, ?
Bahunga F.1.	Kianja	1)Rock rabbit 2)Banana bunches off which the remains of the flower head have fallen. F.2.	Frog	Kiteke	Karagwe		Luboha F.3.	Kyabangabo	Rajege of Muhutwe	Abafura, Abatuare-akanuka, Batwazi	Mpanju of Ushumbo, Kanyakaita of Irama (Ihangiro), Rajege
" (Bakimbili)	Karagwe	Everything tail-less.	Frog	Kaliba	Ntoboro (G.Nyabyonza)	To bury the Chiefs and Bahinda	Wamara	Ntoboro, Kiohuru, Kasinga	Rubuga of Mutaga	?	Kashebe G.Nyabyonza
"	Missenyi	Tailless cow & spotted cow	Frog	Nsinga	Kunana (Bunyoro)	1)Bedmaker to the Chief 2)Body guards (Bumbowa)	Luboha	Kyonyu G.Nsunga	Gaka of Ruhimbazi	Abakagoro, Abakasalila, Abalukaka	Akilewo of Layiye (Nsunga), Daunulila of Gabulanga (Kasambia), Lutwe of Kasambia.

N O T E S Bahunga..

F.1. Col.1. The clan of Kashare, the indigenous chief who was turned out by Kalemera I, the first Hima Chief.

F.2. Col.3. It is forbidden for Bahunga to roast such fruit.

F.3. Col.8. Luboha is the god of hunters.

1	2	3	4	5	6	7	8	9	10	11	12
CLAN = LUGANDA	CHIEFDOM = BUKOMA	TOTEM = MUZIRO	SECONDARY TOTEM = EBINYU EBILI KUGENDA-GENDA	FOUNDER (PATRIACH) = OMUGURUSI	PLACE OF CLAN ORIGIN = ENTABUKO	COURT DUTIES = MWANYA or MURUKA or MWAGA	CLAN SPIRIT = MIZUKA	CLAN VILLAGES = VIJIJI VYA ASILI	PRESENT CLAN HEAD = OMUKULU WA LUGANDA	SUB-CLANS = MAHIGA	PRESENT SUB-CLAN HEAD = OMUKULU WA IHIGA.
Behunga	Kiziba	Tail-less cow & spotted cow	Frog	Kihuja	Karagwe	Court Jesters	Muleguza	Lugaze G.Bwenjal	Lwakatinta of Lugaze	?	Mugiza of Kashasha Kashania of Muzibuko
"	Ihangiro	Rabbit (pimbi)	"	Katalikawe	Kitara	Doctors (waganga)	Lyangombe	Kibondo	Rwakalela of Rutenge	-	-
Behutu	Ihangiro	Enfunzi (a small bird)	Black dog	Nkombya	Ankole	Rain makers Watchmen of inner doors Milkers	Igara F.I.	Mushure G.Mubunda	Ruhanganaza of ?	Abangula Abayozi Abayengo Abasilanga Abenyura	Mbeikya of Bwire G.Kashasha Ruhimbika of Kishoju G. Nshamba Kweyunga of Kabare G.Burabo Tibalibukwa of Makongo G.Bumbire Lwangani of Bwiru
Behutu-Beitira	Karagwe	The milk of a cow whose calf has been covered by a bull.	Enfunzi (small bird)	Rwaktere	Ankole	Keepers of Chief's millet seed (for beer)	Wamara	Kikerere Mugashe	Batira of Kikerere (Kaisho)	-	-
Behutu	Missenyi	Wakonga (?)	"		Kahawa				Waramuno s/o Babeya of Luyiyi	-	-

N O T E S.

Bahutu.

F.I. Col. 8. Spirit of virgin soil.

1	2	3	4	5	6	7	8	9	10	11	12
CLAN = LUGANDA	CHIEFDOM = BUKAMA	TOTEM = MUZIRO	SECONDARY TOTEM = EBINTU EBILI KUGENDA-GENDA	FOUNDER (PATRIACH) = OMUGURUSI	PLACE OF CLAN ORIGIN = ENTABUKO	COURT DUTIES = MWANYA or MURUKA or MWAGA	CLAN SPIRIT = MIZUKA	CLAN VILLAGES = VIJIJI VYA ASILI	PRESENT CLAN HEAD = OMUKULU WA LUGANDA	SUB-CLANS = MAHIGA	PRESENT SUB-CLAN HEAD = OMUKULU WAIHIGA
Baishansa	Ihangiro	Tortoise	Black Cow	Kubungwa	Ankole	1)Cooks (Abanganda ihiga) 2)Herdsmen & milkers (Banyangezi) 3)Hide workers (Banyama) 4)Shield makers (Baheta)	Ruzobo	Mushasha G.Ilemera	Lwabuloga of Bisheke	Abanganda Abanyangezi Abanyama Abaheta	Iramulira of Ulembo Kahuto of Kasharara Lwamboga of Mbatama Lwaneyesha of Mlero
Baihuzi	Kianja	Heart of all animals (Muganya)	Snail	Waihuto (Kaihuzi) F.1.	Karagwe	Furniture makers to the Chief	?		Herman of Katoma dep. in Kianja = Abdalla-hmani Mukungu of Kanyaro	Bagambano Bashamba Barangana Babunga	Herman of Katoma Anatol of Nyanga Kiabiyume of Kayanga Byabangiro of Ilogero
"	Kiamtwara	"	"	Bushaibusha	Bunyoro	1)Bakungu 2)Drumkeepers (Ihiga 3) 3)Milkers & cowherds (Ihiga 1)	Wamara	Katoma	Arkard Nyarushengo of Lukindo Katoma	1)Bagambano 2)Babungo 3)Bashamba of Bagwesa F.3	F.2. Bwegure of Lukindo Kaloho of Ilogero Biendeka of Ilogero F.3
"	Karagwe	Senene	"	Kaihuzi (or Waihuto)	Karagwe	Honey gatherers	Wamara	Kasoni Kimuli	Baguma of Kilifungo	Batongere Balangana	? ?
"	Kanyange-reko	Heart of all animals	"	Kashaija of Bugera G.Ntoma	Uganda	Cooks	Wamara	Bugera G.Ntoma	Miti of Bugera	Bagambano Bashamba	Miti ?

Baihuzi.

F.1. Col.5. On Ruhinda's safari he was greeted by a man called Waihuto (a pole). Ruhinda called him Kaihuzi (the man who wished him a good safari) Kaihuzi then accompanied Ruhinda and became the founder of the Baihuzi clan.

F.2. Col.12. (Some acknowledge the Kianja heads.)

F.3. Col.11. At the time of the Chief Mutashaba there lived an outstanding man of the Bashamba ihiga called Kagwesa, the ihiga took his name as a secondary one and called themselves either Bashamba or Bagwesa.

1	2	3	4	5	6	7	8	9	10	11	12
CLAN = LUGANDA	CHIEFDOM = BUKAMA	TOTEM = MUZIRO	SECONDARY TOTEM = EBINTU EBILI KUBENDA-GENDA	FOUNDER (PATRIARCH) = OMUGURUSI	PLACE OF CLAN ORIGIN = ENTABUKO	COURT DUTIES = MWANYA or MURUKA or MWAGA	CLAN SPIRIT = MIZUKA	CLAN VILLAGES = VIJIJI VYA ASILI	PRESENT CLAN HEAD = OMUKULU WA LUGANDA	SUB-CLANS = MAHIGA	PRESENT SUB-CLAN HEAD = OMUKULU WA IHIGA
Baihuzi	Missenye	Heart of all animals	Snail						Rweswalulu of Itala G.Kasambia	Bamujuzi	Benefansi of Bubare G.Nsunga
										Bamugamba	Byalufu of Lwanyango (Karagwe)
										Bakisa	Zilyaulamu of Mutukula G.Nsunga
"	Bugabo	"	-	Mulimya-nkondo	Katoma	?	Wamara & Irungu	Katale Bushasha Katoma Bugera Maruku	Kikarugaa of Katale	Bagambano Balangara	Kikarugaa ?
"	Kiziba	"	"	Milego	Bunyoro	Cooks & Shield makers	Wamara & Muzola	Mugunga G.Kanyigo	Kikome of Mugunga	? ? ? ?	Kulimbura of Katano Mulekwa of Lukurungo Ntemberehai of Luti Kachumisi of Luti
Bajubu F.1.	Bugabo	Hippo	Bushbuck	Mutange	Muyenje (Ihangiro)	To give the Chief water to wash his face	Kashasira F.3.	Lyendo G.Ibosa	Galaba of Lwagati (Kianja)	Batuku Bajundura	Damazo K. of Ibosa Corner K. of Igombe
"	Kiziba	"	Hippo	Ibanza	Ihangiro	Watchmen	Kashasira	Bugombe	Thadeo Kanagwa	Baihigo -	Bayona of Ibosa -

Bajuba.
  F.1. Col.1. A very old clan of Kiziba.

  F.3. Col.8. An ancestor of the clan.

(13)

1	2	3	4	5	6	7	8	9	10	11	12
CLAN = LUGANDA	CHIEFDOM = BUKAMA	TOTEM = MUZIRO	SECONDARY TOTEM = EBINTU EBILI KUGENDA-GENDA	FOUNDER (PATRIARCH) = OMUGURUSI	PLACE OF CLAN ORIGIN = ENTABUKO	COURT DUTIES = MWANIA or MURUKA or NWAGA	CLAN SPIRIT = MIZUKA	CLAN VILLAGES = VIJIJI VYA ASILI	PRESENT CLAN HEAD = OMUKULU WALUGANDA	SUB-CLANS = MAHIGA	PRESENT SUB-CLAN HEAD = OMUKULU WA IHIGA.
Bajubu	Kanyange-reko	Millet growing out of a rock F.2.	Hippo	Kajuba of Ibosa (G.Kahororo)	Ibosa	To give water to the Chief to wash his face	Kashasira	Ibosa G.Kahororo	Ntangeki of Bibanja	Batuku Bajundule	? Ntangeki
"	Kiamtwara	"	"	Mujumbula	Buzinja	"	Wamara	Kashangati	Seleman of Bukoba	Bajondula Batuku	Seleman Kyabirengo of Birongo
"	Kianja	"	"	Lubango	Buzinja	"	Kashasira	Buhembe (Kiamtwara) Ibosa (Bugabo)	Ntangeki of Bibanja	Bakyama Batuku	Mwota of Kimbugu (Kianja) Katuku of Itare (Bugabo)
Bakainage	Karagwe	Small open basket	Hyena	Isabangere	Kianja	Field workers	Mugasha	Rwambeizi Mabira	? of Rwambeizi	-	-
Bakalaza (Abagabe)	Karagwe	Striped cow (ruzomba)	1)Thunder 2)Franco-lin	Bashaibara	Bunyoro	Drumkeepers	Mugasha	Kakumbio Rwanzira	Baishaijabana ? of Kashasha	Bakihigwa Bakigani Bakyanika	? ? ?
Bakaija	Kianja	Wild cat (orutoni)	Crane (entuwa)	Makakiro	Ruanda	Name the Chief (together with Bayango)	Mwijuka	Kimbugu G.Izigo	Rutanjuki-rwa of Kimbugu	Bugara Bagoma Bamabuye	Rutanjukira Mtafungwa of Kimbugu
"	Kanyange-reko	Millet growing out of a rock	Crane	Kabiito of Kimbugu	Busingo G.Ibuge	To make the Chief's court-yard on the day of his ...	Ishamba F.1.	Kimbugu	Kalabashegye of Kimbugu		

<u>N O T E S.</u>

Baluba.
    P.2. Col.3.   When millet is placed on a rock to dry in the sun some grains may remain when it is gathered up.   These grains often sprout and it is
                   these plants which are meant.

Bakalie.
    P.1. Col.8.   A clan ancestor.

1 CLAN = LUGANDA	2 CHIEFDOM = BUKAMA	3 TOTEM = MUZIRO	4 SECONDARY TOTEM = EBINYU EBILI KUGENDA-GENDA	5 FOUNDER (PATRIARCH) = OMUGURUSI	6 PLACE OF CLAN ORIGIN = ENTABUKO	7 COURT DUTIES = MWANYA or MURUKA or MWAGA	8 CLAN SPIRIT = MIZUKA	9 CLAN VILLAGES = VLIJI VYA ASILI	10 PRESENT CLAN HEAD = OMUKULU WAJUGANDA	11 SUB-CLANS = MAHIGA	12 PRESENT SUB-CLAN HEAD = OMUKULU WA IHIGA.
Bakiyama	Ihangiro	Mobana (a wild fruit) F.l.	Hippo	Kahanantuki (some say Kakiama s/o Yambekwa)	Uzinza	Beramata (see para.22 Customary Law)	Kikuri and Milembe	Muyenje G.Kahangere Iremera	Kamulebwa of Makarwe	Abakyambe / Abankango / Abangaza / Bachambai / Bachambai-Kajure	Bingi of Kabagunda / G.Iremera Rushairwa / Kisma G.Karambi / Ngambeki of Mahane / G.Bureza Katama of Kurugunda / Bishankara of Bumbire
Bakilembo	Bugabo	Bushbuck	-	Katanywa	Makoya	Cooks & Herdsmen	?	Katengwe Butabe	Kajuna of Katengwe	Batanywa / Batabe / Batagya	Kajuna Baitanira of Butube / Mbamanya of Katangwe
"	Kiamtwara	"	-	Kaheji	Buzinja	Cooks & Hunters.	Wamara	Itawa	Mwesiga of Itawa	-	-
"	Kanyange-reko	"	-	Kaheji of Kaagya	Buzinja (Biharamulo)	Cooks	Wamara	Kaagya	Mulegu of Itawa	-	-
Bakoba	Kiamtwara	1)Millet growing from rock 2)Bushbuck 3)Oburo (millet flour)	Stork	Berunga (some say Mukoba)	Isheshe	Honey beer brewers	Kyonya	Bukoba	Clement of Bukoba (others say Karamura of Kaizibaki Viota)	Batakwa / Bagara	Clement Ndekaki of Bunena.

Bakiyama.
  F.l. Col.3. This clan was originally part of the Bajubu, but ate hippo meat and were turned out. They took the mabona as their totem and the hippo as their secondary totem.

1 CLAN = LUGANDA	2 CHIEFDOM = BUKAMA	3 TOTEM = MUZIRO	4 SECONDARY TOTEM = EBINTU EBILI KUGENDA-GENDA AMUZIRO	5 FOUNDER (PATRIACH) = OMUGURUSI	6 PLACE OF CLAN ORIGIN = ENTABUKO	7 COURT DUTIES = MWANYA or MURUKA or MWANFA	8 CLAN SPIRIT = MIZUKA	9 CLAN VILLAGES = VIJIJI VYA ASILI	10 PRESENT CLAN HEAD = OMUKULU WALUGANDA	11 SUB-CLANS = MAHIGA	12 PRESENT SUB-CLAN HEAD = OMUKULU WA IHIGA
Bakoba	Kanyange-reko	Millet growing from a rock	–	Lutakwe of Bukoba		Honey beer brewers	Bwogi F.l.	Bukoba	Lweikiza of Lukindo	–	–
Bakurwa	Bugabo	Bushbuck	Rat (mbeba)	Lwango	Bukwaya (Ukerewe)	Treat & prepare the Chief's coffee (Babona)	Mugasha & Wamara	Itongo Rubafu & Buzi	Butai of Bishaka G.Kaagya	Balumbugu Balala	Batai Bantangya of Kishanje
"	Kiamtwara	"	"	Kanobante	Isheshe	Treat & prepare the Chief's coffee 2)Bearers of the mat on which the Chief sits	Wamara	Kirere G.Itawa	Mbemaara of Kirere	Balala Bambugu Balindamaizi	Mbemaara Kaizamabe of Muyabe Kwass of Muyabe
"	Kiziba	"	"	Kaibare	Ihangiro	Court Jesters	Kiriba	Kigarama	Kigwa of Kigarama	?	Bingile of Kigarama
"	Kanyange-reko	"	"	Ntaraga of Kishanje G.Rubafu	Kitala (Uganda)	1)Treat & prepare the Chief's coffee 2)Carry the Chief's stool	Wamara	Kishanje G.Rubafu	Kabigumila of Ntoma	Bambugu Balala	Kabigumila Constantini of Kahyolo G.Kaibanja

NOTES.

Bakoba. F.l. Col.8. Has been worshipped since the time of Lutakwe.

1 CLAN = LUGANDA	2 CHIEFDOM = BUKAMA	3 TOTEM = MUZIRO	4 SECONDARY TOTEM = EBINTU EBILI KUGENDA-GENDA AMUZIRO	5 FOUNDER (PATRIARCH) = OMUGURUSI	6 PLACE OF CLAN ORIGIN = ENTABUKO	7 COURT DUTIES = MWANYA or MURUKA or MWAGA	8 CLAN SPIRIT = MIZUKA	9 CLAN VILLAGES = VIJIJI VYA ASILI	10 PRESENT CLAN HEAD = OMUKUKU JA LUGANDA	11 SUB-CLANS = MAHIGA	12 PRESENT SUB-CLAN HEAD = OMUKULU WA IHIGA
Bakurwa	Kianja	Bushbuck	Rat (mbeba)	Rwahi	Kitala (Uganda)	Fundis (Kibaija ebyanzi)	Kashasira	Kishanje (Bugabo)	Babara of Kanasi	Baziba	Mwombeki of Ibwera
Bakuma F.l.	Kiziba	Bushbuck Mboga (wild vegetable)	Weaver bird	Ntumwa	Bukuma (Ihangiro)	1)Place Chief's chair at his coronation 2)Ihiga head marks out kikale boundaries 3)lays foundation stones of kikale buildings and starts the planting in its shambas	Nduru	Bukuma (Ihangiro) Ishegangai	Ruberwa of Bukuma	1)Bateke 2)Bakuma 3)Barungu 4)Batimba 5)Baruri 6)Bachoka 7)Babiasa 8)Bakanyisa	Ruberwa Malijo of Bukuma Ntambe of Bukuma Ntabaza of Bukuma Katabaro of Kantale Ishebwata of Inshegenyai Kalokora of Bukuma Karugira of Bukuma
Balenge	Kiamtwara	Blind cow (mpume)	-	Luabawasha	Buzinja	-	Lyangombe	-	Ngirwa-omoi of Msisha	1)Babona 2)Bashamsha	Kente of Katoma Ngirwaomoi
Balenge (or Abagahe) F.l.	Karagwe	Striped cow	Harte-beeste		"	Nshomi(?) of the Chief	"	Kagoro Kishao	Tinatumire of Kishao		

NOTES

Bakuma. F.l. Col.l. them by giving them various privileges. This clan was the most powerful in Kiziba when Kibi I arrived. They refused at first to allow him to become chief but he persuaded (See also "Tribal Structure" p.264).

Balenge. F.l. Col.l. given on this list was received from another informant. In the Karagwe list this clan is linked with Abakalaza and said to share its totems, patriarch etc. The information about the Bakalaza

1	2	3	4	5	6	7	8	9	10	11	12
CLAN = LUGANDA	CHIEFDOM = BUKAMA	TOTEM = MUZIRO	SECONDARY TOTEM = EBINTU EBILI KUGENDA-GENDA AMUZIRO	FOUNDER (PATRIACH) = OMUGURUSI	PLACE OF CLAN ORIGIN = ENTABUKO	COURT DUTIES = MWANYA or MURUKA or MWAGA	CLAN SPIRIT = MIZUKA	CLAN VILLAGES = VIJIJI VYA ASILI	PRESENT CLAN HEAD = OMUKULU WA LUGANDA	SUB-CLANS = MAHIGA	PRESENT SUB-CLAN HEAD = OMUKULU WA IHIGA
Balenge (& Bashambo) F.1.	Kiziba	Bushbuck & Black striped cow	-	Lwashawasha	Mpororo (Uganda)	Soothsayers to the Chief	Lwasha	Kyazi G.Kitobo	Lutahana-ntura of Kyazi	Balasho-ngera Banyibona	Lwabuyo of Bwera Ngirwaomoi of Nsisha (Kienja)
Balenge	Bugabo	Bushbuck	Bushbuck	Lwashawasha	Nsisha (Kabale)	Soothsayers	Lwasha	Kamlibebi Kaagie Nsisha Kitobo	Ndyetabura of Kamlibebi	-	-
Baligi	Ihangiro	Mushroom (nyawasha)	Stork	Kayenge	Karagwe	Fundis	Lyabugando	Mushure	Rubombola of Kakako	Abazigaba	Matazi of Bisheke
"	Karagwe	Bushbuck	Emisibya (a bird)	Ngabona	Mubali (Congo)	Drumkeepers	Mugasha	Kyanika Rukole Masheshe	Ngambwa of Masheshe G.Nyabionza	Bagani Bakyanika Bazigaba	? ? ?
Balisa	Karagwe	Striped cow	Partridge		Bunyoro	Sub-chiefs	Gusimweire	Rugera	Juma Bwikizo of Igona (Kienja)	Bahamira	Rugambwa of Rugera

N O T E S

Balenge (& Bashambo).

F.1. Col.1. In the Kiziba list it is linked with Bashambo.

Bankango.

N O T E S.

F.1. Col.3. Bankango have special customs re twins. A mother of twins may not enter a Mukango's house. A Mukango woman who bears twins must leave the children and her husband.

F.2. Col.5. Nyamwanzi's wife Mukango gave her name to the clan.

1	2	3	4	5	6	7	8	9	10	11	12
CLAN = LUGANDA	CHIEFDOM = BUKAMA	TOTEM = MUZIRO	SECONDARY TOTEM = EBINTU EBILI KUGENDAGENDA AMUZIRO	FOUNDER (PATRIACH) = ONUGURUSI	PLACE OF CLAN ORIGIN = ENTABUKO	COURT DUTIES = MWANYA or MURUKA or MWAGA	CLAN SPIRIT = MIZUKA	CLAN VILLAGES = VIJIJI VYA ASILI	PRESENT CLAN HEAD = OMUKULU WA LUGANDA	SUB-CLANS = MAHIGA	PRESENT SUB-CLAN HEAD = OMUKULU WA IHIGA.
Beami or Bahami	Kianja	The milk of a cow on the day of bulling	Baboon	Nkole	Bunyoro	Blacksmiths		Itojo	Mfuruki of Itojo	Bamiro Babere Bami	Balune e of Muhutwe Kyanante of Kikome Mfuruti of Itoge
"	Kanyangereko	-	"	Kamagyo of Ntoija G.Kishogo	Ankole	Herdsmen	Wamara	Ntoija	Ishewahya of Kanyangereko G.Ntoma	-	-
Banjoju	Karagwe	Striped cow (ruzomba)	Elephant (enjoju)	Kairuntu	Burundi	Firelighters to the Chief	Lyangombe	Kishao Buhimba Kagaruka	Kairuntu of Kishao	Basa Bahara Bakiri Batembeka Batwa	Bwanakapa of Kisao Mutabasi of Kisao Dumebugaga of Kemechumu Musoina of Kisao ?
Bankango	Kiamtwara	1)Semene 2)Bananas joined together F.l.	Hawk (malele)	Mutashaba	Buzinja	Batwazi	Wamara	Itawa	Chief Gabriel of Kabale	Batashaba Bakora Bamuganyi	Mujaki of Nshambia Mitagaywa of Igombe Lugangira of Bulibeta
"	Bugabo	1)Intestines 2) Two bananas joined together	"	Nyamwanzi F.2.	Bunyoro	Batwazi	"		Chief Lweikiza	Barumagi	Chief Lweikiza

1 CLAN = LUGANDA	2 CHIEFDOM = BUKAMA	3 TOTEM = MUZIRO	4 SECONDARY TOTEM = EBINTU EBILI KUGENDA-GENDA AMUZIRO	5 FOUNDER (PATRIACH) OMUGUHUSI	6 PLACE OF CLAN ORIGIN = ENTABUKO	7 COURT DUTIES = MWANYA or MURUKA or MWAGA	8 CLAN SPIRIT = MIZUKA	9 CLAN VILLAGES VIJIJI VYA ASILI	10 PRESENT CLAN HEAD = OMUKULU WA LUGANDA	11 SUB-CLANS = MAHIGA	12 PRESENT SUB-CLAN HEAD = OMUKULU WA IHIGA.
Bankango	Kanyange-reko	1)Intest-ines 2)Two bananas joined together	Hawk (nalele)	Lyangombe of Makongera G.Kamachumu	Bwinai (Biharamulo)	1)To beat the drum called Misheke 2)Milkers	Lyangombe and Mulashani	Katuruka G.Ntoma	Kayungi of Kataruka	Bashamala Bashangwa Bagesi	Karungi ? of Ngarama ? ?
Bunyuma	Kiamtwara	Hearts of all animals	Ant (kinyono)	Kamanyi	Buganda	Barkcloth makers	Mugasha	Bushaza	Kabikwa of Bushaza	Banyaiye Bakamanyi Banume Bahesi Bahigi	Kabikwa Katemana of Bushaza Kagoye of Bushaza Dashwi of Katoma Ichaka of Katoma
"	Kiziba	"	"	"	"	Firelighters to the Chief	Wamara & Mugasha	Bukelele Bwanjai	Bwangwamu of Bukelele	Bajoju Baboga Bajuna Basenene	Kawamara of Kiazi Malege of Kigarama Bwangwamu Kaihura of Missenyi (Minziro)
"	Bugabo	-	"	Kaigi	Kitala (Bunyoro)	-	Wamara	Burugo Katoma	Kaijage of Katoma	Bahigi Banume	Kaijage ?
"	Kanyange-reko	"	"	Mukama of Katoma	Kyasha (Uganda)	Warriors Iron workers	"	Katoma	Patrisi of Kasharazi G.Gera	Bamayi Banyaiye	Patrisi ?

1	2	3	4	5	6	7	8	9	10	11	12
CLAN = LUGANDA	CHIEFDOM = BUKAMA	TOTEM = MUZIRO	SECONDARY TOTEM = EBINTU EBILI KUGENDA-GENDA AMUZIRO	FOUNDER (PATRIARCH) = OMUGURUSI	PLACE OF CLAN ORIGIN = ENTABUKO	COURT DUTIES = NWANYA or MURUKA or MWAGA	CLAN SPIRIT = MIZUKA	CLAN VILLAGES = VIJIJI VYA ASILI	PRESENT CLAN HEAD = OMUKULU WA LUGANDA	SUB-CLANS = MAHIGA	PRESENT SUB-CLAN HEAD = OMUKULU WA IHIGA
Baruwani	Kianja	Cow (kinyai)	1)Lightning F.1. 2)Wild Cat	Munana	Bunyoro	Drummers of the drum 'Mlango' 2)Cooks	Kashasira F.2.	Ibwera	Joseph of Ruhanga	Baziza / Bawere Bakuba	Christopher of Kianguye / – / –
"	Missenyi	Cow (lubombwe)(kinyai)	–	Munana	Kafo (Bunyoro)	Door-keepers	Kashumba	Itala	Kabachwezi of Itala	–	–
"	Kanyange-reko	"	Nungu (a bird)	Komunobi of Kenyange-reko G.Ntoma	Katembe G.Buhe-ndagabo	Cooks Door-keepers to the Bakango chiefs.	Wamara	Katembe (Bugabo)	? of Katembe	Bawelwa / Bazige	Majaliwa of Kanyangereko G.Ntoma / ? of Mahuguru G.Katoma
"	Bugabo	"	Cow	Mugasha	Makongoro (Kianja)	Guardians of the Chief's wives. Cooks.	Kyano F.3.	Mahuguru G.Kamechumu Makongora G.Katoma	Kamushaga of Kigarika	Bawelewa / Bazige	Nturwa of Bukenda Npanju of Bushagara Ifunya of Bushagara

N O T E S.

Baruwani.
F.1. Lightning is the brother of Baruwani.
F.2. See Tribal Structure p.258.
F.3. The god of leopards who can control them. Thus a Muruwani who has a grouse against another man sometimes threatens to ask Kyano to set his leopards on him.

Col.4. Lightning is the brother of Baruwani. No member of the clan can be struck. The Chiefs of Kianja take wives from the Baruwani.
Col.8. See Tribal Structure p.258.
Col.8. The god of leopards who can control them. Thus a Muruwani who has a grouse against another man sometimes threatens to ask Kyano to set his leopards on him.

1	2	3	4	5	6	7	8	9	10	11	12
CLAN = LUGANDA	CHIEFDOM = BUKAMA	TOTEM = OMUZIRO	SECONDARY TOTEM = EBINTU EBILI KUGENDA-GENDA AMUZIRO	FOUNDER (PATRIARCH) = OMUGURUSI	PLACE OF CLAN ORIGIN = ENTABUKO	COURT DUTIES = MWANYA or MURUKA or MWAGA	CLAN SPIRIT = MIZUKA	CLAN VILLAGES = VLIJI VYA ASILI	PRESENT CLAN HEAD = OMUKULU WA LUGANDA	SUB-CLANS = MAHIGA	PRESENT SUB-CLAN HEAD = OMUKULU WA IHIGA
Barwuani	Kiamtvara	Cow (lubombwe)(kinyai)	Porcupine (kishegeshe)	Mugambaye	Bunyoro	Watchmen of the outer gates (Bawabu)	Kyano	Igombe G.Nyakato	Bukende of Kabale	Bawelwa Bazige Barondozi	Bukenie Npanju of Mauguru Lukembe of Mauguru
"	Kiziba	"	-	Kabwenba	Npololo		Kahigi	Kikukwe G.Kanyigo	Bagaesha of Kikukwe	Besha	Ntinabo of Kikukwe
Basaizi	Kianja	Bushbuck	Chicken	Kibi	Bunyoro	Prepare the Chief's throne	Irungu	Kanazi	Kagisa of Kanazi	Babaizi / Busikia / Bagambai Bakweto Babiyetaba / Bakoba	Mkoko of Likonge (Kiziba) / Nshumbe of Kanyigo Kagisa / Nshumba ? / Mpulinai of Kashenye / Ndasirwa of Kasharu
"	Kiziba	"	Mkunia (sand bank in a lake)	Kayanja	Nkole	Spear makers Drummers at the new moon levee	Kara	Luhano	Lwentaro of Luhano	Bakweta / Bagambai / Babiyetaba / ? / ?	Lweyemamu of Kashenye / Ndiamukama of Kashenye / Kabiyemera of Kashenye / Nshumu Kashumbusi of Bukwali / Kawamala of Kyelima.

1	2	3	4	5	6	7	8	9	10	11	12
CLAN = LUGANDA	CHIEFDOM = BUKAMA	TOTEM = MUZIRO	SECONDARY TOTEM = EBINTU EBILI KUGENDA-GENDA AMUZIRO	FOUNDER (PATRIARCH) = OMUGURUSI	PLACE OF CLAN ORIGIN = ENTABUKO	COURT DUTIES = AWANYA or MURUKA or MWAGA	CLAN SPIRIT = MIZUKA	CLAN VILLAGES = VIJIJI VYA ASILI	PRESENT CLAN HEAD = OMUKULU WA LUGANDA	SUB-CLANS = MAHIGA	PRESENT SUB-CLAN HEAD = OMUKULU WA IHIGA
Bassizi	Kiamtwara	Bushbuck	Chicken	Mulimankazi	Bunyoro	Herdsmen	Wamara	Kashenge	Karubandira of Kashenge	Babusaizi	Karubandira
"	Bugabo	"	Bushbuck	Ngobe	"	"	Bwogi & Kimuli	Kashenye Kashengatti Kanazi	Baitubake of Kanazi (Kianja)	-	-
"	Kanyange-reko	"	Chicken	Nyarusaizi of Katoma G.Ibwera	Kitala (Bunyoro)	Milkers	Ishamba	Katoma G.Ibwera	Abdullah Karumuna of Katuruka G.Ntoma	Bebohela Bagwe	Abdullah Karumuna ? of Kitendaguro
Basimba	Kianja	Lung Fish (maamba)	Dog	Mauwa	Bunyoro	Drummers at the new moon levée	Wamara	Itogo Mnifumbo	Iwiza of Butakya F.l.	Babende Batorogo Beteneita Beganga Banguba Basimba	Timotheo of Kaziranfuka Bigirwa of Itongo Iwiza Serugoti of Itoju Misingo of Bute Ndiakowaje of Kimbugu

N O T E S.

Basimba.
F.l. Col.10. Butakya is the ancient village dedicated to Wamara. For this reason the clan head lives here.

1	2	3	4	5	6	7	8	9	10	11	12
CLAN = LUGANDA	CHIEFDOM = BUKAMA	TOTEM = MUZIRO	SECONDARY TOTEM = EBINTU EBILI KUGENDA-GENDA AMUZIRO	FOUNDER (PATRIACH) = OMUGURUSI	PLACE OF CLAN ORIGIN = ENTABUKO	COURT DUTIES = MWANYA or NURUKA or MWAGA	CLAN SPIRIT = MIZUKA	CLAN VILLAGES = VIJIJI VYA ASILI	PRESENT CLAN HEAD = OMUKULU WA LUGANDA	PRESENT CLAN SUB-CLANS = MAHIGA	PRESENT SUB-CLAN HEAD = OMUKULU WA IHIGA
Basimba	Kiziba	Lung fish (mamba)	Kanyoni (a small bird)	Mahaba or Kalija? or Kahanda	Thangiro	Doorkeepers of the drums	Wamara	Rusinga	Kahanda of Rusinga	-	-
"	Kanyange-reko	"	Dog	Iwijage	Ilogero G.Ibuga	Drumkeepers	"	Ilogero G.Ibuga	Balyegashaki of Kabale	-	-
"	Ihangiro	" 2)A species of banana called mamba	-	Kiro	Bunyoro	Cooks Councillors	Wamara & Butuku F.2.	Mafumbo	Mugufu of Rugawiro	Basswe Balkarata Bakisbambo	Mugufu Iharata of Itongo ?
Basingo	Ihangiro	Bugondo (a cow with a stripe along the back-bone)	Siafu ants	Kilabama	Egypt	Herdsmen Milkers Soothsayers Priests	Katondola F.1.	Nshamba	Ruboya of Kihimulo	Bakala Bakima Babairu Bafumu	Mashombani of Bukana G.Nshamba Nsimba of Nahambya Beizi of Bukono Luchwagi of Itongo

N O T E S.

Basimba.
F.2. Col.8. Father of Kiro.

Basingo.
F.1. Col.8. Daughter of Myambi an ancestor of the clan. She died in childhood during a famine.

1	2	3	4	5	6	7	8	9	10	11	12
CLAN = LUGANDA	CHIEFDOM = BUKAMA	TOTEM = MUZIRO	SECONDARY TOTEM = EBINTU EBILI KUGENDA-GENDA AMUZIRO	FOUNDER (PATRIACH) = OMUGURUSI	PLACE OF CLAN ORIGIN = ENTABUKO	COURT DUTIES = MWANYA or .MURUKA or MWAGA	CLAN SPIRIT =MIZUKA	CLAN VILLAGES = VIJIJI VYA ASILI	PRESENT CLAN HEAD = OMUKULU WA LUGANDA	SUB-CLANS = MAHIGA	PRESENT SUB-CLAN HEAD = OMUKULU WA IHIGA.
Basingo	Kiamtwara	Mfuru (fish)	Siafu ants	Musirika	Igara	Prophets	Kashasira	Kyasha G.Nyakato	Kyabukoba of Kyasha	Baira Babasi / Bagaju Bashayo / Bahima	Kyabukoba Masinjagala of Ibaraizibu Bebutunika Panda of Kitwe Makasi of Kabale
"	Kanyange-reko	Bugondo	"	Mulima of Itawa	Itawa	1)Prepare skins for clothing. 2)Prophets	Wamara	Itawa	Lawrence Kachume of Busingo G.Itawa	Basingosingo Basingohina	L.Kachume Barongo of Katuruka G.Ntoma.
" (Barondo)	Karagwe	Cow with spine stripe (omurara)	"	Ntenda	Karagwe	Cultivators	Wamara Rusingo	Ruanda G.Bugene	? of Ruanda	Barondo Batazindwa	Ntanda of Ruanda Kirwa of Nyamuhingo G.Igurwa
Basingo	Bugabo	"	"	?	?	Tanners milkers & butchers Soothsayers (Bafumu)	?	Kyamange	Babara of Kyamarange	Babairu Bahima Bafuma	? Babaro ?
"	Kanyange-reko	"	"	Mulima of Itawa	Itawa	Prepare skins for clothes 2)Witch doctors (Bafumu)F.2.	Wamara	Itawa	Lawrence Kachume of Busingo G.Iguba	Basingosingo Bahima	L.Kachuma Barongo of Katuruka G.Ntoma.

NOTES

Basingo.
F.2. Col.7. Bafumu. In the old days of trial by ordeal the bafumu conducted the ordeal.

1	2	3	4	5	6	7	8	9	10	11	12
CLAN = LUGANDA	CHIEFDOM = BUKANA	TOTEM = MUZIRO	SECONDARY TOTEM = EBINTU EBILI KUGENDA GENDA AMUZIRO	FOUNDER (PATRIARCH) = OMUGURUSI	PLACE OF CLAN ORIGIN = ENTABUKO	COURT DUTIES = NWANYA or NURUKA or KWAGA	CLAN SPIRIT = MIZUKA	CLAN VILLAGES = VIJIJI VYA ASILI	PRESENT CLAN HEAD = OMUKULU WA LUGANDA	SUB-CLANS = MAHIGA	PRESENT SUB-CLAN HEAD = OMUKULU WA IHIGA
Basita	Karagwe	Obulunga (thorn tree)	Endabi (a hare)	Nyakika	Ankole	Cultivators	Mulindwa	Bukura Bugara	Rwankenge of Bugara	Bagwe	?
"	Missenyi	Bushbuck	Stork	Kanagwa	Birundugu	Drumkeepers of the drum Nkonge	"	Kitobo	Aligawesa of Kiteimbwa G.Kipanda Koki (Uganda)	Bakesi / Bakenyana / Balwasibagu / Baigurukila / Bamgeleka / Bakanpera	Tinkananyire of Kitobo / Kalwani of Kayanga G.Nsunga / Mubi of Bunazi / Mushanda of Bwera / Miganyia of Bwera / Ngimbwa of Kashenye
Bashambo	Karagwe	1)A burnt out house 2)An unmarried pregnant girl.	1)Dog 2)Wag-tail	Kigari	Mpororo	Herdsmen	Lyangombe	Masheshe Kichwamba	Kigari of Kichwamba	Byakahaya / Bashambo	? / ?
Basindi	Ihangiro	Otter	Dog	Mbohyo	Egypt	Cooks	Wamara	Mushure G.Mubunda	Balimujula of Itongo	Babanga / Basimba	Lyakahande of Buhimba G.Bureza / Kanobwa of Kashasha (Ihangiro)
"	Kanyangereko	Liver	Spotted cow	Bitaba of Lundu G.Mwinutwe	Omulukiga (Kigezi District)	Interpreters for the soothsaying chickens	Lwasha F.l.	Lwiza G.Bibanja	Nickolas Kabologoto of Lwija	-	-

<u>N O T E S</u>

<u>Basinde.</u>

F.1. Col.8. Iwasha is sacrificed to when chickens are killed for soothsaying.

1	2	3	4	5	6	7	8	9	10	11	12
CLAN = LUGANDA	CHIEFDOM = BUKAMA	TOTEM = MUZIRO	SECONDARY TOTEM = EBINTU EBILI KUGENDA GENDA AMUZIRO	FOUNDER (PATRIARCH) = OMUGURUSI	PLACE OF CLAN ORIGIN = ENTABUKO	COURT DUTIES = MWANYA or MURUKA or MWAGA	CLAN SPIRIT = MIZUKA	CLAN VILLAGES = VIJIJI VYA ASILI	PRESENT CLAN HEAD = OMUKULU WA LUGANDA	SUB-CLANS = MAHIGA	PRESENT SUB-CLAN HEAD = OMUKULU WA IHIGA
Bashasha	Bugabo	Heart of all animals F.1.	Omuhasha (a tree)	Iyele	Mpororo (Ankole)	Firelighters to the Chief (Lwigo)	Ishamba (a snake)	Kayungwe G.Buhenda-ngabo Kanahunda (Kiamtwara)	Samwel-Belenge of Bumai G.Bashasha	Babeta Baihima Baziguza Basisi	Terugwa of Lwangono Samwel B. Juma Nd. of Lwangono Bashalita of Bumai
"	Kiamtwara	"	-	Muganja	"	Milkers	"	Kanahunda G.Itawa	Ndyema of Kanahunda	Bawimla Basisi Bajundura	Ndyema Kasiga of Kibeta Kahinga of Katoma
"	Kiziba	" 2.Bush-buck	" 2.Small black ant (ekinyomo)	Kashasha		Prophets to the Chief	Mugasha	Kantare	Yabu of Kantare	Bakuba ? ? ?	All of Ilundu Bigilura of Bwera Musa of Kikukwe Bihanda of Buyango
"	Kianja	Heart	"	Ndolaki who emigrated from Bugabo	Bugabo	Shield & spear bearers to the Chief			Kanyaruju of Kagondo	Baihwa	Kanyaruju
"	Kanyange-reko	"	Nzonso (a bird)	Mbeihywa of Katoma	Mpororo	Baramata	Wamara	Bushasha	Bakengi of Kanahunda G.Itawa	Baihura Basisi	Bakengi ?

Bashasha.

N O T E S.

F.l. Col.3. This clan originally had an empty basket, olugegalusha, as a totem as well as the heart. When they emigrated to Bugubo they began

1	2	3	4	5	6	7	8	9	10	11	12
CLAN = LUGANDA	CHIEFDOM = BUKAMA	TOTEM = MUZIRO	SECONDARY TOTEM = EBINTU EBILI KUGENDA-GENDA AMUZIRO	FOUNDER (PATRIARCH) = OMUGURUSI	PLACE OF CLAN ORIGIN = ENTABUKO	COURT DUTIES = MWANYA or MURUKA or MWAGA	CLAN SPIRIT = MIZUKA	CLAN VILLAGES = VIJIJI VYA ASILI	PRESENT CLAN HEAD = OMUKULU WA LUGANDA	SUB-CLANS = MAHIGA	PRESENT SUB-CLAN HEADS = OMUKULU WA IHIGA.
Bashonde	Kiziba	Cow called kinyai	Nkwaju (bird)	Buroja F.1.		Cooks		Karamira Bukwari	Kemigani of Karamira	Batalengia Batunzi Bajoju Barokozi	Kemigani Kaboneka of Bukwari Kato of Karamira ?
"	Kanyange-reko	May not kill with a spear F.2.	"	Kilema of Ibaraizibu G.Itawa	Makongo G.Kahororo	Blacksmiths	Nyaibunga	Ibaraizibu	Tibanganyika of Ibaraizibu G.Itawa	-	-
"	Kiamtwara	Tailless cow	Entalago (? an animal)	Mugasha	Ankole	Fishermen	Wamara	Makongo G.Kahororo	Byembona of Kisinde	Bashonde Babolomo	Marselli Karekoma of Kitara Byembona
"	Bugabo	"		Kilema	"	Agents of the Chief (Ntunwa)	"	Makongo Mibaya Katare Rushasha	Tirutoijwa of Makongo	-	-
"	Missenye	"	-	Kigufa	Kilima Musaja-mukulu (Bunyoro)	Court jesters	Katege	Ngando G.Nsunga	Kibundi of Kasozi G.Kasambia	-	-

N O T E S.

Bashonde.

F.1. Col.5. Iyenda, great grandson of Buroja, was the first settler in Kiziba.

F.2. " 3. The reason given is that the Bashonde clan were the police (msimamizi) at the Chief's court of Law. A chief may not kill a man with a spear during the hearing of a case and nor may an official of the court.

1	2	3	4	5	6	7	8	9	10	11	12
CLAN = LUGANDA	CHIEFDOM = BUKAMA	TOTEM = MUZIRO	SECONDARY TOTEM = EBINTU EBILI KUGENDA-GENDA AMUZIRO	FOUNDER (PATRIACH) = OMUGURUSI	PLACE OF CLAN ORIGIN = ENTABUKO	COURT DUTIES = MWANYA or MURUKA or MWAGA	CLAN SPIRIT =MIZUKA	CLAN VILLAGES = VIJIJI VYA ASILI	PRESENT CLAN HEAD = OMUKULU WA LUGANDA	SUB-CLANS = MAHIGA	PRESENT SUB-CLAN HEAD = OMUKULU WA IHIGA
Bashosi	Kianja	Bushbuck	Francolin	Ntai	Mwega (Ruanda)	Coffee preparers	Mugunya	Itonga Kigarama (Kianja)	Lukabuka of Kigarama (Kianja)	Babona Babogo Bahangi Banshwi	Ndiakowa of Kigarama Rukambona of Itonga Karumuna of Itonga Lwenza of Kinoni G.Muhutwe
"	Bugabo	Rain water	Bushbuck	Lwabugage	Kigarama	-	Wamara	Ibosa Kigarama Kanyange-reko	Zeimanya of Ibosa	Bashosi Babukera	Zoimanya Muzee of Ibosa
"	Kiamtwara	Bushbuck	Francolin	Rwajabwa	Buzinja	Drum keepers	"	Kiziru G.Kitwe	Baelejanyia of Kiziru	Bashosi	Baelejanyia
"	Kanyange-reko	"	"	Amumi of Katunguru Karagwe	Bunyoro	Bed makers of the Chief	Kimuli F.l.	Rwagati	Fredrick Nyakarre of Maruku	Basi	Fred. Nyakarre
Batagarwa	Kiziba	Bushbuck	Siafu ant	Kishwa	Bunyoro	Batalela (body F.l. guard)	Kagoro	Kishenge	Kazoba of Kantare	Barwaza Bataihuru-lwa Beiririza Bandekwe	Lutaiwa of Luganjo ? Kazoba Katabaro of Kantare.

N O T E S.

Bashosi.
    F.l. Col.8. Kimuli is their spirit because this clan are the Chief's agents.

Batgarwa.
    F.l. Col.7. See note to Bagombe.

1 CLAN = LUGANDA	2 CHIEFDOM = BUKAMA	3 TOTEM = MUZIRO	4 SECONDARY TOTEM = EBINTU EBILI KUGENDA-GENDA AMUZIRO	5 FOUNDER (PATRIACH) = OMUGIIRUSI	6 PLACE OF CLAN ORIGIN = ENTABUKO	7 COURT DUTIES = MWANYA or MURUKA or MWAGA	8 CLAN SPIRIT = MIZUKA	9 CLAN VILLAGES = VIJIJI VYA ASILI	10 PRESENT CLAN HEADS = OMUKULU WA LUGANDA	11 SUB-CLANS = MAHIGA	12 PRESENT SUB-CLAN HEAD = OMUKULU WA IHIGA.
Batundu (or Baheta)	Karagwe	1)Rain water 2)Prey of a leopard	Leopard (engol)	Njujuma	Bunyoro	Brewers	Irungu	Nyakagongo Katahoka	? of Kayanga G.Bugene	Baishanza Baganda Bahungu / Batahoka / Bahindo / Bachungu / Banyakahana	? / Kwezi of Kisao / Bugongoro of Kayanga Katesumbwa of Kayanga / Dukoko of Kisao / Rwamahuru of Kayanga
"	Kiamtwara	Prey of leopard	Leopard	Lushembo	Indigenous	Baharambwa	Wamara	Kabale G.Kitwe	Kamgisha of Kabale	Bafubwe / Banyama Bakomela	K.Kyoshe of Kitwe Kangisha Karuhandira of Rubumba
"	Bugabo	"	-			Cup bearers or food bearers to the Chief	Mugerwa F.l. (a leopard)	Ibosa, Kaato, Maruku Bwigula (Kianja)	Bandihai of Kaato	Banyama Bakomera / Bafubwa	Bandihai Katabara of Iyando Iwamalaba of Kaato
"	Kanyange-reko	"	"	Bwemelo of Bunyonya (Bugabo)	Bunyonya (Bugabo)	1)Herdsmen 2)Bakungu	Wamara & Irunga	Bunyonya	Lweikiza of Itawa	Banyama / Bakobe / Balamba / Bafubwa	Domissian of Maruku G.Bibanja Lwenyagira of Bujogero G.Bibanja Mwombeki of Ibaijo. G.Ntoma Lwabyo of Kabale.

N O T E S.

Batundu.

F.l. Col.8. A mythical leopard who lives in the forest near Bunyonya which the Bugabo Batundu have taken as their clan spirit.

1	2	3	4	5	6	7	8	9	10	11	12
CLAN = LUGANDA	CHIEFDOM = BUKAMA	TOTEM = OMUZIRO	SECONDARY TOTEM = EBITU EBILI KUGENDA-GENDA AMUZIRO	FOUNDER (PATRIACH) OMUGURUSI	PLACE OF CLAN ORIGIN = ENTABUKO	COURT DUTIES = MWANYA or MURUKA or MWAGA	CLAN SPIRIT = MIZUKU	CLAN VILLAGES = VIJIJI VYA ASILI	PRESENT CLAN HEAD = OMUKULU WA LUGANDA	SUB-CLANS = MAHIGA	PRESENT SUB-CLAN = OMUKULU WA IHIGA
Batundu	Kiziba	Prey of leopard	Leopard	Munjagi	Bunyoro	Cooks Name the Chief at his coronation	Irungu	Kashenye G.Kanyigo	Kigoye of Kashenye	Bafubwa Bashumba Banyama	Ndibaza of Lugando Kawa of Lwamshango Lubunda of Bwere
"	Misenye F.2	"	"	Mulinda	Bwende Buddu (Uganda)	Bahambansi (Baharambwa)	Mkulo	Nganda G.Nsunga	Mashanda of Nganda	? ?	Kabumbire of Kituntu Mashanda
"	Kianja	Otter (kaishe-ikogoto)	"	Mukuba	Bunyoro	Tanners Fishermen	Mugasha	Kabale (Kiamtwara) Lyanda (Bugabo)	Libarie of Kamuri (Kianja)	Banyama Bakorela Bafubwa	Libario of Kamuri ? Mugenyi of Bwigiru
Bayango	Kianja	Monkey (tumbili)	Sungasunga ants F.1.	Muyango	Abyssinia	Lay out the new Kikale Spear makers Name the Chief at coronation (together with Bakaija)	Kimuli F.2.	Ilingero	Kaimba of Ilingero	Bahizi Bejura Balibata	Tinshange of Kisindi Kaimba of Ilingero ?

N O T E S.

Batundu.

F.2. Col.2. This is an old established clan in Missenyi; when Kakolo, who was the first alien chief, arrived he found them living at Ngando.

Bayango.

F.1. Col.4. Sungasunga are supposed never to hurt a clan member. Children are said to be able to play with them.

F.2. Col.8. Kimuli son of Kalemera Megango who was poisoned in childhood by his father's jealous wives.

1 CLAN = LUGANDA	2 CHIEFDOM = BUKAMA	3 TOTEM = MUZIRO	4 SECONDARY TOTEM = EBINTU EBILI KUGENDA-GENDA AMUZIRO	5 FOUNDER (PATRIACH) = OMUGURUSI	6 PLACE OF CLAN ORIGIN = ENTABUKO	7 COURT DUTIES = MWANYA or MURUKA or MWAGA	8 CLAN SPIRIT = MIZUKA	9 CLAN VILLAGES = VIJIJI VYA ASILI	10 PRESENT CLAN HEAD = OMUKULU WA LUGANDA	11 SUB-CLAN = MAHIGA	12 PRESENT SUB-CLAN HEAD = OMUKULU WA IHIGA
Bayango	Karagwe	Monkey (tumbili)	Sungasunga ants & lion	Bigerera	Ihangiro	Traders	Ruhinda	Nyakashashe Kabalala G.Bugene	Kabazana of Nyakahenga	Nyakatura	?
"	Nissenyi	"	Lion		Kabonua				Walabyeki of Itala G.Kusembla	Bamunana / Babwensekere	Kalongo of Kabakasa G.Nsunga / Kakuma of Kaiga (Ankole)
"	Kiamtwara	"	Sungasunga	Ilesa	Bunyoro	Guardians of the Chief's wives	Wamara	Kisindi G.Nyakato	Karugwe of Kisindi	Balibata / Baesi / Banyaluahao	Karugwe Mutalogwa of Katoma / Kashaga of Kabale
"	Bugabo	"	Monkey	Nyakabaka	"	The ihiga Baesi gives the sign to start culti-vating again at the end of mourning for a late Chief by removing dead banana leaves in the new Chief's shamba			Kayango or Kanyange-reko (?) of Kyanyonyi Kianja ?	Bagoma / Balibata / Baesi	Kayango Banyanza of Kyaya / Muziribi of Kabale

1	2	3	4	5	6	7	8	9	10	11	12
CLAN = LUGANDA	CHIEFDOM = BUKAMA	TOTEM = MUZIRO	SECONDARY TOTEM = EBINTU EBILI KUGENDA-GENDA AMUZIRO	FOUNDER (PATRIARCH) = OMUGHUSI	PLACE OF CLAN ORIGIN = ENTABUKO	COURT DUTIES = MWANYA or MURUKA or MWAGA	CLAN SPIRIT = MIZUKA	CLAN VILLAGES = VIJIJI VYA ASILI	PRESENT CLAN HEAD = OMUKULU WALUGANDA	SUB-CLANS = MAHIGA	PRESENT SUB-CLAN HEAD = OMUKULU WA IHIGA.
Bayango	Ihangiro	Monkey	Sungasunga	Kiyango	Egypt	Assessors	Ankiri	Mushure G.Mibunda	Kyakuru of Itonga	Bazilenkende Baijanamikira Bagome Bagaju	Mafente of Itonga Balsaliza of Itonga G.Bureza Kabamanya of Kijwire G.Bureza Biliimu of Itonga
"	Kanyangereko	"	Monkey	Kayango of Kibona Karagwe	Toro (Uganda)	1)Hand the Chief his spear at coronation 2)Name the Chief 5)Firemakers to the Chief	Kimuli	Kibona (Karagwe)	Kayango of Lwazi G.Ntoma	Baesi Bakelebi Bakweba	Kayango Kyaya of Kahohoro Mbuga of Kanyangereko G.Ntoma.
Basigaba (or Abalagi)	Karagwe	Bushbuck	Bird called Emisiliya	Ngabona	Mubeli (Congo)	Kabaligi(?) Drumkeepers	Mugasha	Kyanika, Rukole & Mashesha	Ngambwe of Mashesha G.Nyabionza	Bakihigwa Bakigani Bakyanika	? of Bigene ? ?
Basirambogo	Kiziba	Buffalo	Buffalo	Mugasha	Bunyoro	Batalala F.1 (bodyguards Drumkeepers	Kiyondo	Mitagal	Kasumaino of Mitagal	Bazima Bolozi ?	Mazima of Katashana Mwolozi of Bushoza Igololo of ?

N O T E S.

Basirambogo.

F.1. Col.7. See note to Bagombe clan.

1	2	3	4	5	6	7	8	9	10	11	12
CLAN = LUGANDA	CHIEFDOM = BUKAMA	TOTEM = MUZIRO	SECONDARY TOTEM = EBINYU EBILI KUGENDA-GENDA AMUZIRO	FOUNDER (PATRIACH) = OMUGURUSI	PLACE OF CLAN ORIGIN = ENTABUKO	COURT DUTIES = MWANYA or MURUKA or MWAGA	CLAN SPIRIT =MIZUKA	CLAN VILLAGES = VIJIJI VYA ASILI	PRESENT CLAN HEADS = OMUKULU WA LUGANDA	SUB-CLANS = MAHIGA	PRESENT SUB-CLAN HEAD = OMUKULU WA IHIGA
Basiba	Kiamtwara	Bushbuck	Bat	Luahunda	Kiziba	Fundis	Kahigi	Busimbe G.Kitendaguro	Babutunika of Busimbe	Bagaju Bashayo Bakuma	Babutunika Panda of Kitwe Mulaki of Katale
"	Bugabo	"	Bushbuck	Magembe	Kigarama Kiziba	Hunters	Kahigi	Busi, Bwanjai & Yombe	Kempanju of Busi G.Bushasha	-	-
"	Karagwe	"	-	-	Kiziba		-	-	Katsliwa of Rwambare	-	-
"	Kanyange-reko	"	-	?	Bwanjai Kiziba	Cooks	Gahyoile	Bwanjai	Tibangayuka of Kigusha G.Ntoma	-	-
Basiba (Balinda)	Kiziba	"	Siafu ants	Kyato	Ishosho	Batalala (Bodyguards)	Kachwankizi	Kishenge	Kiti of Kishenge	-	-

1	2	3	4	5	6	7	8	9	10	11	12
CLAN = LUGANDA	CHIEFDOM = BUKAMA	TOTEM = MUZIRO	SECONDARY TOTEM = EBINTU EBILI KUGENDA-GENDA AMUZIRO	FOUNDER (PATRIACH) = OMUGURUSI	PLACE OF CLAN ORIGIN = ENTABUKO	COURT DUTIES = MWANYA or MURUKA or MWAGA	CLAN SPIRIT = MIZUKA	CLAN VILLAGES = VIJIJI VYA ASILI	PRESENT CLAN HEAD = OMUKULU WA LUGANDA	SUB-CLANS = MAHIGA	PRESENT SUB-CLAN HEAD = OMUKULU WA IHIGA.
Bakoma (Bayanja)	Karagwe	Heart of all animals	Bush pig	Muhima	Karagwe	Cultivators	Kagoro	Katwe Kibuga	Rwakitembe of Kibuga G.Bugene	Bayanja	?
Balebeki	Karagwe	Bushbuck	Baby bushbuck	Kizimya	Koki (Uganda)	Door keepers	Mayanja	Nyarwere Kihanga	? of Nyarwere G.Bugene	Byankuma	?
Bapina	Missenyi	Cattle (Ng'obe)	-	Kachocho	Mbale Mahokolo (Uganda)	Keepers of the spear called Kinegena	Wamara	None F.l.	Batunde of ?	-	-
Bashaigi	Missenyi	Heart of all animals	Nyange (Bird)	Nyinamaiso	Busaigi F.l. (Bunyoro)	Shield carriers to the Chief when he goes to war	Kagolo	Miajwa G.Nsunga	Bernardi Kasangaki of Gabulanga G.Kasambia	Babala / Batagubya	Kaibiba of Kagondo G.Kasambia Yowana of Simba G.Katoko Uganda.

N O T E S

Bapina.

F.l. Col.9. Because they lived with Chief Kalolo at the village of Mutukula and were not given villages of their own.

Bashaigi.

F.l. Col.6. A village on the hill Musajamukulu.

1	2	3	4	5	6	7	8	9	10	11	12
CLAN = LUGANDA	CHIEFDOM = BUKAMA	TOTEM = MUZIRO	SECONDARY TOTEM = EBINTU EBILI KUGENDA-GENDA AMUZIRO	FOUNDER (PATRIACH) = OMUGURUSI	PLACE OF CLAN ORIGIN = ENTABUKO	COURT DUTIES = MWANYA or MURUKA or MWAGA	CLAN SPIRIT = MIZUKA	CLAN VILLAGES = VIJIJI VYA ASILI	PRESENT CLAN HEAD = OMUKULU WALUGANDA	SUB-CLANS = MAHIGA	PRESENT SUB-CLAN HEAD = OMUKULU WA IHIGA
Banjenje	Missenyi	Lung fish (maamba)	-	Maluboga	Busekere (Bunyoro)	Herdsmen	Buye	Kyalukolongo G.Nsunga	Lukabaza of Nganda G.Nsunga	-	-
Beginu	Missenyi	Small buck (ngeye)	Kanyonyi ke Bunyoro	Munana	Kafo (Bunyoro)	1)Prophets 2) Name a new Chief.	Muwazi	Kabakesa G.Nsunga	Ivembya of Kabakesa	Bankambe Bakatwire	D.Lwalanda of Kabakesa Zibaili of Mutukula G.Nsunga.
Balenzi	Missenyi	Bushbuck	Kitwatwa (Bird)	Kwanda	Kilima Mubendi (Bunyoro)	Basabadu (Assessors)	Ndaula	Nongo	Kijuta of Bunazi G.Kasambia	Bakasanya / Bakibalan-gulo Badungu / Bankakya	Kasanya of Gabulanga G.Nsunga / Binamungu of Kasambia Benedicto of Mutukula G.Nsunga / Balidukao of Nakawanga G.Minziro
Baitira F.l.	Missenyi	Wakonga (a small animal)	Nfunzi (small bird)	Kinga	Kafo (Bunyoro)	House builders of the house called Kavamala where the body guard lives.	Kyomya	Part of the village of Ngando	Luuki of Luyiyi G.Nsunga	Bakanyambo Bakachope	Kasimbasi of Kasosi C.Kasambia Babala of Kayanga G.Nsunga

N O T E S.

Baitira.

F.l. Col.l. This clan was almost wiped out in battle with Chief Nyamutula.

1	2	3	4	5	6	7	8	9	10	11	12
CLAN = LUGANDA	CHIEFDOM = BUKAMA	TOTEM = MUZIRO	SECONDARY TOTEM = EBINTU EBILI KUGENDA-GENDA AMUZIRO	FOUNDER (PATRIACH) = OMUGURUSI	PLACE OF CLAN ORIGIN = ENTABUKO	COURT DUTIES = MWANYA or MURUKA or MWAGA	CLAN SPIRIT = MIZUKA	CLAN VILLAGES = VIJIJI VYA ASILI	PRESENT CLAN HEADS = OMUKULU WA LUGANDA	SUB-CLANS = MAHIGA	PRESENT SUB-CLAN HEAD = OMUKULU WA IHIGA
Bamiro	Missenyi	Spotted cow	Tortoise (kobe)	Kamiro	Mubendi (Bunyoro)	Blacksmiths	Bwiula	Mabuye G.Kasambia	Kyomya of Mabuye	Batumunya / Bayambya / Balikambi / Byamanyi	Ziryaulamu of Nsambia (Buddu Uganda) / Banalekaki of Bulongo (Uganda) / Kalekezi of Mabiro (Karagwe) / Lutenta of Lusahasha (Kiziba)
"	Ihangiro	"	Baboon	Rugaju	Ankole	Prepare skins	Kihazi	Bukaija	Bagayoire of Nshamba	Baami / Bakala	Nshongo of Kitnutu G.Iremera / Mashombeni of Bukara G.Nshamba
Bajwala	Missenyi	Otter (ngonge)	Kikonai (bird)	Brire	Bunyoro	Drumkeepers of the drum Ngonge	Gwabo		Kisigula of Kasozi G.Kasambia		
Bayenja	Missenyi	Heart of animals	Kinyira (snail)	Katula	Bunyoro	Keepers of the house called Rwabanyoro	Gwabo Kairurankwa		Zilyaulamu of Mutukula G.Nsunga	Bajuzi / Begamba	Benefansi of Bubaro Lwesululu of Itala
Bachwerera	Missenyi	Spotted cow	?	Kyabugulu	Bunyoro	To spit every morning into the mouth of the Muchwerwa and the man who sat at the table 2)Set traps in the river at the village Lwakalisa.	There are none left in Missenyi today.				

1	2	3	4	5	6	7	8	9	10	11	12
CLAN = LUGANDA	CHIEFDOM = BUKAMA	TOTEM = MUZIRO	SECONDARY TOTEM = EBINTU EBILI KUGENDA-GENDA AMUZIRO	FOUNDER (PATRIACH) = OMUGUREISI	PLACE OF CLAN ORIGIN = ENTABUKO	COURT DUTIES = MWANYA or MURUKA or MWAGA	CLAN SPIRIT = MIZUKA	CLAN VILLAGES = VIJIJI VYA ASILI	PRESENT CLAN HEAD = OMUKULU WA LUGANDA	SUB-CLANS = MAHIGA	PRESENT SUB-CLAN HEAD = OMUKULU WA IHIGA
Bachwezi	Missenyi	Lugave (a buck)	Mfunzi (small bird)	Kachope	Bunyoro	House builders of the house Kawanala where the bodyguard lives	Gwabo Kyomya		Babala of Kangundu G.Nsunga	Babira	Yozefu of Kampangi G.Minziro
Batwa	Kiziba	To milk cows (?)	Enkunia a bird follows the women when they cultivate)	Lulinga	Karagwe	Nobles Wise men	Lyangombe	Lwamachui	Mugoa of Lwamachui	? ?	Lweshabura of Bugombe Kagoza of Kyelima
Bagesho	Kiziba	May not look at an empty basket	?	Tabaro	Bunyoro	Doorkeepers	Wanara	Ilundu G.Buyango	Lukagula of Ilundu	Babende Bassa Banyolo Bajwangya ?	Lwabwera of Lushasha Ishabakaki of Kaina Kelya of Ilundu Mushumbusi of Ilundu Kachumisi of Ilundu
Bamwri	Kiziba	Buffalo	Small grass-hopper	Mugasha	Mabira (Karagwe)	Herdsmen	Lyangombe & Kagoro	Luija G.Buyango	Mibarulo of Luija	Baraukwa	Igurugati of Bugandika
Bashongya	Kiziba	Black cow	White bird (enyange)	Lwakajumba	Bunyoro Bwera	Herdsmen	Wanara & Mkaue	Bukabuye	Mwombeki of Bukabuye	? ? ?	Mbalilwa of Buhekera Ngimbwa of Nyabiolwe Mucikula of Lwamachui.

1	2	3	4	5	6	7	8	9	10	11	12
CLAN = LUGANDA	CHIEFDOM = BUKAMA	TOTEM = MUZIRO	SECONDARY TOTEM = EBINTU EBILI KUGENDA-GENDA AMUZIRO	FOUNDER (PATRIACH) = OMUGURUSI	PLACE OF CLAN ORIGIN = ENFABUKO	COURT DUTIES = MWANYA or MURUKA or MWAGA	CLAN SPIRIT = MIZUKA	CLAN VILLAGES = VIJIJI VIA ASILI	PRESENT CLAN HEAD = OMUKULU WALUGANDA	SUB-CLANS = MAHIGA	PRESENT SUB-CLAN HEAD = OMUKULU WA IHIGA
Bashamia	Kiziba	Bushbuck	Siafu ant	Lukonyla	Bunyoro	Priests of Kiziba	Kiziba	Kigarama G.Kanyigo	Kyaruzi of Kigarama	Batokolo Bashambe ?	Katana of Bukwali Kyaruzi of Kikukwe Mwanika of Bukwali
Balondo	"	Black cow 2)Fish	Chameleon	Mbalaluju	Karagwe	Herdsmen	Lyangombe & Mudgala	Musibuka Kitobo	Bulazi of Musibuka	Bazigwa ? Basigo	Kaluzigwa of Igurugati Kente of Ishozi Kswe of Kashasha
Batabazi	"	All animals	Stork	Katabazi	Ishesho	Milk vessel makers	Wamumi	Nshumba Byazi	Kyaruzi of Byazi	Bakele	Kalokola of Lushasha
"	Kiamtwara	Emparara (large grass hopper)	Stork	Kakozza	Rwanda	Fundis	Mwijuka	Nshambia	Kabanuka of Nshambia	-	-
Babiki F.l.	Kiziba	Bushbuck	Siafu ant	Kintu	-	(Once the rulers)	-	Kigarama	Mugasha of Kishenge	?	Mabaruri of Kigarama

N O T E S.

Babiki.

F.l. Coll. This is a very old established clan.

1 CLAN = LUGANDA	2 CHIEFDOM = BUKAMA	3 TOTEM = MUZIRO	4 SECONDARY TOTEM = EBINTU EBILI KUGENDA - GENDA AMUZIRO	5 FOUNDER (PATRIACH) = OMUGU RUSI	6 PLACE OF CLAN ORIGIN = ENTABUKO	7 COURT DUTIES = MWANYA or MURKKA or MWAGA	8 CLAN SPIRIT =MIZUKA	9 CLAN VILLAGES = VIJIJI VYA ASILI	10 PRESENT CLAN HEAD = OMUKULU WA LUGANDA	11 SUB-CLANS = MAHIGA	12 PRESENT SUB-HEAD CLAN HEAD = OMUKULU WA IHIGA
Bakiyaga F.l.	Kiziba	Bushbuck	-	Nkonge	Uganda	1)Staff makers to the Chief 2)Fire lighters to the Chief	Wamara	Mifumia	Kalokola of Mifumia	-	-
Bawende	"	"	Chicken	Nyamwimba	Bunyoro	The model of a Chief's new house is built upon the head of a Muwende F.l.	Irungu	Nshumba	Kamugisha of Nshumba	? ? Bashwaimi ?	Kiajurga of Kyolima, Kamzola of Bwoki, Mwembeki of Kafunjo, Lusiga of Kashasha (Kibumbiro)
Bashaga	"	Semene	Nyange (white bird)	Tabaro	Bunyoro (Galla)	Herdsmen Milkers of the Chief's own Milk.	Kagoro	Kashasha Bukabuye	Mutayabarwa of Kashasha	Bagoysnante Banyaigana	Muteyabarwa ? s/o Kata-boro of Bukabuye
"	Ihangiro	"	Hyena	Kashohera	Nkole	Herdsmen	Kagoro	Bushara	Rugiga of Mubunda	-	-

N O T E S.

Bakiyaga.
F.l. Col.l.   There are very few of these people.

Bawende.
F.l. Col.7.   When the Chief's house is built a Muwende stands and they build a model house on his head before beginning the real house; i.e. the
Chief's house must stand many days upright as does a man.

1 CLAN = LUGANDA	2 CHIEFDOM = BUKAMA	3 TOTEM = MUZIRO	4 SECONDARY TOTEM = EBINTU EBILI KUGENDA–GENDA AMUZIRO	5 FOUNDER (PATRIARCH) = OMUGURUSI	6 PLACE OF CLAN ORIGIN = ENTABUKO	7 COURT DUTIES = MWANYA or MURUKA or MWAGA	8 CLAN SPIRIT = MIZUKA =MIZUKA	9 CLAN VILLAGES = VIJIJI VYA ASILI	10 PRESENT CLAN HEAD = OMUKULU WA LUGANDA	11 SUB-CLANS = MAHIGA	12 PRESENT SUB-CLAN HEAD = OMUKULU WA IHIGA
Baahaga	Kiamtwara	Two bananas joined together	Senene	Mushaija	Buzinja	Milkers	Wamara	Kangabushalo	Mwombeki of Busimbe	-	-
Bananai	Kiziba	Bushbuck	Hyena	Kayanja	Uganda	Doormakers to the Chief	Muzola	Katoke Buyango	Bingileki of Katoke	Bakaina Bamwanza	Kato of Lutara Bwesha of Buhanga
Basigu	Kiziba	"	Enyawewa (stork)	Mtungillia	Itawa	-	Kakile	Kigelela Buyango	Katabaro of Katoke	F.l.	-
"	Kiamtwara	"	Editwatwa (bird)	Balindwa	Ruanda	Blacksmiths	Wamara	Bulyampuro G.Itawa	Laurien of Bulyampuro	-	-
"	Karyange-reko	"	" (a bird with a crest on its head)	Ndugaala of Mibale (Karagwe)	Mibale (Karagwe)	Cooks Drumkeepers of the drum Kyegenywa	?	Mibale (Karagwe)	Byeaburilo of Mahiga G.Bibanja	Bazigaba	N.Rwakatare of Maruku G.Bibanja
Bagayia	Kiamtwara	Lung fish (Maamba)	-	Kikanya	Buganda	Baharambwe	Wamara	Lugaze G.Kitwe	Nyamwihula of Lugaze	Bainiga ?	Nyamwihula Kamanyi of Kagondo

NOTES

Basigu.

F.l. Col.11. No mahiga because the omugaruzi had no sons.

1 CLAN = LUGANDA	2 CHIEFDOM = BUKAMA	3 TOTEM = MUZIRO	4 SECONDARY TOTEM = EBINTU EBILI KUGENDA-GENDA AMUZIRO	5 FOUNDER (PATRIACH) = OMUGURUSI	6 PLACE OF CLAN ORIGIN = ENTABUKO	7 COURT DUTIES = MWANYA or MURUKA or MWAGA	8 CLAN SPIRIT = MIZUKA	9 CLAN VILLAGES = VIJIJI VAY ASILI	10 PRESENT CLAN HEAD = OMUKULU WA LUGANDA	11 SUB-CLANS = MAHIGA	12 PRESENT SUB-CLAN HEAD = OMUKULU WA IHIGA
Begavia	Kanyange-reko	Bushbuck	Akafunzi (small bird)	Kajeema of Bugera G.Ntoma	Kingo G.Kitenda-guro	Brewers	Mgumia	Bugera G.Ntoma	Anatol Bwezile of Bugera	-	-
Bagwe	Kiantwara	Bushbuck	Chicken	Kabembula	Uganda	Make sacrifices to overcome enemies	Wamara	Kitendaguro	Tibakweitila of Kitendaguro	-	-
"	Ihangiro	Copper (Omurigga)	Hyena	Muganda	Egypt	Watchmen	Katanga	Kitobo G.Kanengere	Marwa of Kasilantemwa	Basita Balende Bahigiza	Mutengerekwa of Nshisha G.Kahengere Katorogo of Ihunga G.Kishanda Mufuruki of Ihunga G.Kishanda
Babenge	Kiantwara	Monkey (Tumbili)	-	Ibona	Kiziba	Soothsayers	Wamara	Nshisha G.Kitwa	Ngiromo of Nshisha	-	-
Bahuge	"	Millet growing out of a rock	Omusibya (bird)	Kagarami	Mpololo	Iron workers	Wamara	Ibaraizibu G.Itawa	Ndyegemdezaa of Ibaraizibu	Bakuntuzi Bagisa Bakanguta	Mbarabara of Kibuye Mwijage of Kibuye Batela of Kibuye

1	2	3	4	5	6	7	8	9	10	11	12
CLAN = LUGANDA	CHIEFDOM = BUKAMA	TOTEM = MUZIRO	SECONDARY TOTEM = EBINTU EBILI KUGENDA-GENDA ANUZIRO	FOUNDER (PATRIACH) = OMUGURUSI	PLACE OF CLAN ORIGIN = ENTABUKO	COURT DUTIES = MWANYA or MURUKA or MWAGA	CLAN SPIRIT = MIZUKA	CLAN VILLAGES = VIJIJI VYA ASILI	PRESENT CLAN HEAD = OMUKULU WALUGANDA	SUB-CLANS = MAHIGA	PRESENT SUB-CLAN HEAD = OMUKULU WA IHIGA
Bahuge	Kauyange-reko	Intestines of a cow	Hawk	Kinyomo of Buhesi G.Izigo	Uha	Ironworkers	Irungu F.l.	Buhesi G.Izigo	Lukantanga	-	-
Balungika	Kiantwara	Fish	Buffalo	Rutemba	Bunyoro	Soothsayers	Wamara	Ijugaryoado G.Kitendaguro	Karyankole of Muyaba	-	-
Bahembe	"	Bushbuck	Fish	Mbeo	Buzinja	Fundis	Wamara	Buhembe G.Nyakato	Ndyagati of Buhembe	-	-
Baganda	Ihangiro	Tortoise (kobe)	Chirku (a finch)	Rubire	Egypt	Cooks & personal servants	Kabogyo	Mushasha G.Bisheke	Rwabutoga of Bisheke	Baheta / Banyama / Banyangezi / Bajolobwa / Batama	Rukabuka of Mulela G.Kishanda / Bahangarwa of Katale G.Bureza / Kanahaiga of Buhimba G.Bureza / Rutakangwa of Bureza G.Bureza / Kikwasi of Bureza G.Bureza.

NOTES.

Bahuge

F.l. Col.8. Irungu because he is the guide of iron workers.

1 CLAN = LUGANDA	2 CHIEFDOM = BUKAMA	3 TOTEM = MUZIRO	4 SECONDARY TOTEM = EBINTU EBILI KUGENDA-GENDA AMUZIRO	5 FOUNDER (PATRIACH) = OMUGURUSI	6 PLACE OF CLAN ORIGIN = ENTABUKO	7 COURT DUTIES = MWANYA or MURUKA or MWAGA	8 CLAN SPIRIT = MIZUKA	9 CLAN VILLAGES = VIJIJI VYA ASILI	10 PRESENT CLAN HEAD = OMUKULU WALUGANDA	11 SUB-CLANS = MAHIGA	12 PRESENT SUB-CLAN HEAD = OMUKULU WA IHIGA
Baamwena	Ihangiro	Runye (a cow)	Rabbit (Sungura)	Rwemiganda	Egypt	Witch doctors	Wamara	Mashure G.Mibunda	Muhikira of Kisana	Bagara	Belwegilira of Kabare G.Burabo
										Bahyo	Rwanyakwisa of Kabare G.Burabo Ndimo of Kaina G.Bureza
										Beilili	Kasanene of Kyamahoga G.Nahamba
										Bashagu	Tirwebwa of Musinga G.Nahamba
										Basha	Rubingabikara of Itong G.Nahamba
										Bagahi	Rwabukoba of Katwelele G.Kahangere
										Bazila	Ijunga of Rwazi G.Kahangere
										Balwani	Byandwano of Buhimba G.Bureza
										Bashengya	
Babago	Ihangiro	Bushbuck	Francolin	Nyaibunga	Kitara	Personal servants to the Chief	Ntane	Kagarama	Rwabunywenge of Rubya	Baziba	Kaiza of Rwanganilo G.Kahangere
										Bakulwa	Bachuba of Kikuku G.Kahangere
										Bebogo	Tiruhongerwa of Kitoko G.Mibunda
Bakombe	"	Civet cat	Squirrel	Muhambi	Egypt	Cooks	Muhaya F.l.	Mushure	Rushabari of Bushegeshe	Batundu	Kangabwa of Karambi
										Bakolansi	Kakyoo of Iremera

N O T E S.

Bakombe.

F.l. Col.8. Muhaya d/o Muhinda Mahule who was turned out by her father and died of sorrow at Ijumbi.

1	2	3	4	5	6	7	8	9	10	11	12
CLAN = LUGANDA	CHIEFDOM = BUKAMA	TOTEM = MUZIRO	SECONDARY TOTEM = EKINTU EBILI KUGENDA-GENDA AMUZIRO	FOUNDER (PATRIACH) = OMUGURUSI	PLACE OF CLAN ORIGIN = ETTABUKO	COURT DUTIES = MWAMYA or MURUKA or MWAGA	CLAN SPIRIT = MIZUKA	CLAN VILLAGES = VIJIJI VYA ASILI	PRESENT CLAN HEAD = OMUKULU WALUGANDA	SUB-CLANS = MAHIGA	PRESENT SUB-CLAN HEAD = OMUKULU WA IHIGA
Bateneita	Ihangiro	Cow (bihogo)	Dog	Kakarenge	Egypt	Herdsmen	Wamara	Kagogo	Manunga of Kagogo	-	-
Bajolwa	"	Olukyanya (a tree)	Elephant	Mworo	Kagarwe	Watchmen	Wamara	Kishao	Rugembe of Kitoko	-	-
Bagobela	Kanyange-reko	Millet growing out of a rock	Ekitwatwa (a bird)	Nyakulioki of Lwasi G.Ntoma	Kamesi (Ukerewe)	Drummers of the drum Buchwankwanzi (Kabandae)	Wamara	Lwazi G.Ntoma	Mohamed of Lwasi	-	-
Babende	"	Rain water	Dog	Baboko of Maruku	Businja	Priests of Mugasha	Wamara	Maruku G.Bibanja	Byabaranzi	-	-
Babwongu	"	The milk of a cow which has been covered by a bull	-	Njoju of Katuruka G.Ntoma	Ishango (Uganda)	Soothsayers of the oracle Kagwi	Wamara	Katuruka G.Ntoma	Mutagwaba of Rwiga G.Itawa	-	-
Basira	"	Striped cow	Wild oat (enjangu)	Kazira	Ankole	Prophets	Wamara	Izigo	Lukeisa of Izigo	-	-
Bayeyego	"	Goat skin	Small ant	?	Katoke	None	Kimuli	Katoke G.Izigo	Wamara of Kilele G.Minazi	-	-

1	2	3	4	5	6	7	8	9	10	11	12
CLAN = LUGANDA	CHIEFDOM = BUKAMA	TOTEM = MUZIRO	SECONDARY TOTEM = EBINTU EBILI KUGENDA-GENDA AMUZIRO	FOUNDER (PATRIACH) = OMUGURUSI	PLACE OF CLAN ORIGIN = ENTABUKO	COURT DUTIES = MWANYA or MURUKA or MWAGA	CLAN SPIRIT = MIZUKA	CLAN VILLAGES = VIJIJI VYA ASILI	PRESENT CLAN HEAD = OMUKULU WA LUGANDA	SUB-CLANS = MAHIGA	PRESENT SUB-CLAN HEAD = OMUKULU WA IHIGA
Bayeyego	Bugabo	Millet growing from a rock	-	Bwesha	Kahumuro (Kianja)	None	Kimuli	Kishanje, Kayungwe Iyanda	Kutulilire of Kishanje	-	-
Balomo	Kanyange-reko	-	-	?	Ankole	None	Wamara	Kahororo	? of Kahororo	-	-
"	Bugabo	Millet growing from a rock	-	Tabaro	Ankole	Baramata	Wamara	Makongo Bunyonya Buzi	Mitabuko of Makongo	Baiule Bagoma	Mitabuko ?
Balasa	Kanyange-reko	Lung fish (maamba)	Lung fish	Nganzi of Kanyan-gereko	Kiawani (Bihara-mulo)	Nobles	Lyangombe	Kanyange-reko G.Ntoma	Benzi of Karyange-reko	Bamuzira-lushanju Bachwan-kwanzi	Benzi G.Mutakyawa of Kabale G.Kitendaguro
"	Bugabo	"	-	Kitwara	Bunyoro	Drum keepers	Kalemera	Kishanje Kyamarange G.Rubafu & Ndama G.Kabilizi	Bugage of Ndama	Balago Bachwan-kwanzi	Kyasheme of Bumai Gadiozi Mutakyawa of Kabale
Bakongo	Kanyange-reko	Heart of all animals	Baboon	Mulinga	Mukongo G.Kishogo	Cast out devils (Basiliki)	Wamara	Kanyange-reko G.Ntoma	Ali Kasha-nda of Kanyange-reko	-	-
Bagaya	Bugabo	Lung fish (maamba)	-	Bwelunge	Uganda	Herdsmen	Nkuro	Ishozi Mayondwe G.Muhutwe Kaagia	Bakanoba of Kaagia	-	-
Babuta	Bugabo	Buffalo	-	Kanyara	Isheshe	Baramata	Kabanga & Wamara	Rubafu Kyamarange Kaagia	Tilmeorwa of Rubafu	-	-

			Page
Mwami	...	...	116, 155, 157,234, 237, 270, 275, 276
Mwana wa bisisi see Bisisi			
Mwana wa luhoire	...	...	32, 33, 34, 38, 62, 105
Mwate	...	...	113, 121
Ninarumi	...	...	4, 5
Nsika	...	...	124, 125
Ntegeka	...	...	230, 234, 235, 236
Ntekwa	...	...	167, 168
Ntumwa	...	...	237
Ntungwa	...	...	169, 170
Nyarubanja	...	...	4, 123 et seq., 146, 147, 156, 157, 159, 164
Oath	...	...	239
Obuchweke	...	...	3, 7, 8, 18, 19, 23,39,76, 119, 120, 121, 124, 125
Obwiko	...	...	89, 91
Officials	...	...	155, 157
Omugurusi	...	...	255, 256, 257
Ordeals	...	...	240, 241
Plantation	...	...	55, 56, 92, 121, 122, 124, 136, 138, 140, 141, 142,144, 155, 157, 162, 164, 189, 191
Pledge	...	...	121, 132, 140, 219 et seq.
Plural wives' tax	...	...	102
Polygamy	...	...	92
Priest	...	...	159
Property	...	...	110, 113 et seq.
damage to	...	...	181, 206, 251
division of	...	...	20, et seq.
of married women	...	...	6, 7
sale of	...	...	188 et seq.
Prostitution	...	...	100
Rape	...	...	231, 252